Christmas, 1953: While the rest of Philadelphia sings Jingle Bells, Thomas Grubb gets his first taste of a cop's life. Before he cashes his first paycheck he encounters: a man gutted by a knife-wielding mugger, a fighting-mad mental case intent on destroying a hospital emergency room and the hushed-up shooting death of an undercover cop. That first week is nothing compared to what lies ahead. Working as a street cop, an undercover officer, a detective and finally in gang control, Grubb will spend the next thirty years going toe-to-toe with all the fast-changing and sometimes violent events that have rocked American society. A Cop's Life: The remarkable story of a truly remarkable man.

A Cop's Life won many accolades, but the most prized were the good opinions of police officers themselves. Here are just a few of the comments: "A must read by anyone who ever wore the uniform or badge!" - Robert V. Eddie, Recording Secretary Philadelphia Lodge #5 Fraternal Order of Police; "If you like the inside story, if you like dealing with facts and not fluff, then you will love reading A Cop's Life!"- Michael G. Lutz, President, Pennsylvania Fraternal Order of Police; "I thoroughly enjoyed A Cop's Life. It was both witty and right on target." - Bill Pawley Inspector, Retired, Philadelphia Police.

**For Cassie - A True Cop's Wife
And
Kathryn - Who Made This Book
Possible**

A Cop's Life

Philadelphia, 1953–1983

by
Thomas M. Grubb
and
Allan "Lucky" Cole

Table of Contents

Table Of Contents
(Continued)

List of Illustrations

MAPS AND PHOTOGRAPHS

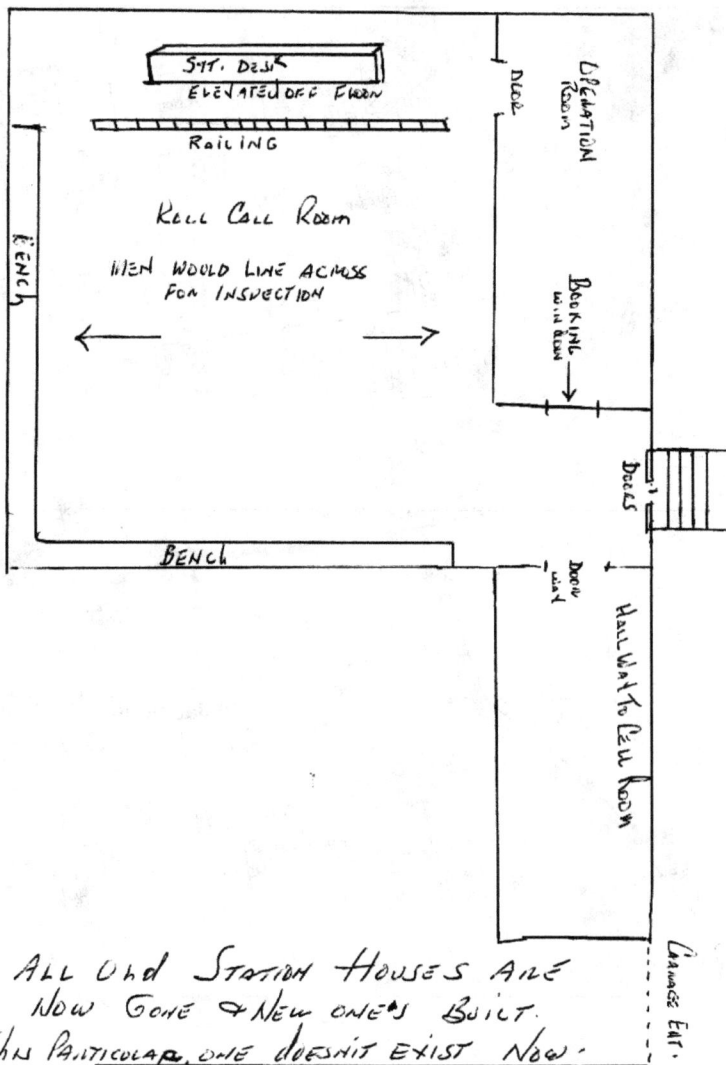

SGT. DESK
ELEVATED OFF FLOOR

RAILING

KELL CALL ROOM

MEN WOULD LINE ACROSS
FOR INSPECTION

BENCH

BENCH

OPERATION ROOM

DOOR

BOOKING WINDOW

DOORS

DOOR WINDOW

HALLWAY TO CELL ROOM

GARAGE ENT.

ALL OLD STATION HOUSES ARE
NOW GONE & NEW ONE'S BUILT.
THIS PARTICULAR, ONE DOESN'T EXIST NOW.

An Old Station House (Chapter 4)

The Ninth District (Chapter 5)

Thomas Grubb (at right) and partner with "The Wagon" (Chapter 6)

Thomas Grubb with his children while recuperating
from accident
(Chapter 12)

Thomas Grubb during his plainclothes years
(Chapter 18)

Thomas Grubb (far right) with some of the members
of the Special Investigation Squad (Chapter 19)

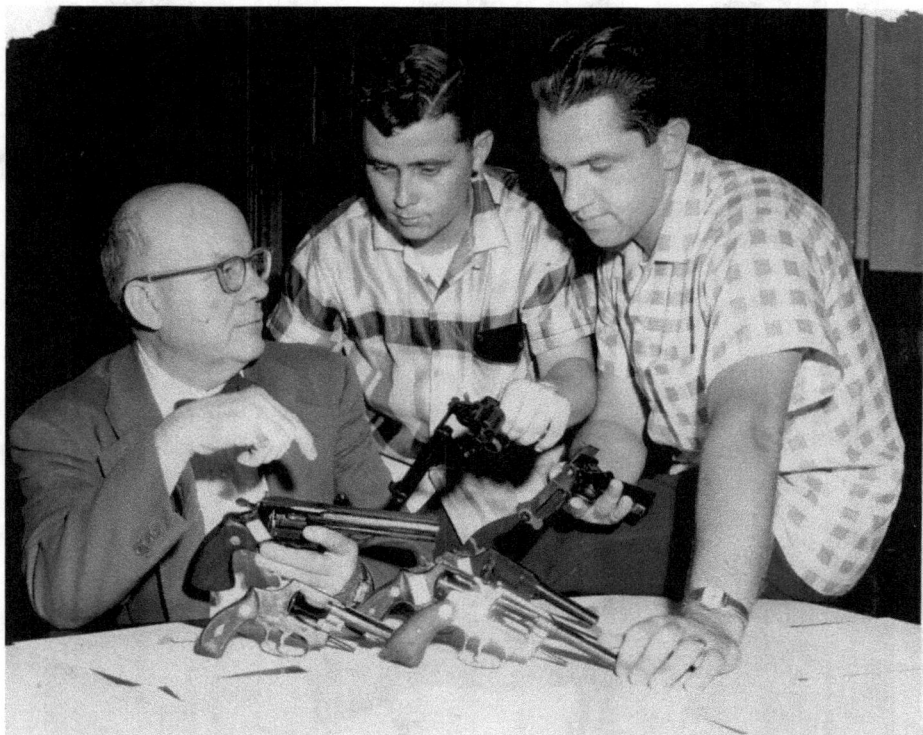

Thomas Grubb (at right) with partner and captain
after the "Thirty-Six Hour Marathon" (Chapter 25)

Thomas M Grubb (Jan. 6, 1929 - Feb. 20, 2005)

Foreword

DEAR READER: The late Thomas M. Grubb - Uncle Tommy to me — was one of those larger than life characters who stand out even in a very large, very colorful family.

I had listened intently to his stories about his experiences in the Philadelphia Police Department ever since I was a boy. They were so thrilling, so real — and sometimes quite comical — that I'd always yearned to put them in a book. A novel or a movie, I thought, based on a character very much like him. But I'd never had the nerve to ask him about it. He'd always made it plain how disdainful he was of most fictional efforts to portray a policeman's life. So I never said anything about it.

Then a few years ago I visited with Uncle Tommy and my Aunt Cassie in Philadelphia. It had been quite some time since I'd seen them and once again he regaled me and my wife, Kathryn, with some of his choicest stories.

This time I didn't remain silent. I told him about my lifelong desire to write a book about him. To my surprise, he not only listened but warmed to the idea.

And before I left he promised me he'd start taping some of his stories and send them me to do with as I wished.

Not too many weeks later, I received the first installment. To my amazement, he'd gone far beyond his initial promise, and I found myself listening to the autobiography of a remarkable cop. He kept it up, month after month, until the entire story was complete.

The tapes were so good, so well organized, I could see right away that this would make a remarkable book all by itself.

This is that book.

Kathryn and I edited the tapes, condensed and rearranged incidents to keep the narrative flow, plus the names have been changed to protect the innocent — and guilty. But out main objective was to retain the warm conversational tone of his narration, which was addressed directly to me, his nephew "Lucky." That's is my childhood nickname, and how I'm know to all in the large Philadelphia Irish family I was fortunate enough to be born into.

The book covers my Uncle Tommy's thirty-year career with the department. During that time he witnessed incredible changes in our society. But at heart, the job of fighting crime isn't that much different today than it was in 1953 when he started out. As you'll see for yourself when you turn the page. - Allan Cole

Part One - Patrolman

CHAPTER ONE
The Beginning

HELLO, LUCKY THIS is Uncle Tom. This is the first of the tapes I'm going to send you and I'm going to relate some of my experiences during my thirty years in the Philadelphia Police Department.

I'm going to start when I was strictly in uniform, Lucky, and kind of give you a picture of what it was like in those days, and go on from there.

And I can't use the right names of people, I'll just use some names that I make up as I go along.

Lucky, you gotta realize that this is not gonna be one of these shoot 'em ups like you see in the movies or on TV, or all that nonsense. That's not really the police department.

They may put a movie together for an hour or so of something that took ten years to get together. This is just gonna be what it's like to actually be a police officer.

It's not the excitement or anything, it's the absolute boredom and expectations of what could happen.

It's a funny thing. When you're out on patrol, you don't know what's gonna happen and you're expecting everything to happen and nothing happens. And then you get very careless and bored.

I'm gonna start by trying to explain to you just what it was like and the funny things that happen as a rookie cop during your six months' probationary period.

Y'know, this is the time, if you look sideways at anybody or do anything the slightest bit wrong, you're fired. There's no question about that.

So you just gotta kinda lean back and try to do everything that you're supposed to.

CHAPTER TWO
Training

OKAY, LUCK, LIKE all stories start, I was accepted to the Police Academy for training. Now at the time I went into the business, there were various amounts of training time, depending on how badly officers were needed out on the street.

My experience at the Police Academy was very short. I had exactly eight — no, ten days training. That was two weeks — ten days — and that time was supposed to prepare me to go out and handle the general public.

I'll just tell you a few of the things we were taught in those ten days. We were taught how to fill out a traffic violation ticket. We were taught a few of the traffic laws.

We were taught how to fill out papers for the Widow's Pension Fund. That was a big thing then, y'know. You get knocked off, you wanta have your pension go to your survivor — your wife or mother, whomever.

And then, of course, we were brought down to the pistol range. This was a joke. We were issued the oldest weapon I've ever seen in my life.

It was called an Iver Johnson breakdown. This is the type of gun that you broke in half. The bullets that were inserted looked like they came from the Civil War.

We were allowed to point them down the range and actually fire five shells that were given to us. Most of them did not fire. The ones that did fire, the projectile just about rolled out of the barrel of the gun.

I guess we were fortunate that they didn't blow up on us. This was the extent of our pistol training on the range.

Then we were issued gray uniforms. By uniforms, I mean gray working pants, the khaki type, and a matching shirt. We were also issued our badge, and that was the kicker.

We had this badge on these working clothes, and we didn't even have a hat, y'know, that would identify you as a police officer. You wore a jacket of your choice. They requested that it be somewhere in the blue or black color area. This was a joke in itself.

Then we were assigned to various districts. It was only two weeks before Christmas. That's why we were needed outside on the streets so quickly.

I was assigned to a Center City district, along with two other rookies — Jerry Rivers and Eddie.

We came into this district and looked around and you could just see, like in church, they had the pulpit where the house sergeant would stand and conduct roll call.

And we even went there a couple of days early so we could check and see what was going on, because nobody knew anything about it. We barely knew where the district was.

Well, right away we bumped into this old, nasty house sergeant.

Now, a house sergeant isn't like a street sergeant. A street sergeant goes out in the patrol car, kinda looks after the men in the street, where a house sergeant always remains in the house — the house meaning the district or the station house.

He handles the arrest book and nobody touches it or writes in it but him. You just tell him what you want and he'll put it in there.

Well, we reported to this old house sergeant, Francis was his name, McFall. He was a grumpy old son-of-a-gun. And us being rookies, he let us know where we stood.

So, we got to talk to a street sergeant and we were assigned to a squad. I was assigned to Two Squad, I believe. There were seven squads in those days, and you always worked with a different squad during the week.

I was told by the sergeant that I was to report for duty for the "last out shift." Now "last out," I didn't know what the hell that meant. Last out of the station house, last out of — what does it mean?

He said, "well, red ass," he said, "that means you report in here at twelve o'clock or before. Last out is twelve at night till eight in the morning."

I learned real quick what "last out" was.

CHAPTER THREE
First Day

WELL, I DID report to the district as I was instructed. I came in my gray work clothes, which was my "uniform" and my Navy peacoat, and I just sat there.

The other guys went into different squads, so I sat there by myself, not knowing what to expect. I was supposed to be there at midnight, but I got in there like, eleven thirty. I wasn't gonna be late on my first night.

No need to say that I watched the men coming in and they were all different shapes and forms. None of them looked happy, they were all bitchin' or gripin', y'know, workin' last out. Some looked like they were half loaded, but then you never could tell with some of them.

I neglected to say that this night was a rainy, slushy, snowy night and it was really a bitch. Freezin' with the goddam clothes we hadda wear.

But anyway, in the district I got introduced as the new man in the squad. Well, that means, y'know, you're the ass, you get all the dirty jobs — anything that comes up, you'll get it, and I went through roll call.

Well, I didn't have a gun. Only that Iver Johnson I told you about, because we didn't have time to really get pistols, which you bought yourself, by the way. So I kept the Iver in my pocket, because I didn't have a holster.

When I took that out — the duty sergeant who was conducting the roll call walks up and down the aisles of men, be there fourteen men to a squad or what, and he inspects their uniform and their revolver, and so forth.

And when he came to me and he looked at that thing that I was holdin' in my hand, he told me, he says, "Boy, don't try to shoot.

"If you've got to, hit 'em with it. Use it as a club. Don't try to shoot it."

And everybody had a big laugh out of that. And I just put it back in my pocket — I mean, it was only about six inches long; the barrel.

After roll call, the sergeant, who was a pretty nice guy, really, he told me, he said, "Hey, kid, you're up here," he said, "you're gonna work with Tim."

Well, Tim I didn't know. That was Dewey, that's his last name, Dewey. I looked at him, he's about six foot five, maybe two fifty, wearing one of the long overcoats down to his ankles, and I thought, "Oh," you know, "this looks like a real big cop to me."

He says, "You'll be assigned to him for this tour of duty."

O.K., that was it. We had an assignment, a certain car, and we left the roll room.

Well, we went out and got into a patrol car, oh, I think they were Chevy's at that time, '53 Chevy's or something of that nature. And we got a sector to patrol. I forget right now what it was, C Sector, we'll say.

Sectors are bordered by streets. You work so far into the sector and you don't leave it, you don't go into another guy's sector. You remain in your own.

We left the station house, must've been, oh, 12:00, and we hit the bricks, y'know, we relieved the guys that's comin' in to check off.

Usually there's a little joviality between the guys comin' in and the guys goin' off, like, "Did'ja get enough sleep for tonight?" or "Whattya gonna do tonight, ya gonna stay awake?"

And you gotta exchange the little quips with the men, but I had nobody to exchange anything with 'cause nobody even knew me, and I didn't know them.

We went out to our assigned sector. It must have been 12:15, we get a call. Disturbance In A Restaurant.

Well, this is all new to me. I was riding as the recorder in the patrol car. You've got the operator and you've got the guy sitting on the other side of the seat with the clipboard and the forms. He's the recorder. He writes down all radio messages.

So we get this assignment and naturally, Dewey knows where this 19th and Nectarine is located. Matter of fact, it was only a few blocks from the district.

Thomas M. Grubb & Allan "Lucky" Cole

So we go up there, and we walk into this place, and it's more or less a luncheonette type of situation, with a long service counter, some tables against the wall. Like, these tables for two people, and it's a very narrow place. It couldn't have been any wider than eight feet. But long. Had to be like forty, fifty feet long.

Naturally, I'm the young man, I'm walking behind the experienced officer. And we go in, and here's this guy standing at the end of the counter and I didn't know it at first, but he's standin' there with a gun in his hand.

I can't see anything. I can't see around Dewey 'cause he's so goddam big in front of me.

And we get to the end of the counter and it spread out then a little bit, the tables weren't there, and then I saw this guy lyin' on the floor.

Dewey goes over to him and what I really saw mostly was this pool of blood. It was huge.

And his head was in the pool of blood. And Dewey spoke to this guy behind the counter and it didn't seem to be nothin' serious, y'know, just talked to him.

Then he goes over to this man lyin' on the floor. And he takes his foot and he kind of rolls this guy's head so he could get a look at the face. 'Cause the guy was more or less down on the floor, face down.

And he looks at him, and to tell you the truth, I got a glimpse of him, I thought it was a black man. He had very short hair and he looked black to me. Not knowing any better, I kept my mouth shut, the senior officer's gonna handle this matter.

Well, Dewey takes a look at the guy, gives a couple of grunts, turns around to the man standing behind the counter, wants to know what happened.

He said, "Gimme something to write on."

They got a paper bag, I'll never forget this, a brown paper bag, and he wrote down the guy's name, and he didn't write nothin' down about the corpse lying on the floor.

And he asked the guy what happened and the guy said, "He walked in here," he says, "I saw him with a gun and I shot him."

That was about it.

24

So I just looked at him, keepin' my mouth shut.

He said, "O.K.," he said, "Gimme the phone", he says, "No, better I'll go out and call from the police radio. Get me a supervisor."

That is what he calls the sergeant.

And shortly thereafter the sergeant arrives. We didn't do nothin', stayed in the place. Matter of fact, Dewey had a cup of coffee while he was in there.

The man's dead, lyin' on the floor, blood's running all over.

Well, lo and behold, the sergeant came. Then the detectives were notified, and so forth. By then they told us, y'know, "You can leave."

We were there, like, forty-five minutes. I knew nothing more when the forty-five minutes was over than I did when I walked in. It's just — a guy got shot, that's it.

But I did learn one thing. The guy had been shot in the temple and in the neck, and I overheard one of the detectives talking and one of the guys from the police lab that came said that when you're shot like this, you discolor.

And with this, I learned the guy on the floor was a white man, not a black man. But that didn't mean nothin' to me one way or the other.

So out we go, and back on the air, on the radio. See, whenever you get a radio call, Lucky, you know, you pick up the mike to acknowledge the call, repeat the location, then tell 'em you're taking the call.

When you get done with the job, you got to get on the radio and put yourself back in service. That was the terminology. Like, you say, "98 Car, back in service," so they know you're available for more calls.

So we left that place and we started to tour around our sector. Now mind you, I said the weather really sucked. It was bad. And it was cold and, y'know, it was just a miserable night.

So we're goin' into the night, and all of a sudden Dewey pulls up beside this bar. It was closed — it was after hours. He goes to the door, bangs on the door, goes inside.

He's in there all of maybe ten, fifteen minutes. Then he comes back out to the car and he's O.K., but I can smell the booze on him.

He rides around, we get around a couple more hours. Then we get another job. Investigate a prowler, I think that's the way it came out from the radio.

And we went up to Broad and Mellon Street and we get out of the car. Like I said, it was a nasty night.

And I see this fella backed against a wall and he's leaning forward. And I can't figure what's the matter with him, maybe drunk, or what?

But Dewey, the big gentleman, he says, "Hey, red ass, go see what that guy's doin'."

So I went up to talk to the man. Well, the guy is up against the wall, flat, so I start talking. It's a black guy, young man, and he's tellin' me, "I'm hurt, I'm hurt."

I'm lookin' at him and he doesn't look hurt to me.

I'm looking at his face, naturally, and I say, "Come on, pal," I said, "you'd better come back to the car."

I put a light on him to see if he's hurt or not, asked him where he's hurt.

Then he says, "I can't move."

I was gettin' a little upset because I didn't know what to do. He's telling me he can't go and I'm telling him to come to the car.

Well, the guy starts to walk and he leans over and I look. He's got like a leather jacket on, and down the back of the jacket there's these two — slash marks, is what they are.

And, man, when he bent over to walk, they just opened up and the blood just flowed out like you wouldn't believe. Somebody actually got up behind him and slashed him, probably with a razor.

Well, that was it. We hadda carry him to the car and take him down to the hospital. And they start workin' on him, y'know, just cut the clothes off of him and start sewin' him up.

And that was more or less my first night on the job.

I didn't particularly care for this guy Dewey I was with, because during the early night he stopped at a couple of places — the bars — and hit the booze. That was it, he hadda have his booze.

Thomas M. Grubb & Allan "Lucky" Cole

So we went back into the district and as you — check off is what they call it — as you check off duty, you return to the district and you go in, your squad sergeant's there and you check off to him.

That's more or less to make sure the guys got back to the district all right. Nobody was missing, or anything.

And the sergeant said to me, "How did'ja make out with your partner? Everything all right?"

Well, I knew enough that you don't complain. It's just like the service, you work it out yourself.

So I said, "Oh, sure, Sarge, everything's great."

And that was it for the first night on the street.

Then it was the following night I came in and the sergeant said, "Kid," he said, "I want you to tell me what happened up there at Nectarine Street."

This was the shooting that we went in on.

I related to the sergeant exactly, y'know, what I did up there.

He said, "Did you know that fellow was a police officer?"

I said, "No, how would I know?"

And here, the guy that was shot was a plainclothes police officer. He worked for the captain or the inspector, and that meant like certain times they would go out in just civilian clothes and do police work. More or less like undercover guys, if you wanna use that term.

Somehow he got mixed up with this guy in the restaurant and the guy blew him away. But that was all, he just wanted to know if I knew he was a cop. No, I didn't know.

So that's the first night on the job. I'm goin' in where a cop's murdered, actually, and the other guy got sliced almost in half.

Lucky, that morning I was very disillusioned about the job, and when I got home, or I should say on my way home, I decided that I wouldn't ever tell your Aunt Cass any of the bad stuff that I saw or what happens on the job.

I knew, soon's I got in, she's gonna want to know, "Gee, how was your night?" and "What went on?" and all this.

I decided then that I'd just tell her, "Very quiet night, Cass," and "We really didn't do that much but ride around."

I did that for the thirty years I was in the police department.

Thomas M. Grubb & Allan "Lucky" Cole

The only time I'd tell your Aunt Cass anything is if something funny, comical, occurred that I could elaborate on. She would ask me almost every night, "How was the night?" or "How was the day?"

So that's what I decided I'd work with, with the comical stuff, but nothing serious.

Unless I came home bleeding, and then she would know.

Thomas M. Grubb & Allan "Lucky" Cole

CHAPTER FOUR
Probation

I GUESS IT was the second night that I went on duty, again it was "last out."

I'll try to explain to you how the shifts work. You work seven days on each shift, and after, like if you were working day work you would have the day off, or if you were working four to twelve you'd have the next day off.

And it would come around every seven weeks you would have a weekend off. And this was called "The Big Apple."

You would work from midnight Thursday till eight o'clock Friday morning, and then you would be off Saturday and Sunday and come in on four to twelve on Monday.

So they figured it was four days that you had off, so they called it "The Big Apple." And like I said, this occurred every seven weeks.

During the week you had alternating days off. A Monday and a Tuesday, then a Tuesday and a Wednesday, and so forth. But that was your scheduled time off.

I want to describe to you the district that I worked in. It was at 20th and Buttonwood, and it was the Ninth Police District.

It was an old, old house — police station. You came up a flight of steps through a double door.

You came into a room and there was a bench that stretched all the way around the room. And it was like a wooden paneled room with the old, German siding wood up.

And then there was the bar and what we called the pulpit where the sergeant stood, bringing the men on duty and taking them off duty. And it was picturesque, if nothing else, kind of like the ones you see in old movies.

But anyway, on the second night I came into work, and the same thing happened. I sat on that bench that stretched all the way around the room. The other guys came in and they had their conversations and b.s. among themselves until there was roll call.

We went through the roll call again and the sergeant told me I would be working with a different man each night, y'know, and sorta familiarize myself with the districts, learn the streets, and then we'd go on.

And that made sense to me. And that's exactly what I did.

The following nights were rather uneventful except for the sleeping part. These guys, they didn't trust me, of course, so they wouldn't wanna sleep in the cars. But I knew they did.

I knew it simply because I watched other guys actually bring a pillow into the police car with them. You don't bring that in unless you want to lay your head on it.

That was kind of funny, and the guy I would work with, he would be pissed off because he couldn't do too much with me because he didn't trust me. At least he thought he couldn't trust me.

They didn't want you to drive so much 'cause they didn't even know if you could drive that well.

But anyway, we went through the next week or so and I did learn the district, riding all the various sectors. Each night I was assigned to a car that rode a different sector, different guys. And very little talk. Y'know, common things: "Where are you from," maybe, "What's your name?" and that's about it.

So two weeks passed by. And now we're really into the holiday time of the year. But in this period our sergeant got transferred, and we got a guy that was an acting sergeant. A guy right from the squad.

Now, he used to be a steady man on 95 Car. So that night that he would be leavin' 95 Car and goin' to the sergeant's car. And the sergeant used to get a chauffeur, y'know, it was one of those deals.

He left his partner, so when this guy was appointed acting sergeant of our squad, I was the newest man there.

Like I told you, the young guy gets the bullshit.

He called me, he said, "Grubb," he said, "I want you to work 95 Car," he said. "You will be working with Mike Finney."

That didn't mean nothin' to me. O.K., Mike Finney.

He said, "You'll get along good with him," he said, "you'll be workin' this car steady."

I liked that. I figured you don't go bouncin' around in different cars, different people.

Well, I didn't know Mike Finney. And I'm tellin' you he was one strange man. Luck, the sergeant who introduced me to Mike, he was part Cherokee Indian, I believe. Big guy, stone face.

But Mike was quite the opposite. Mike was a little, fat Irishman. He fit the name Mike Finney very, very well. Round face, reddish complexion — ruddy, I guess you would call it. Blue eyes, and the nastiest disposition you ever wanted to see.

So I went out and I got in 95 Car. Mike Finney came out. Never said a word to me.

He said, "Come on," and that's it.

We went on.

Well, 95 worked down Market Street, Chestnut Street, in around that area. Mike didn't talk much. Didn't say anything to me. What he would say when I got in the car, he'd say, "Drive."

You'd drive.

And when he wanted you to turn, he'd just say, "Turn here, stop here, go here, stop," and that was it.

He never held a conversation, and, y'know, after a night or two of this you get pretty disgusted.

And I asked him one time, I said, "Mike, is there somethin' wrong?"

"Just drive the car."

Well, that went on for a while, and let me tell you, you're workin' with a guy, be it day work, night work, last out, and he doesn't talk to you at all, it makes that eight hours like sixteen hours.

You're too new on the job to tell him just what you think of him or anything else 'cause you need the job — you don't want to screw it up.

And that's the only reason I ever went into the police department. I made four times as much money at Dupont's, where I worked prior to the police department. I only took the police department because I got laid off once at Dupont.

That was frightening, when you have a family and you're trying to live as well as you can, and I got bumped out of my job by a more senior man in the laboratory. I was a chemist's assistant. And that was scary. Honest to goodness, that was scary.

31

And that's why I took the examination for the police department. Not knowing what the job really was, but I knew it was a steady job and you'd have to screw it up yourself to get canned.

Whereas, in the other way, if somebody had more seniority, they just bumped you out of a job.

So I just kept thinkin' about all this and I just kept my mouth shut with Mike. After a month of this, I finally — Monday when I came in — I went to Garry Hudson, who was our acting sergeant. And Mike's former partner.

I told him, I said, "Sergeant," I said, "There must be a problem. I can't seem to get along with Mike."

I said, "It's personal," I said, "maybe he's, y'know, I don't know what's wrong. He never says a word to me."

The sergeant turns around and he says, "Kid," he says, "Y'know what they call Mike? They call him Iron Jaw."

I said, "What?"

He said, "Yeah. Iron Jaw Finney."

I said, "I heard that."

A couple of guys asked me, "How ya gettin' along with Iron Jaw?"

I never knew what they meant.

He said, "Mike does not talk very much."

I said, "No, Sergeant, Mike don't talk at all."

He said, "Look, you stay with him," he said, "y'just stick it out a little longer," he says, "I'll take care of you when the time comes."

So I figured, well, the sergeant is a nice guy. I'll stick it out with this man.

Another couple of weeks passed, different tours. Now this night, it's four to twelve. That's the shift we're working. In every district there's an assigned hospital where you take injured people. Ours was the Hahnemann.

Well, we get a call, a "Hahnemann Hospital Disturbance." It could be anything.

So we go over and we pull into the hospital, go around to the emergency ward, which consisted of three rooms: reception, the middle and the back room. And they had doors connecting.

Thomas M. Grubb & Allan "Lucky" Cole

When we get in there, soon as we pull into the driveway, here's the doctor standin' outside and the nurses and the orderlies.

I said, "Who the hell's watchin' the store?"

Y'know, I'm a big-timer now, I got about six weeks in the business.

I follow Mike. Mike puts his stick under his arm, he's talkin' to the doctor, I don't know what the hell's goin' on, he just says, "C'mon, red ass, with me."

Well, we go into the hospital and I walk in the first door. And here's this guy in there. He's throwin' a rant. He's a psycho.

He's throwin' the stuff all over and, Christ, he's bleedin' from cuts and everything else. And I don't know what to do.

I stand there, and Mike says, "I'm goin' around behind him," and I said, "O.K."

Soon as I step in the door of the emergency room, this guy comes at me. And I got this stick they issued at the academy. Believe me, that's all they were — sticks. No kind of a club.

And I bounced the guy on the head and it just bounced back off of him. And he's grabbin' me and down we go.

Well, we're rollin' on the floor, in the glass. He had grabbed these gallon jugs they keep the alcohol and swabs and everything in and was throwing them around the room.

Needless to say I'm gettin' cut, rollin' on the goddam floor, and I can't hit this guy with the stick because I lost it somewhere in the melee — slid outta my hand. So I relied on the oldest thing that I knew.

I got him in a hold, I stood him up, and I gave him a right hand with everything I had on it, Luck.

And I hit him — he traveled across the room. And just at that time I saw Mike Finney comin' in the back door to the emergency ward. But he didn't come in, he just stood there at the doorway.

So this guy, whatever he was on, he bounced off the wall and came back at me, and I gave him a few more shots. And he grabbed me and down again we go on the floor. Then when I got him on the floor I laid a few on him and that was it.

He kind of, was subdued. To say the least.

33

Thomas M. Grubb & Allan "Lucky" Cole

After I got this guy out, I'm gettin' up and I'm bleedin' from the face, I'm bleedin' from the hands, and my legs, and my ass. Because I'm rollin' around in this glass.

Then Mike comes in, he says, "You awright?"

And right then and there, my blood was up, I guess the Irish was up, and then and there I wanted to punch him. I really did. But I figure, you don't do that unless you wanna get fired.

I told him, "Yeah, I'm all right."

He goes out, he gets the people back into the emergency ward. And naturally the doctor comes in, he sees I'm cut.

He says, "C'mon, we'll take care of you."

And Mike puts — I don't know what the hell — we didn't even have handcuffs in those days, Lucky. I don't know how he secured that guy. But he did. I don't know if he used a belt, or what. He secured him, and the doctor took me in and gave me a few stitches and shit.

That was the first time that Mike ever talked to me. By sayin', "Are you all right, now?" And that in itself, which I didn't realize at the time, was something.

Well anyway, we get that settled out there, and we go out and we get in the car. It was funny. Mike jumped in the driver's seat. That was unusual.

We pull around to Broad and Race, the side door. On Broad and Race was — on the corner there — I think it was the Newtown Tavern.

He tells me, "C'mon. C'mon with me."

That was another new thing. To go with him. We go in and he just puts his hand up like with the "V for Victory" — coupla shots. Bartender comes back with two doubles.

He says, "Go ahead, kid, have 'em."

Bam. I drank 'em down because I was kind of shaky, y'know. It was the first, so-called "action" I had in the police department.

From then on, Mike and I, we got along good. We got along real good. I'd have guessed maybe it was to see if you weren't a coward or if you had any heart or you could keep your mouth shut or anything like that. But it took several months before this happened.

Thomas M. Grubb & Allan "Lucky" Cole

And after that I liked Mike. He was a real good cop and a darned good teacher.

See, that's the only way you learn, is from the old timers. But the old timers would teach you, or they would not teach you. It was up to them.

The teaching — you learned so much. And you take one hundred per cent of what some tell you, fifty per cent of what others tell you. But Mike, you always listened to him. He was good.

And we had those whiskies and from there on Mike and I were really tight.

Other little things that went on — He used to leave the car, go down a subway for maybe five or ten minutes, then come up and just get back in the car and never say a word. Well, after we got straight, I learned what those little things were.

He'd offer me something but I wouldn't ever take. I just couldn't do that. But I wouldn't criticize him in any way, 'cause what he did was his business. And like I say, we got along good.

And Mike was a darned good teacher. I use the words darned good teacher, but it was more than that. As a matter of fact, some of the things that he taught me actually saved my life further on in my career in the department.

I guess I worked with Mike for about six months, or maybe a little less, and each day was like going to school with this man.

He would tell me different situations that an officer could get into. Also, the situations that he would not want to get into. And then he would quiz you on what he said.

Actually I enjoyed it, because he was a teacher, and his experience in the police department was his greatest gift to give to a young police officer.

Besides teaching me all the things that would help me in the P.D., Mike also told me the things that would get you jammed up. He used to have a saying— "No booze, snooze, or cooze."

This meant you shouldn't be drinking on the job, don't sleep on the job and don't mess with some of the women that you'll meet on this job.

Thomas M. Grubb & Allan "Lucky" Cole

Mike made this very clear, because I know two of the items he told me he was very strict about. The third I had learned about earlier while we were working together during our silent months.

I took notice that when we worked the four to twelve shift, oh, I'd guess it would be around nine, ten o'clock at night, we would always get this call of a prowler at this certain location.

Well, the first time it came out, like I said, I used to be the driver.

We would go to this location and he would tell me, "Tom, wait in the car."

O.K., I figured he knew what he was doing. And he would go into this house, it was like a three-story apartment building, and I thought he was going to go look for this prowler.

I just sat in the car. Maybe fifteen, twenty minutes, half an hour would pass. Then Mike would return to the car.

And I'd say to him, "What's goin' on?"

And he'd say, "Nothin' to it. False alarm. Unfounded."

That was our thing — "unfounded" — meaning that there was no incident at the place where we got the assignment.

So I'd just say, "O.K., Mike," and we'd just go back on the air and wait for our next assignment.

Well, this used to happen on every four to twelve shift that we worked. It was odd the first time it happened, didn't mean much to me. The second time it happened it still didn't mean much to me, but I began to wonder.

We got the same call of a prowler at the same location, and like I said, you learn to keep your mouth shut and your ears open.

And again Mike would spend a half hour in the place and come back to the car and say, "O.K., nothin's in there, kid. It's unfounded."

All right. This used to go on. Then, when I got in good standing with Mike, we got to be friends. Mike got another job at the same location, and it was on South 21st Street.

And we pulled up — the prowler call — and then he said, "Look," he said, "I'm gonna be a little while, Tom."

He said, "Let me tell you what's goin' on."

Thomas M. Grubb & Allan "Lucky" Cole

Because I figure he's gettin' out of the car and, God, if there is a prowler in there, I don't know if he's gonna get shot or hit in the head or hurt or what and I'm gonna be sittin' in the patrol car.

Now mind you, this is when I start to learn a little about the police department. Like always back up your partner, for sure. Even when he tells you not to.

Well, Mike told me there were two lady friends in there that used to work for the Bell Telephone Company. They were from upstate and evidently they got to know Mike somewhere along the line.

And Mike used to go in and actually service one of these ladies. Later on, he introduced me to them.

That was about the end of that. Any time there was a prowler call there, Mike would handle it. I wasn't into that. But those were some of the things you learned as you went along. And I didn't criticize the man. His business was his business.

It was during the period that I worked with Mike that these men used to come around to these districts, and they were salesmen.

They sold you shoes, you got measured for your uniform, and so forth. And you got a clothing allowance of a hundred dollars a year, and you purchased clothing up to a hundred dollars.

By then I had my uniform. And in that time we went and bought our pistols. We were told where to buy them and what to buy. You paid for all of this equipment.

Blackjack, handcuffs if you wanted to buy them, and your pistol, and whatever else you needed. Flashlights and so forth. Well, working with Mike I finally got to look like a police officer. And that was a big help.

Mike was the kind of cop, he minded his own business. He didn't look for trouble but he could certainly handle it when it arose.

I got a picture of him in a situation where there was a disturbance in a house, and it was kind of a party type of thing and it was in a black area. And we went in and it was a rowdy party.

Mike told me when you get into a domestic situation, the first thing you do is separate the man and the woman or whomever, and take them into other rooms and talk with them.

Thomas M. Grubb & Allan "Lucky" Cole

And try to be realistic in seeing what's going on, and how you can resolve it without actually arresting a person.

Mike was very good at this.

He used to have a lot of sayings like, "You don't want me to arrest your husband or your boyfriend because he's gonna be in jail. He ain't gonna be workin'. He can't take care of you."

Believe me, most of the time this would work.

And if this wasn't the clincher, he would take out this complaint that we had and he would tell 'em, "Now, c'mon, if you want him in jail, you gotta sign this complaint."

That wasn't realistic, but most of the people didn't know that. And as soon as they saw the paper, they wouldn't sign it. They would start mumblin' and grumblin', but they would not sign. So I learned that's the way to settle a lot of domestic arguments.

Thomas M. Grubb & Allan "Lucky" Cole

CHAPTER FIVE
The 24th Street Dukes

AFTER THIS I was pretty well on my way to becoming an officer. I had my six months' probation in. I stayed in the same squad. We did get a new sergeant, and it happened to be one of the fellas that was actually from one of the squads that we worked with.

When this occurred, Garry went back on the car with Mike Finney and I was kind of alone again.

When this new sergeant took over the squad, by then some other new men had come in, and I was assigned to a car with a fella that had a few months more than me in the business.

In other words, we were two rookies just past our probation period, and the sergeant liked us, and he put us on the car. This was Fred Cooper. He was our new sergeant. Our new street sergeant.

Like I said, by then a car had opened up. The regular guys that were on it either retired or were transferred to other units. But Fred put me and Johnny Bennett on this car together.

We were assigned to 97 Car. Now, 97 Car was the car that worked the Sixth Sector in our district. This sector went from Spring Garden Street up to Poplar Avenue.

In between there was Ridge Avenue and so forth, which were the worst places in the district to work, because it was primarily slums up in that area. And we had a lot of transients.

Like I said, it went from Spring Garden to Poplar, and from 20th Street back to the Schuylkill River. This also at this time included the abandoned car lot.

Part of our duty on this car was to check the abandoned car lot every couple of hours or so to see that nobody went in there and stripped the cars or what have you.

Also, to check on the officer that was assigned to the abandoned car lot. I learned that this was a black officer named Dave Dutton, who later became a very good friend of ours.

Like I mentioned, this particular sector that we worked was just about the worst sector in the district to work. You had all the lowlifes in there — Green Street, Mount Vernon Street, Wallace Street. These were the transients.

And just at the opposite side of the coin you had some very big hotels along the Parkway, where very prominent people worked. Such as your City Manager, your lawyers, doctors, and so forth. And you figure you're handling entirely different types of people, so you had to adjust your gears when handling them.

Also, I learned quickly that there was a gang of young men that used to hang out on 24th Street, which was part of our sector. And these guys used to just raise hell generally — stealing cars, fighting, bothering the residents of that area. And they were a very mixed group — blacks, whites, Puerto Ricans.

And they had a name. They called themselves "The 24th Street Dukes."

Now like I told you, Lucky, in the City of Philadelphia at that time there was only one radio band for all police cars. No matter what part of the city you worked. So whenever a call would come out, everybody in the city would hear that call.

Well, it just happened that we used to get calls, we'd be working like four to twelve particularly, we would get like three to four calls up to this corner. Just Disturbances, that would be the call. And when you went there the first time, you didn't know what to expect.

And we got these rowdy guys. And you would calm 'em down and tell 'em, "O.K., move on," and you would take a lot of static from them, y'know. But it got to be pretty repetitious, and the other squads that worked before us or after us, they used to get the same kind of calls.

It was actually a very, very hot spot on this corner, and everybody used to get the troubles that were caused up there. So we kinda got to know the different ones in the group.

We went up there a number of times and you tell 'em to move — y'know, you can't just take all the static from them, and you gotta get a little pushy, and you keep them off the corners.

As I said, every time you get a call to a location you would respond, your car number and where you were going. Well, this got to be so repetitious that there was what they called a jacket "good on the corner."

Thomas M. Grubb & Allan "Lucky" Cole

This means that any time, anybody on that corner, you would have to move them. And like I said, the other guys in the district also had this problem.

Well, it got so — it was in the summertime was the worst. And we would be up there every tour of duty, three, four times. And I didn't like it, 'cause you had to take the static from these guys, and Johnny didn't like it either.

So this one particular night, we went up on one of these calls, disturbance, fighting, so forth, in the street. Well, we went up there, and this was at 24th and Parrish.

And right on this corner was a place where we liked to eat. It was an Italian restaurant. Small place, but they served the pizzas and the macaroni and so forth.

I guess it was about six thirty, seven o'clock, we get up to this corner. And lo and behold, the same characters are out there, maybe 15 of them, 20 of them, raisin' hell.

So we went in, we put our gorilla suits on, y'know, start movin' 'em. And you could actually see the people in the neighborhood kinda watchin' what you're doing to see if you really do your job and kinda' cause a little peace in the area instead of these bums carryin' on.

Well, there was this one particular guy about my size, and he had the most mouth.

And the old thing used to be, "Aw, you guys ain't nothin', take them guns away and you ain't shit."

So I had just about as much as I could take, and I had Johnny beside me, and I took off my pistol and I gave it to Johnny.

And I grabbed this one punk and I told him, "You and me," I said, "C'mon. You're so bad. We're gonna try it. Now I don't have my pistol, I don't have my partner," and I said, "Just me and you. I don't want any of your boys."

And he, y'know, thought he was tough. "O.K., O.K.," and mutterin' and cursin' and so forth.

So we went off the corner. And right behind this corner started, like, the old factories and stuff, and we went up this side street between two factories. Well, Luck, we got it on.

Thomas M. Grubb & Allan "Lucky" Cole

And we were up there, barrelin' away, and I'll tell you, this kid was tough. He was a tough-ass. He was as tough as he talked.

But from Grandpop Guinan bein' a fighter in his old days — and I don't know if you know it or not, but I used to go to the gym myself when I was a kid.

I got a call, and we went down to the 48th Ward. That was the police station, 24th and Walton. And we learned to box. And I had some time in the ring, I had a few bouts. And actually, it was your Grandpop Guinan that got me to do this.

So when I had this kid on my hands up there, he was a street fighter. The kickin', the buttin', the this, the that, the other thing. The only way I could get off him was to actually box him.

And when I got to boxin' him, and he couldn't get to me, he really lost his head. And that's when I got to him. Well, it went on for a while, and after a while, after I knocked him down five or six times, he figured that he wasn't tough enough to stand up.

I grabbed him, we were kind of punched up, and I took him by the back of the neck and I drug him around the corner.

And there's all his friend standin' there.

And I told 'em, "Now. He's had his. Which one'a youse are the second-toughest in this gang?"

Lucky, nobody stood up. Nobody said a word. And I looked at Johnny, and Johnny was there just more or less holdin' them off so they wouldn't come around while we were doin' our thing.

And nobody said a word. That was it.

And I told 'em, I said, "When I work, this corner belongs to me." I said, "I don't wanna see any of you around or you get the same as him."

Lucky, that was the best thing I ever did in the police department. But if I ever got caught I would'a been fired. See, you just can't do those things, but this was the only way to resolve a situation like this.

I got back in the car, they all took off. I don't know if the neighbors saw us, or what, or anything. I tried to keep it very private. And I was lumped up a little bit.

So we just got in the car, I went over to Hahnemann, got cleaned up a little bit. I was scraped up and stuff. And not another thing was ever said about it.

We just went along with the job after that. And we would patrol our area, like I said, and whenever we went by this particular location, this group was not there. And actually, you could hear things from the neighbors.

Like, "Gee whiz. There's been no problems on the corner here."

The guy in the store I told you about, the Italian restaurant there, he was very, very friendly to us after this. 'Cause, y'know, they used to hang out in his joint, and they didn't hang out there any more.

So this went on and maybe, oh, a month or so passed by, and, this day, we're called into the district. Now this is funny, this is what I wanted to tell you. We had a captain that got transferred in just after Christmas. His name was Abe Gold.

Well, Abe Gold was about five foot tall. And four foot wide. And he was Jewish. And Abe Gold, although he was the most belligerent, nasty talkin' man, insult you up and down, he would never hurt a cop. When I say hurt 'em, like, suspend 'em.

His theory was, "I could get to you and do this, but who would it hurt? It would hurt your family. And you ain't worth it."

So I liked the man for that reason.

But my partner Johnny was scared to death of Abe Gold. Why, I don't know.

When you would go to roll call — like I told you, it's twice a day, you went on in the morning or evening, and then you hadda check off. Well, Johnny had this habit. He used to always hold the front of his cap with his thumb and forefinger, and the thumb would be right over his nose. And it was like he was hiding.

Whenever Johnny hadda go near the captain for any reason, he would practically wet his pants. Why I don't know, but he was definitely afraid of this man.

So after this incident occurred, like I said, a month or so later, we're out in the street and we get a call to come into headquarters to see the captain. Well, when we got calls like that, any time, for headquarters, Johnny would say, "Go ahead, Tom, you go in."

Thomas M. Grubb & Allan "Lucky" Cole

And it didn't bother me any, 'cause I knew I didn't do anything wrong, I thought, and I would go in. Well, Johnny never would.

But this day, the captain wanted to see both of us. So I went in and I talked to the captain for a minute, and he says, "Where's Bennett?"

"He's out in the car."

Says, "Go get him."

I went back out to the car to get Johnny. And when I told Johnny, "The captain wants to see you," he says, "Ah, you're kiddin'. You've gotta be kiddin'."

I said, "John, he wants to see you."

He wouldn't believe me. He thought I was kidding with him. And I'll tell you why, later. Well anyway, I finally almost hadda pull him outta the car to go in and see Abe Gold, the Captain.

Well, we get into the captain's office. And the captain wants to talk to us and he's got our patrol logs.

Now I didn't touch much on this, but you have a patrol log when you go on duty. And every radio call you get is listed on your patrol log. And every place that you had to check, or anything, you kept the time of everything you did in your eight-hour tour.

I went in, and lo and behold, the captain's sittin' on his desk, and he had these logs on his table.

He says, "I want to see you first, Grubb."

I said, "Yes, sir."

And Johnny went out into the outer office.

The captain says, "What's goin' on out there, at 24th and Parrish?"

At first I thought, "Oh, Christ, I'm caught."

I said, "Nothin' that I'm aware of, Captain."

He said, "Well, I've been checkin' your logs, here," he says, "I see you check the corner. But you've got no radio calls there."

I said, "That's right, sir."

He said, "Well, how come everybody else gets radio calls to that corner, and when you and Bennett are working you don't get any calls to that corner?"

He said, "I've checked the logs for the last month or so, and you just never get calls there." He said, "Is there a reason?"

Well, I didn't know if he knew what happened up there, but I wasn't going to admit it. If he found out, he was gonna have to tell me.

So I just said, "No sir, Captain, we had no problems up there. We just don't get any calls there."

He looked at me, like sayin', "O.K.," and nothin' more. Must'a known what happened, but he didn't say it.

He said, "Well, we got a Commissioner's Jacket on that corner," he said, "but now I'm gonna raise it, because it seems to be under control."

I said, "Whatever you think is best, Captain," and that was it.

That was my conversation with him.

Well, then Johnny went in. And if you've ever seen a guy frightened half to death, it was this guy, Johnny Bennett. He just could not be around the captain. He would shake, and he would hide under his thumb.

Actually, it was funny. It was really comical. I couldn't understand it. Johnny went in, and Johnny wasn't in there three minutes.

And the captain threw him out of the office. I guess he knew that it wasn't Johnny's thing to take care of that corner.

But that was our first big thing in the district. And I think we got a little reputation from that, because if you could clean a corner off from these gang guys it was a big thing, and we never got calls.

And the captain wanted to know, "How we didn't get 'em and everybody else gets 'em?"

I said, "I don't know, Captain. I guess we're just around there when nobody else is."

So that was the end of that. But it was quite an experience, and that's when I started to like the captain. If you could get a job done, any way you'd do it, he wasn't gonna rat on you. 'Cause no doubt he had heard what had happened up there. P

Thomas M. Grubb & Allan "Lucky" Cole

CHAPTER SIX
Patrol (I)

SO THAT WAS the beginning of our partnership on that car, Johnny and me. And we got along well. Johnny actually only lived around the corner from us, when we lived down on 28th Street. Johnny lived on Marsden Street. And we got to be good friends. I mean socially as well as working together.

Your Aunt Cassie became friends with Jimmy's wife, Dee Bennett, and they used to spend time together. So it was a nice situation. And off duty we would play with the ball team and stuff like that. So our working relationship was great and we were getting to learn how to be police officers.

Johnny had some funny ways about him, but he was a good partner. I decided that most of the time I would do the driving and Johnny'd be the recorder. In that period of time, that was our first thing that we got some recognition for with the captain.

The other guys in the squad used to come up when we'd change squads, and ask what the hell happened up there that we don't get calls to that corner and they do.

Nobody ever said a word. Johnny never opened his mouth, nor did I.

But time went on and we became a little more seasoned. One thing I wanted to mention, we used to cover that lower sector where the abandoned car lot was. Dave Dutton was assigned down there.

Well, the reason I learned Dave Dutton was assigned there, 'cause Dave was a drinker. He was the nicest guy you'd ever wanta meet, and we would go down there during, like, day work or four to twelve. It was desolate.

And we would shoot. And we would shoot the rats, or we'd set up targets and shoot. Johnny was a good shot. I guess he learned it in the service like I did. We used to go down there and Dave Dutton used to set up targets and we'd shoot 'em down.

We used to tease him, y'know, tell him, "Dave, you gonna shoot us?"

"Hell, no, I ain't shootin' nothin'."

All we would do with Dave was feed him outta the jug, we would pick up a jug for him to, y'know, have his "taste" down there. And he was really a good guy to know.

Later on, we used to have what they called "subway duty" together.

The sergeant used to tell us, "Well look, I don't wanta break you guys up, so both of you will pull subway duty the first day of every tour."

And he said, "Since you've become friends with Dave Dutton, I'm gonna put him with you, too."

That was kinda lousy duty. You walked the subways all night. And you didn't walk together. At Broad and Race the subway used to split out and go in three different directions. We patrolled these different areas.

And of course, at maybe an hour or two intervals, you would meet where you started out from. And we'd sit and talk for a few minutes or have a smoke or whatnot.

After a while, when we started to pull this pretty steady, Dave Dutton's girlfriend used to come down to the subway. This is when we would be on twelve to eight or last out.

And this lady used to bring down lunch. And when I say lunch, I mean a real lunch, like a picnic. She brought down a basket.

And in that basket would be the chicken, or the chops, collard greens, everything you could think of. She'd bring down the collard greens, and they were hot, and she'd also bring down chitlins. Well, I had heard of chitlins, but I had never tasted them.

And we used to sit there, and she'd have the bowls and stuff, and we would eat. I mean we would eat for a half-hour.

And then she had the taster, too. She'd always bring down a little bottle for Dave. And that got to be routine. Really, it was something you kinda looked forward to. And we did that for two years.

After several of these midnight dinners, Dave's lady friend realized that I wasn't drinking, or Johnny, so she would bring down sodas for us, or some lemonade, or whatever. It really got to be a welcome and an anticipated affair every time we pulled the subway duty.

47

Thomas M. Grubb & Allan "Lucky" Cole

Maybe I haven't been really specific in some of these tapes, but at that time there were officers known as "ginks." These ginks were created by Internal Affairs just to catch officers off base doing the wrong thing. By the wrong thing, I mean in my day it was very strict in the police department.

Be it whatever, cold or hot, Number One, there were no air conditioners in your patrol cars. Two, you wore a uniform, and when I say a uniform, a complete uniform.

You wore your tie up to the collar. You always wore your cap. If a gink caught you with your cap off or your tie down, you went to the front.

Now, the front was an expression they used when they take you to suspend you. And for each of these varying offenses you could be suspended for a week or ten days or two weeks. And of course you received no pay while you were suspended.

So the ginks were something you always had to keep your eye out for while you were on duty.

Also, there was a smoking ban while you were on duty. You could not smoke from sunup to sundown. And this was strictly enforced, be it you were on the street, in the car, or out on patrol.

Well as you can guess, when you're on the twelve to eight shift — three, four o'clock in the morning, you're tired. You might wanta sit down or whatever, and that's when these ginks would show up.

Sometimes they worked in pairs, other times alone. And at my time, they were all sergeants. Prior to this they were lieutenants or captains or even inspectors. But in our case it was always sergeants.

And there were two infamous ginks known as Dunny and Getman. They seemed to be the ones that could get the most officers off-base and have them suspended.

Well, as a young officer I never saw these guys. I just didn't know who they were. I just knew their rank, and that they did wear a uniform.

On one of these occasions I was down the subway and I forget which area I happened to be working. But I had been sitting, like, on the turnstile, because I'd covered the subway maybe six times, I was a little beat.

I just had gotten up, and as I got up I turned around, and lo and behold here's this uniformed sergeant. And I looked at him and he looked at me and I was in full uniform the way you should be.

He approached.

"What's your name, officer?"

And being's as he was a sergeant, I gave him my name. He already had my badge number.

And I asked him, I said, "Anything wrong, sergeant?"

He said, "No, not this time," he said, "but I'll tell you who I am. I'm Sergeant Getman."

"Sergeant Getman," I said, "nice to meet you."

I knew who he was. But I knew that I hadn't done anything wrong, so he couldn't do a thing to me.

He took out a log and he asked me, "Do you have your log, officer?"

Which I did. I had it folded up in my pocket. And that son-of-a-gun, he signed my log. So that was the first encounter I had with the ginks.

Later in my career I learned a lot about them. But that was it for the first time.

And if I didn't mention it, Lucky, with the log, it was a sheet of paper which you kept on a clipboard in the car. This was prior to us ever having incident reports, which came out the next year or two.

What you did, you'd get a call, you'd mark the time you got the call in your log. You would take the assignment, and when you completed the assignment and went back on the air by radio, you would mark in the time. So everything was documented in your log — what you did on your tour of duty.

Also I should indicate that you had to mark your starting mileage on your log, and your completed mileage at the end of your tour of duty.

Now according to sectors, it pretty much standardized the amount of miles you had traveled. And if you didn't have a lot of assignments, you wouldn't travel as many miles.

Since I'm telling you about the subway detail that we pulled once each week at the first day of our tour of duty, there was also another detail known as "the windows." This was in the Center City

Section on Chestnut Street. Say from Broad to, oh, 18th or 19th Street.

And this was to check on the windows to see that they weren't broken, no places were burglarized. And you could check front and sometimes in the rear of these various business locations.

We didn't get the windows that much, because like I told you, we had this new sergeant, and he liked us, and he liked to keep us together. And the windows was only a one-man assignment, so usually we didn't pull that, except in extreme emergencies.

Also, Luck, I'll tell you that we didn't have many men in the district at this time. And a lot of times you would work what they would call a "one man car."

That would be if your partner was off, or perhaps another team didn't show up, and you or your partner would be asked to work another car. So from time to time we worked one man cars.

Now this isn't a very enjoyable thing. First, all the nights are very long and so are the days. Nobody to talk to. And also, it was dangerous in a lot of ways.

Big things at this time were car stops, where you would stop cars for some reason — suspicious, not being where they belonged — just any reason that you thought was reasonable cause to stop that vehicle. One man in a car at this time was a dangerous situation.

There was one way to compensate for this. Your squad would know who's working one man cars. So what would happen is that, maybe the car from the adjoining sector, if you had the right kind of guys in it, would go over to where you got the call.

Now this wasn't entirely authorized. You were not supposed to leave your sector, but sometimes the guys would do it.

Secondly, we had two wagons in the district which were always two men. What would happen would be, the wagon that was working your sector or near your sector would come in to make sure you were all right or to back you up. This was good in many a way.

Thomas M. Grubb & Allan "Lucky" Cole

CHAPTER SEVEN
The Wagon (I)

LIKE IS SAID, Johnny and I worked together, and for some reason, some guy screwed up or something on a wagon. So our sergeant, Fred Cooper — like I said, he took a liking to us, he knew we did our job. And he assigned us to this wagon — often referred to as the "meat wagon."

In a case like this, this wagon came from another squad. So what would happen is that half the week we worked the car, and half of the week we worked on this wagon.

Well, this was the best of two worlds, because the car worked the upper end of the district and the wagon would work the lower end of the district.

Now, we had two wagons. The borderline was Spring Garden Street, which was the center of the district from river to river.

And one wagon worked south of Spring Garden, the other worked the north of Spring Garden up to our outer borders, which in one case was Chestnut Street, the other case it was Poplar Street.

So we had a very good thing going there, 'cause you weren't bored, you were doing actually every job that could be handled in the district in one manner or another.

You know, as usual in any organization, when something like this happens, there were other guys that wanted to have these jobs, specially the wagon. And they would gripe and bitch.

And the sergeant that we had, like I said, he was a good guy, and when he'd hear the grumblin' he'd just stand up at roll call and he'd tell 'em why he had put us on the car.

And he told 'em, he said, "These are the guys that do the job. There's no job too big or too small for them to handle."

Again, when he said this, it was a boost up for us, and a lot of guys didn't particularly care for it, but they got over it.

And also, with the sergeant's faith in both of us, we would handle any job that was, y'know, a little off-color or somethin' for him, because it was him that asked us. He didn't have to ask us, he could order us, but he wasn't like that.

I'll explain a little bit to you about the wagon. The wagon was manned by two officers. In the wagon, you did have handcuffs. They were bolted to a section of the front of the dashboard.

Like I said, we never had handcuffs, and at that time money was too tight to even buy them.

I figured, if I couldn't hold the bums, I would take care of them in another way.

A wagon's duties is primarily to handle hospital cases of all natures, or transfer various things such as barricades, red lights, and what have you, to the different locations where they were needed.

Personally, I enjoyed working the wagon simply because you always had your partner with you. Only some of the cases you would get on the wagon would really turn your stomach and others, y'know, were just normal.

Ill — sick people — would make a call to the radio central and a wagon would be dispatched to take 'em to the nearest hospital in your district. Of course, there were elderly people who needed hospital attention.

They would have a heart attack, a stroke, or any of the various illnesses they needed to go to a hospital for. We got many, many of these. Working a wagon you were usually pretty busy.

I found as time went by one of the things that Iron Mike told me about was, "Kid, always look to see if there's gonna be a full moon," he said, "If there's a full moon out, you're gonna get every kook, nut, lunatic that's out there calling for some reason or another, and you're gonna bust your hump your tour of duty."

Well, he didn't exaggerate one bit. When that full moon came out, you got all the nuts around. Now we both know that lunatic is a name from Luna, the moon. And when the moon came out, all the lunatics came out with it.

This was also a thing: that the district cars used to like to call the wagons. They weren't permitted to transport a pregnant woman, or anything of that nature, or a bleeding victim, to the hospital.

Anything of that nature, they would call for the wagon. Or when they had to transport a person they had arrested to the district, nine times out of ten they'd ask for a wagon.

And of course we would take 'em to the district, or to City Hall, or Central Detective Division, whatever was required.

Also I learned, in a wagon, you used to compete with the adjoining district, which was the Sixth District, which was exactly in size the same as our district, the Ninth.

The Ninth District used to operate west of Broad Street, while the Sixth District operated east of Broad Street to the Delaware River.

If you were working four to twelve, and something happened at say, eleven thirty, quarter to twelve, a radio call would come out for a wagon from the Sixth District. Somehow, they'd all be busy.

They were busy, so that meant the adjoining district wagon would have to take the assignment. Well, I got stuck many a time like that until I learned how to play the game.

Now when we went to the Sixth District, it was usually down to what they used to call Skid Row. This was where all the derelicts used to be in the flea bag hotels, you know, fifty-cent-a-night flops. Well, when you got down there, you knew you were, you were gonna have a problem of one nature or another.

Usually it was the older men, that's all that stayed in these flophouses, and they were filthy. The body lice you could actually see jumping off their bodies. And many a time Johnny and I went down there, and that was the reason I learned that you'd better wear gloves.

'Cause I used to see some of the other guys wearin' 'em, but at that time I just didn't wear them. But I learned.

We used to go into these flophouses, and these guys laid on cots in little cubicles five feet wide, eight feet long. And they were older men, like I said, and the clothes they wore they, y'know, they coulda' been years and years old.

Well, they would mess themselves and what have you, and on one occasion we went in to extract a man from this place, Johnny and I.

As we got near him, you could actually see the body lice jumping off his body, jumping up. And body lice, if you don't know it, they're bad characters. You don't want to get 'em on you.

53

And what we would do, is we would transport these poor souls to the hospital.

Now we'd be past our tour of duty, mind you, we're over at midnight. But we would get 'em to the hospital by midnight or quarter after, and they would be lying on a stretcher in the back of our wagon.

Well, soon as the orderlies found out what we had in the wagon — we'd go in and tell 'em — they used to come out with a can of ether, and actually spray the wagon after they removed the person.

And they'd throw a blanket over him immediately. That's so the lice wouldn't get on them, and they'd take him in, and it was the oddest thing, you couldn't get your stretcher back.

And you knew every wagon had to have a stretcher. So we'd have to leave the stretcher there, and what they would do, they would disinfect the stretcher with ether. Ether somehow killed body lice. But it would also knock you out if you stood around it too long.

So we had to let the wagon air out for ten or fifteen minutes before we could get back in and proceed to headquarters and check off.

Many a night when gettin' bagged on one of these jobs that should have been handled by a different district, we wouldn't get off duty till maybe twelve thirty, one o'clock.

These are some of the things you learn as a young officer. Still a rookie, actually. And we remained rookies for five years.

You're no longer considered a rookie after five years, 'cause that's when you've got full pay. Which wasn't that much money, I think it was five thousand dollars at that time.

Thomas M. Grubb & Allan "Lucky" Cole

CHAPTER EIGHT
Patrol (II)

LUCK, I ALWAYS like to say this. Although you were a policeman — you had your uniform and badge and carried a gun — that did not make you a tough guy. A lot of officers didn't realize that and they thought those things could get them through any situation, but to their regret they found out that it didn't.

Well, my partner Johnny, like I said, was a great guy and I loved working with him. Johnny was great at makin' up our reports, fillin' out our logs, and things of this nature. But Johnny wasn't a fighter. By nature he just wasn't a fighter.

But he was good company and I couldn't ask for a better partner, because I knew whatever situation we got into, he was there behind me. He may not be able to do much, but I knew he was there, and a lot of times this deters a lot of trouble.

And, just — some of the things we did, I'll relate a few incidents.

We used to get a disturbance in a house, oh, often. Quite often. And it was the oddest situation. We'd get up to this particular house, I think it was on either Wallace or Mount Vernon Street.

And when we'd go in, this older woman, I mean an older woman, used to answer the door, and she was always banged up.

Bleeding from the nose and her mouth or whatnot, and the first time we went there she said, "My son, my son, you've got to take him out. You've gotta take him outta the house."

I looked at the lady and I said, "Your son?"

Well, I met her son. This happened to be a black family, and her son was — demented, I guess, is the best word to say.

He was slow, he was retarded, but God Almighty, he was built like a bull. I mean, he had shoulders and a chest that you could hide behind.

We used to go in there, and the first time I was — "Gee, this guy beat his mother up. He's gotta be a real creep."

And we went into the living room of this place, and here he was, he was in there.

I said to Johnny, "C'mon, we've gotta take this guy out."

Well, he got up, and that's when I saw what he looked like.

I told Johnny, I said, "This guy scares me, man."

We tried talking to him. Well, to make a long story short, that didn't get us anywhere.

So I told Johnny, I said, "Go ahead, go over there and c'mon, we'll grab him, get him in the car, take him out."

Well, that was a big mistake.

He grabbed Johnny and threw Johnny from the living room out into the hallway. Then I made my grab at him, and he threw me against the wall.

So then, it's a different story. He's assaulted us. Well, we started on this guy, and let me tell you we hit him with everything but a chair.

And we couldn't get to him, and then finally I was able to get my arm around his neck. And, Lucky, in my younger days, I don't think there was anybody any stronger than I was. I held him around the neck so long and so tight, I thought I was chokin' him to death.

Anyway, he went down to his knees. And that was it. Temporarily, I cut off his air, and people go unconscious. Well, that was it.

By this time, Johnny was bleedin', I was bleedin', I'm sore all over. And we got this bum out. And we got him into the car.

We got him into the district, and in the district he started again. A couple of guys from the house that were in the district helped us get him in the cell room. Well, this guy was like an animal. I swear to God, Mike Tyson was a saint compared to him.

Then we kinda got a history from the mother, that another car brought in. And she told us he's the nicest guy most of the time, but every so often he goes off his rocker and he beats her up. And the woman said it's a wonder she wasn't dead from him.

Well, Lucky, that was our first encounter with this individual.

After a while, we got to learn that this was a regular call that we would get to go to this location and it was always the same thing.

Now you didn't get him every week, but it wasn't much longer than that. If you happened to be on the tour of duty when this guy flipped out, you would get the assignment. Well, we got to learn about him pretty good.

56

I learned that this guy usually went berserk and beat on his mother when there was a full moon. And if you were workin' the four to twelve, because they lived in our sector, I believe it was up on Mount Vernon Street or Bowers Street, we would get the call.

And you knew just what to expect.

We did have to go back to this place one evening and it was the same thing. The mother called, and again we saw this lady. She was kinda beat up, bleeding.

And we went in.

This character was sitting on the stairway. Like I said, he wasn't too tall, maybe five eight, five nine, but he was strong as a bull. He hadda weigh a couple hundred pounds, easy.

And this time, instead of fightin' him, I realized the guy was psycho, so the best thing to do in a case like this, which I learned from my instructor, Mike Finney, was try to talk to him. We could always "stick" him later.

We went in and I stood there, and I just talked to the man, and I talked to his mother, and didn't make any aggressive moves toward him.

Well, first thing I thought was, "Christ, how'm I gonna get this guy out of here without him and me goin' to the hospital?"

I looked at Johnny and I said, "Johnny, we ain't gonna go through this again."

And I got to learn from his mother, talking to her, that he liked ice cream.

So I kinda got closer to him, talkin' with him and everything. And I talked to him about ice cream.

The funniest thing was, he didn't jump off the stairs on us like I expected him to do. He remained kinda cool, but just lookin' into his eyes you could see that the man wasn't right. So what was I going to do?

I looked at Johnny and I told him, "Ice cream, Johnny, this guy goes for ice cream."

I asked Johnny, I said, "Where the hell's the closest place you can get some ice cream?"

This was Doc's Pharmacy up at 20th and Fairmount.

Thomas M. Grubb & Allan "Lucky" Cole

So Johnny left. He was back in a couple of minutes and I occupied this guy talkin'. And Johnny come in with this big double-decker. And he just stood there.

And the guy was lookin' at him, lookin' at the ice cream, lookin' at me, lookin' at him, and Johnny was kinda eatin' the ice cream and the guy was watchin' very carefully.

I took the ice cream from Johnny and I asked him, "Hey, whattya say? Would you like some ice cream?"

I said, "C'mon, we'll go get some ice cream. You and me and, y'know, we'll get some for your mother, too."

He just gave me a look like, he didn't know if I was tellin' the truth, or lyin'.

So I took the ice cream and I said, "Here, pal."

I gave him the ice cream. And like you would see a child, I mean a little child, he got his whole face down into it.

And, Christ, before you knew it, the ice cream was gone.

So I told the mother, and I asked Johnny, I said, "Whattya say, Johnny, we try to get him out now?"

I told the guy, "Hey, we got more ice cream out in the car." I said, "You want to come with us and we'll get you some more?"

Lucky, it was like a miracle. He got up from the steps and he walked out with us. No fightin', no bouncin' off the walls, nothing.

Because we had gone through this once, and boy, believe me, it wasn't a pleasure.

We got him outside and like I said, we didn't have handcuffs. So we got him into the car. And the first thing we did is, we went right around to the drugstore and got some more ice cream for him.

And he wanted to get out, but I left Johnny in the car with him to hold him there. I got him ice cream. I don't know if I got him a half-pint or what. And then we drove him right in to the district. And we booked him for assault and so forth.

That was the beginning of learning how to handle certain individuals that you get to know that are on your sector or on your beat. And instead of fighting all the time, you handle them in different ways. Different strokes for different folks, as the saying goes.

Thomas M. Grubb & Allan "Lucky" Cole

I want you to go back and listen to what I told you about when we used to have to go to the flophouses and get these street people, as we call them today. In our day, we just called them bums. And what we used to do after we'd get them over to the hospital and get them de-loused.

When I used to go home, I would go in the back alley and the gate would be open, and your Aunt Cassie would open the gate for me.

And what I used to do, we'd decided on this much earlier, Cass and I, I would go out, and I would just change my whole uniform out in the yard, even though it had ether on it and everything else. To kill what might be on the uniform.

She would throw me out soap, a towel and a robe, and I would change out in the back yard. And then I would go into the house and have another shower. This was almost a constant thing, at least once a month.

I guess the neighbors figured I was nuts, because every morning they'd see a uniform hangin' up on the clothesline.

As time progressed, we got to be a little better than rookies, and we were accepted by most of the fellas that we worked with, because we worked with different guys each week. Changing of the squads, and so forth. And we got to know a lot of the other fellas.

This in itself was an experience because, believe me, Lucky, cops can be the weirdest son-of-a-guns you can ever come across.

There were the braggarts, and the drunks, and the ones that weren't too honest. You would just have to know who was who, and what they were liable to do, and thank God you didn't have to work with them too often.

There were some who always told you their prowess with the ladies and liked to brag about things that men shouldn't really talk about.

Then there were the ones that always talked about where you could get the free booze at any time, and so forth, the free food. This was just something, it was natural for them, but it was all new to us.

And then you had the other ones that would tell you how you could actually shirk your duty and kind of get over on your supervisors.

59

Thomas M. Grubb & Allan "Lucky" Cole

Like I said, you learned these things and you judged for yourself what you would do in any of the given situations.

It just happened one night during the rather cold weather, Johnny and I were patrolling and we saw an elderly man, what you would call a bum, and he was asleep on the bench in one of the areas by the district.

I mean it was really cold, it was like ten below, or something of that nature.

So figuring this poor guy's gonna be a stiff by morning, we picked him up.

It was almost a common thing with some of the good cops that they would take a drunk into the district even if he wasn't drunk, and put him in a cell where he'd at least stay warm for the night and survive the weather.

Well, on this one particular occasion we brought this guy in and he was rather a young man. And he was kind of rammy from the booze, and we took him in and we booked him for DK, which is drunk and disorderly.

That wasn't a big charge, because usually in the morning they would stand them up before a magistrate who would discharge them.

But before they'd get out of the place you'd have them sweep up the whole district and wash down the cell room and some things of that nature, y'know.

When we brought this guy in it seemed that two of these cops took a dislike to him. And after he was out of our custody, they took him back to the cell room and they kind of put a hurtin' on the man for no obvious reason that I knew of, because I wasn't there.

I didn't learn about it until the next morning when I saw the guy with his fat lip and eyes swollen and what not. And he told me, you know, what had occurred, which was uncalled for.

I couldn't do anything at that time, but I just remembered it. If you arrest somebody, you take him back to the cells yourself.

You see, when they were stood up before the magistrate in the morning, you were the arresting officer and had to be there. And more or less explain the situation, why you brought them in, and that would be it.

Well, when the magistrate looked at this guy, kinda punched up, and then he looked over at Johnny and me, he kinda wondered, "Christ, what the hell's going on?"

He didn't say too much, but it was just his attitude — "Boy, this guy musta really resisted you fellas."

And we let it go at that.

Later on I learned who it was that walked him back to the cell room. And, just a coincidence, we were working the wagon this evening for the Twelfth and we were up on the Ridge, which is Ridge Avenue.

And this particular cop was in the car by himself. Like I said before, you would usually go up when you knew it was a one-man car to make sure the guy didn't get into trouble or get involved in something that he couldn't handle, where a few more cops on the scene would be very beneficial.

Well, we pulled up to this guy and Johnny leaned out the window and he just said to him, a phrase we used to use, "Are you awright?"

This guy come back at Johnny with a lot of static, and "You guys think you're hot shots," and "God damn it, I'm all right and I don't need you, get out of here, you're off your sector." All this nonsense and that.

This rubbed me very wrong.

I got out of the wagon and I told him, I said, "You don't need to act like this," I said, "We're here to help you."

He gave me a lot of bullshit, and pushed me. Now we're out in the street. You don't disgrace yourself out in the street with another officer.

So I told him, I said, "Look. You want to settle this?" I said, "You see me back in the garage."

Well, that was it. We went back and we went into the district and parked the wagon. And this guy, who was an arrogant sucker, he came into the garage and well, me and him had it out there.

And we made it very clear to each other just how we felt. No need to say I was fortunate enough to come out on top of the situation.

And he was unconscious in the garage.

61

Thomas M. Grubb & Allan "Lucky" Cole

After that, Lee, the turnkey, must've gone in and said somethin' to the house sergeant, 'cause he came out and they got this guy on his feet and kind of straightened him out. And the sergeant wanted to know what was wrong.

The only thing I could say was, "Sergeant, you ask this guy what was wrong and perhaps he'll tell you."

That was more or less the end of that, because a sergeant's a smart man, and all I meant was, "It's a personal matter."

And they like you to settle personal matters among yourselves and not involve any of the Higher Authority.

That was the end of that situation. And Johnny and I went back on patrol and more or less finished up our tour of duty.

From time to time you would come across some of the officers that were, y'know, they were just out of line and weren't doing what they should be doing.

But you kept your mouth shut unless it became a personal thing between you and this other guy. All too often it did get that way.

Lucky, 'member I told you I worked just about the whole district between being in both the patrol car and the wagon. This particular Friday or Saturday evening it was, we got a call down to this hotel on Arch Street.

And we knew that it was, not a flop joint, but a place where the cheaters used to go. And on the weekends it was always full up.

Well, it seems that the captain made the call for us to meet him there. Right away, I pretty much smelled what it was.

This was a raid, Lucky.

If you've ever seen it on TV or anything, you go in, and of course there were other officers there. Our wagon was merely for the transportation of who was going to get arrested.

They go to the floors and knock at the doors and various men and women come out and there's hundreds of excuses why they're there, and what they're doing, and they're not doing anything, and all this sort of stuff. Well anyway, we arrested quite a few people.

The funniest thing was, when we brought 'em into the district, they arrested all the men and they sat all the women outside in the roll room. Then the captain instructed the house sergeant to call the spouse of each married person that was there.

Well, there were several of the women that were married. And we, as transportation for the prisoners, were ordered to stay there and guard them.

Lucky, it was a shame and yet it was funny. The husbands started to come in. Some husbands kept it under control. Some didn't. And the women were in various modes of dress. Some had clothes on, some were nude under their coats.

And it was really pitiful. I didn't like the thing at all, but I was under orders and I did what I was told.

Well, we watched these husbands come in. And a few of them were pretty angry, but they held it in and they didn't get violent.

This one man came in and he didn't look too angry at all. And he went up to the desk and the sergeant gave him the copy, what was going on and all this and that.

And he turned around to his wife very nonchalantly and he hit her a shot and drove her halfway across the goddamn roll room.

Right away Johnny grabbed him and I went to see if the woman was conscious or unconscious. I got her up to her feet and this was one that was wearing the fur coat and she was nude. Well, she was split open, all her mouth and everything else, and that was a hospital case and we knew it.

The house sergeant just said, "Call the captain."

The captain was in the back room, and he came out and he looked at this woman, and what he said was not very nice. And the husband was really angry.

So he said, "Lock him up. Lock him up for assault."

And that's what we did. We charged the husband with assault.

The house sergeant says, "Well, Captain, what about her?"

He says, "Let her go."

And that was it. We locked the old man up and let her go. We didn't even take her to the hospital.

The next morning I couldn't help but stand there and wait for those hearings, because it was really a riot.

This woman was back in there and her face was like black and blue and puffed up. And the husband was there and we had to charge him with assault and battery.

And the magistrate in those days was really comical. He wanted to know the whole story, and we told him our part of it. And he didn't do nothin' to the guy, he just let him go, really.

He told him, "You can't do this stuff," and blah, blah, blah. But he let him go.

It wasn't until quite a while later I understood that a young woman who was workin' outta this hotel had come in and was yellin' murder, that she was raped — that's why we were there.

Well, when I got the whole story, I found out that she was a prostitute. That she went in there with a guy, and the guy didn't give her all the money that she wanted. So she figured she's gonna yell rape.

That was just a joke. We checked her out and she had three or four prostitution arrests. And the guy was just a rather young fella and we talked to him, and that was it. Nothing else ever happened about that.

But the point was, we never, ever, used to bother the people in those hotels. It was a very quiet place, but we knew what it was used for, mostly. They had regular tenants in there, also.

But that was my first raid, as you might call it, on a house of ill repute.

I neglected to say that, while we were going through the place, a number of people slipped by us, perhaps with help or without help, but I just couldn't see people gettin' arrested for that.

They all consented to be there, and this was just a bitch of a thing to do.

Still and all, we arrested quite a few people there, including the owner of the hotel and the manager and so forth.

Thomas M. Grubb & Allan "Lucky" Cole

CHAPTER NINE
The Wagon (II)

WE LEARNED THAT that while you're working the wagon, usually around three o'clock in the morning, you would get a radio call which would be, these are the exact numbers, "5292," then, "Contact the medical examiner's office."

Of course, the first time we heard this it was all new to us. So we went over to the hospital and we contacted the coroner's office, medical examiner, whatever you want to call him, and they instructed us to pick up a body and bring it to the morgue. Well, that we did.

We had to pull around from where we normally pulled into the hospital to the morgue area. They'd have a body in there, and we'd go in and we'd sign for the body and then we'd remove it to take it to the morgue.

In our day they'd just wrap these bodies up, not in sheets, but in kind of a, oh, butcher-type paper that they used to wrap meats in and so forth, like a brownish wrapping paper.

So they would take the body out on their gurney and we would put it on the stretcher and take it into the wagon. And then we'd proceed to the morgue.

We're at the morgue, at three o'clock in the morning, four o'clock in the morning, a very desolate place. It was only, God, a ten-minute ride from the hospital, fifteen at the most if you went slow. And we would back the wagon up into the loading dock of the morgue and buzz the attendant out.

Then we would take the body and bring it into the morgue, have the papers signed, and release the body to them. That was about the size of it and the normal transportation job.

Well, no need to say, the first time I went to the morgue it was a hell of an experience and we had a kind of a weirdo that worked in there and he knew right away.

"Say, I never seen you fellas before."

And y'know, you just said, "Yeah, that's right."

And he would commence to show you the various parts of the morgue. Like what they did with the bodies, and then he'd pull you into the, what they called the refrigerator room.

And he'd show you the different stiffs in there and they had 'em layin' out on slabs and whatnot. Well, this wasn't very exciting, but it was educational.

In the course of time in uniform I transported a lot of bodies, and to say the least, there were some very, very comical experiences while transporting them.

This one instance, we took a man, he was at a wedding, and he just dropped dead, no doubt from a heart attack or whatever. And we picked him up at the hospital, and we get him into the wagon, and usually I drove and Johnny would be the recorder.

Well, we're en route to the morgue when I heard these sounds in the back of the wagon. I didn't know what they were.

They were sorta like groans or "umms," this sorta thing, and then the next thing I know, this body sat straight up on the gurney in the wagon.

I look in the rearview mirror, and I see this stiff sittin' up and the paper musta fallen off his face. I'm gonna tell you, Lucky, I got scared as hell. I didn't know what was going on.

And I practically hadda hold on to Johnny, so that he didn't jump outta the wagon. We were not too far from the morgue, and the doors were closed, so we got to the morgue.

And after we got the body into the morgue, the morgue attendant explained to us what it was.

I said, "This son-of-a-bitch sat right up while we're bringin' him here."

He said, "That's not uncommon," he said, "This happens every so often. Either rigor mortis doesn't set in or it has set in and they react to it."

Something with the nerves in the body. And the noise that we heard was the gasses escaping from the body. Rectally or through the mouth or whatever.

Well, that was an experience in itself, and let me tell you, three, four o'clock in the morning, that scared the hell outta me. And we just let that go as an experience.

Put it back in the, y'know, back in the memory drawer of your mind.

And said, "Christ, I hope this never happens again."

Thomas M. Grubb & Allan "Lucky" Cole

Like I said, we got many of these runs working a wagon. And like I told you, it always came out at three o'clock in the morning or so. On this one occasion, we got the same kinda' call, we knew what it was, we knew the procedure.

We went to the hospital, picked up a body. Put the body in the wagon. Johnny secured the back of the wagon, or at least I thought he secured it, and we commenced to go down Broad Street towards Wood en route to the morgue.

Very uneventful. We get to the morgue, pull up, and we go to the back of the wagon. Well, the door isn't open, but the latch isn't secured. We look in — no body.

There's no body in the goddam wagon.

Well, I start to panic.

I said, "How could this happen?"

And after the last experience with this guy that sat up I said, "Could this bastard still be alive?"

Well, y'know, we're still rookies, we still can get fired.

You're not allowed to lose dead bodies.

I told Johnny, "C'mon, quick. Let's get back in."

So we get back in the wagon, we start backtracking the way we came. And sure's hell, we're on Broad Street, and we're looking and looking and looking.

And I see this body lying up against the curb, in the street. And it's half wrapped in the paper and half not wrapped in the paper.

Well, we scooped it up, and of course the paper's all ripped and, y'know, half of the body was hangin' out. We got it back in the wagon and brought it to the morgue.

And the funniest thing was, when we got to the morgue, the morgue attendant, who was a weird, weird character, said, "What'd you fellas do, decide to take a look to see who it was?"

And that was it.

He says, "Ahh, nothin' to it," y'know, 'cause the paper was all ripped and dirty and everything else.

So we dropped the body off and that was the end of that.

But it was something — to make sure you had the goddam doors locked and bolted on the outside. So nothing like this could ever happen again.

Thomas M. Grubb & Allan "Lucky" Cole

Believe me, Lucky, it sounds silly, but that was one of the times I was the most frightened. To lose a body out of the wagon! I didn't know how I could explain that to my supervisors.

I'll go on to tell you some of the nasty details you got being a wagon driving officer, or working a wagon.

Many times we got called for these jumpers. And normally that is a mess. Somebody decides they're gonna commit suicide.

They go out a window, five or six stories up or more, and when they come down, I mean they just splatter.

And you've got to help the coroner's office to get 'em on the stretcher or get 'em into a wagon. Well, there were some instances that, y'know, were really messy.

There was one guy that went out of a Center City building and I could never, ever understand it. He came down flat on his face, but when we picked him up, his glasses weren't even broken.

It was very odd. But that was just another strange thing that occurred.

We used to get these people that stepped in front of subways. Now that is really a mess. And when you get the job, you've gotta go down the subway.

Of course the train moves, and you extract the remains of what is under the train or lyin' on the tracks or whatever.

This is scary, because you have that third rail down there, and they've gotta cut power and everything before you get down.

Well, I don't know, I guess we got two of them at least. And the funniest thing is, when you get the body, you've gotta get all parts of the body.

We transported one body to the morgue, and like I say, it was really a mess. The coroner's guys got down and got that one. We just had to transport it. And we did that, took it to the morgue.

And then we got a call to go back. It seems that part of this guy's head was missing. And we hadda actually go down on the goddam tracks with flashlights and look for the top of this guy's head.

And we found it.

It was just like an Indian scalp, only the skull was there with it also. Nothing there, just the bone fragments and the hair.

Thomas M. Grubb & Allan "Lucky" Cole

We didn't like that at all, but that was part of being the wagon crew.

Also, as people like to commit suicide, they jump off of bridges and whatnot. They could be in the river anywhere from two, three, four days to a month.

And when a body was found — we called them "floaters" — they would ask for a wagon.

The motor harbor men would get them out with a small boat, I should say a rowboat, when they were out in the middle of the river, and so forth.

But when they brought 'em into shore they would need a hand. They'd ask for the wagon guys.

I remember this particular day when Johnny went over to give 'em a hand and they got the body and went up to the shore.

And Johnny reached down and took this body's arm, took it by the hand, and by Christ, when he started to pull, the whole skin of the arm came off.

Well, that was a sight to behold, and no need to say, Johnny threw the goddam thing back in the water, and it was recovered by the motor harbor guy.

This is the kind of thing that you really get sick of and you start to learn, you gotta do everything one time, and you learn better than to do it the second time.

Thomas M. Grubb & Allan "Lucky" Cole

CHAPTER TEN
Patrol (III)

WHEN YOU'RE A patrol officer, you patrol for weeks at a time, never really getting a job that commands any police work. You may get auto accidents, you may get minor disturbances, but nothing that really requires a great deal of police work.

The biggest enemy of being a cop is boredom. And I mean, you can get bored. You travel four to twelve, twelve to eight, with or without a partner, and you just don't know what to do. You just go patrolling around, looking and looking, and nothing happens.

And from time to time you get careless. And I think that's with every police officer. You know what to do if you get into a situation, but all too often it's carelessness that gets an officer hurt.

As a police officer, when you're at roll call your sergeant tells you, "Well, the squad needs to get tickets."

So he's advising you to write tickets.

Also, there was a procedure known as "car stops," which meant that each squad is judged — their activity — by the amount of car stops they make. Now you have to have reasonable cause to stop a car. Well, you could always find reasonable cause if you wanted to.

Stopping cars was a very, very dangerous procedure. You were taught by your instructors in the district, like I had Mike Finney, who I told you was great at tellin' you how to do things.

He said, "Always be alert. You never know what to expect."

Well, this was the solid truth.

You stop cars, you don't know who you're stopping, you just know why you're stopping. Some with bad lights, some with turn signals that don't work, anything that's reasonable cause, you stop a car.

And then of course you've gotta ask them for the normal things — your driver's license, your registration card — and then you tell them why you stopped them.

Ninety per cent of the people that you stop, you only detain for less than five minutes, if that. And you might even ask them to open their trunk to see if their wiring is correct, because a taillight is out.

Most people have nothing to hide, and they cooperate with you, and they're on their way.

Well, you always get the wiseguys that don't want to cooperate, and they give you a hard time. So you merely take them into the district and detain them until you have them open their trunk.

Because you can't do it on your own, and if something's illegal in there, you have to get a warrant to open the trunk. Most people would gladly open the trunk when they weren't wrong.

Like I say, the procedure for this is one guy would walk up to the driver's side of the vehicle, stand just behind the driver's door and talk to the driver, while the second officer stood at the right rear corner of the car so he could observe who was inside, through the windows.

That way it gave you a measure of safety, so if anything happened, you could handle it.

These were the normal duties of a patrol officer — stop cars, write tickets, check your area, your sector, make sure there's nothing wrong. If you could determine there was something wrong, it's good. If not, you just patrolled, and filled out your log as such.

The worst thing is when you're patrolling your area, and in the morning you find out there's been a burglary or a rape or a robbery. That's when you wonder, "Did I do my job right? Was I drivin' with my eyes closed?" or "What the hell happened?"

I remember one occasion, we were working twelve to eight, and I guess we were a couple of hours into the shift. And we're rolling along, checkin' things out. You actually get to know every car that's in your sector and the people that own them.

Strange cars kind of send up a red flag, and you usually take the license number and try to get a license check on them to see if the people belong there or not.

Well, we're ridin' along one night, and we see this fairly young black woman coming down the street, and her clothes are kind of ripped off her and everything else.

She runs right up to the car and says, "I've just been raped."

Well of course, that was it. And she told us about the guy that raped her — she gave us a half-assed description of him — and she told us which way he had run.

He had come into her house through a back window, and she believed that when he went out, he went into a house just a few doors down.

Johnny and I, we got her into the car, and we pulled up to this other house. We go in, and as we're tryin' to get into the house, somebody hollers, "There he goes, out the back."

We're in the middle of the block, so I tell Johnny, "Wait here, I'm shootin' around the back."

So I get around the back of the place, and I'm lookin' up alleys and yards and what have you. And it's funny, I see these clothes on the line are movin' around.

I figured, "This is it. I'm goin' in here."

Well, it was a house that was occupied. People lived in there. But this sucker, whoever he was, he ran in and went right down to the basement.

Johnny came around with the car and finds me in the alley. I flash the light at him and he comes down. Now, we go down to this basement. And we're lookin' around, and it's a big, old basement.

I mean big. Christ, these homes musta been 60 feet long and 20 feet wide. And there's all kind of cartons and boxes and everything down there.

I told Johnny, "Well, I'm down here. You go up on the first floor and check with any of the people, if they heard anything, or this or that."

In ten minutes or so he came back, he said, "Yeah, they heard somebody runnin' down the cellar steps."

We figure we got this guy in there, 'cause there's only one way out and that's the front window. And these are those small, cellar windows. And I got up there and I checked, and they're nailed shut.

I said, "That sucker's gotta be in here somewhere, Johnny."

And we start goin' behind these boxes and everything. And there was this big, old-fashioned furnace with those huge ten, twelve inch vent pipes. So I even looked in the goddam furnace for him. And nothing.

And here's a cardboard box. Just a box on the floor.

And I'm lookin' at it, and I'm sayin', "Could this be it?"

Well Lucky, I kicked the box over and here's this bastard crouched in the box. I had my pistol out and no need to say, the best thing I did, is I gave him a shot in the head with the pistol. And, of course, down he went, and the blood squirted out, and everything else.

This was our, really our first felony arrest. And we drug his ass out, and the girl in the car identified him immediately. In a situation like that, you've got the prisoner and you've got the victim.

So what we did, we called for a wagon, transported the prisoner into the district, and took the young lady to the hospital.

We got her information and so forth, then we went to the district. In the district, right away, when you get a felony arrest, you don't handle it. They told us to bring this guy down to the Central Detectives. Well, this was something. It was a great big new experience to me.

So we drove him down to Central Detectives. And we got in there.

Detectives are sittin' there, "Whattya got?"

And we told 'em.

"You got 'im here, you got the victim, you got an I.D.?"

"Yeah. We got all'a that."

We told 'em where the girl was, and so forth, and right away they dismissed us.

This one detective says, "Look, guys," he said, "when you made this pinch," he said, "just remember that you called for us and we were in the back of the house. And we assisted in the arrest," or, " we made the arrest and you assisted," and all this bullshit.

I said, "We never called for you guys. We got 'im ourselves."

Guy said, "It don't work that way."

To tell you the truth, the way it turned out, Lucky, when the arrest came in, we didn't even book him with our house sergeant, they booked him at Central Detectives. They made the arrest and we were on there for an assist.

Right away I learned you can't screw with these guys. They're a little higher than you in rank, more experienced, so to speak, and that's the way the game is played. They put themselves right on the arrest, like they made the arrest. And you assisted, instead of vice versa.

That was another learning experience for me. I knew how to handle it better the next time.

Got to understand, Lucky, at the time I went into the police department, we didn't write incident reports when something occurred. It was a year or two later that they came out with these, what they called a 7548 Form, that you filled out for any police action that you took.

With this, it made it more evident who were the arresting officers and who had participated in the arrest. These forms were known as Incident Reports.

Like I said, we were still rookies, in the learning process, but the point is, you have to learn before you can do things the right way and protect yourself.

There were many incidents after this that got the adrenaline running, and I'll try to relay them to you as I recall them.

All too often I worked the patrol car by myself, because there really weren't that many men in the squad. And with days off and various other sick time and things, that was the reason you worked by yourself.

The only time we always worked two-man cars was when we were assigned to a wagon. And as I told you, we split up our week — half on a patrol car, half on a wagon.

Well, it was this particular day, oh, it was in the summertime, July or August, Johnny and I were working, and it was a real quiet day. And it was like, one, two o'clock in the afternoon. And we're going up Green Street, and we're just gassin' to each other in the car.

And I saw this woman up on the steps, about halfway up the block.

And I said to Johnny without knowing for sure, "Johnny, I bet you we got a job here. We're gonna get stopped by this woman."

Sure as hell, we pull up, and just as we're getting up to the house, the woman came down the steps and started waving to us and so forth. So we stopped. This was an older woman, and she was quite upset.

She told us that one of her boarders, she hadn't seen him for several days. And that he was the kind of man that always had a steady routine — go out for his newspaper and so forth. And she always managed to see him once or twice a day. She hadn't seen him and she was quite upset.

She asked us to come into the house and go back to his apartment. She directed us through the house, and like I told you, these were big, old homes. Row homes, but very, very large. She directed us up to the first floor, all the way back to the rear apartment.

Well, we got there, and the door was locked.

I asked her, "Well, ma'am, you got a key?"

No, she didn't have a key.

I said, "Well, if you don't have a key," I said, "there's only one other way to get in here and that's to break the door down."

She said, "I don't care," she said, "You go right ahead, Officer."

Johnny and I got together and gave it a few kicks and actually, we kicked the lock off. Those old locks, they weren't that strong, anyway. We did that, we entered the apartment, and went all over the apartment and — nothing.

The apartment was clean, neat, and it was just odd that there was no one there. And she told us she hadn't seen this man go out. She mentioned his name, but I can't recall it at this time.

So like I say, it was very bright, sunny outside, and when we went in it was pretty dark, 'cause we're just coming in from the sun into a dark hallway and so forth.

I looked out, I told Johnny, "Go ahead, you keep lookin' around."

I recalled when we passed by there was this cellarway, a door that led down to a cellar. And the woman was out in the hallway.

I said, "Does this gentleman use the basement for any reason?"

She said, "No, he doesn't."

But something was telling me I should go down that basement. I switched on the light — didn't work, naturally. So I had my flashlight with me and I went down.

Thomas M. Grubb & Allan "Lucky" Cole

And I get down, oh, about three-quarters of the way down the steps. And I see these legs, like somebody standing just below the bottom of the steps. And I'm looking and I can't really see.

As I'm talkin', I'm sayin', "Yo, pal. You awright?" and this and that.

And then the strangest thing happened, Lucky. I saw the body just starting to turn.

I said, "Oh, Christ," and I got up closer to him, and here, this man had hung himself in the basement.

Well, I didn't know he'd done this, because he used some sort of a wire, like a cable or a lead from an iron or something. It was coated, y'know. And I looked at him, and the wire had pulled into his throat, you hardly saw it. His flesh hung over it.

And he must've stepped off this little stool that was standing there. It was so small that he just — his feet were touching the floor, practically.

Well, this gave me a shock when I saw him. It's not that I hadn't seen a body before but, y'know, when you walk in outta the sunlight and — shit, it's a little frightening.

I said, "Oh, Christ, how 'bout this. Here I am, talkin' to a dead man."

I'm thinkin' to myself, "I gotta do somethin' about this." So I turned around and I walked back upstairs.

Then I call, I said, "Hey, Johnny," I said, "C'mere a minute," I said. "There's a guy down there."

I said, "The son-of-a-bitch won't talk to me," I said, "I don't know what's wrong. I don't know if he speaks English or not. Give 'im a shot."

So Johnny says, "Sure."

And Johnny, he walked down the cellar stairs. And it was a minute or less — seconds, and I heard him holler, "Aahh, Christ sake."

And he came up the stairs.

Well he, y'know, he gave me a few choice names and told me, "Christ, don't do that. You scared me to death."

This was typical. We liked to play a few jokes on each other now and then.

Thomas M. Grubb & Allan "Lucky" Cole

After this, we know we've got a suicide. And not knowing as much as I should, I cut the guy down. Y'know, the man was stiff as a board, rigor mortis had set in.

So I took out my pocketknife and I cut the goddam wire. And the guy came down, and again, we went out t'the car, called police radio, told 'em what we had.

Immediately they dispatch a detective car up to us. Told us to stand by.

I learned another lesson. Yes, it was a suicide. But this detective came in — "Who cut 'im down?"

And I said, "I did."

He said, "Don't you ever, ever do that again."

Evidently I cut the line too short, but it wasn't that much of a line to begin with, because the guy was almost standing on the floor when he hung himself. And I learned a lesson — in a suicide, just like a homicide, you don't touch anything.

When I cut him down, if I was gonna do anything, I should have cut the longest section of the cord that he hung himself with.

The detective knew that we were pretty new on the job and he said, "Look," he said, "Never do that," he said. "Y'know, for the future. If you come across somethin' like this again, you leave him for us."

So we went out, and they did their thing, and then we were called back to transport the body to the morgue, and that was that. But the point was, you learn a lesson with everything you encounter. Don't jump the gun. Don't do what you're not sure of.

Well, things went along again, time passed by, and this time we were working last out. And it was a bitchy night. It was pouring rain. And, you know, you just hate to get out of a squad car. You can't sit in there with a raincoat on, and you sure as hell ain't gonna carry an umbrella.

And we're rollin' the district in our sector and just goin' up and down the streets as we normally did. We used to always reverse our pattern, though.

We tried to not keep the same pattern of patrolling, because if anything's going on out there and if you pass a guy that's doin'

77

something wrong and he knows your routine, he'll wait till you go by and then do his thing, whatever he's intending on doing.

But we were smart enough — like I said, Mike told me about this, what to do. Up the street, then down, then instead of going up and down the next one come back to that first street again. And this is what we more or less did in our normal patrolling.

This particular night, we're comin' up the street and, like I say, it was pourin' rain, Luck. And in the street we see a body, so I pull up. And the headlights are on the body.

Not wanting to get out, but knowing I have to get out, I get out. And I'm getting soaked. And I run up to the body. And I turn it over, it was lying on its face.

Here, it was a young woman. As a matter of fact, even with the rain pourin' on her and everything, it was a rather attractive young white woman.

I look at her, and I check her out, and I see that she is breathing. And you don't know if she got hit in the head, or hit with a car, or what.

We kinda pick her up, take her into the car. And she's moaning, now, and she's blabbering, y'know — doesn't make a lot of sense, but she's talking.

So we take her into the district. I'm trying to get information from her — who she is and whatnot — but she's just not making much sense.

We go into the district, and I really wanted to get the house sergeant out to see her. He wouldn't come out in all that pouring rain, so we more or less helped the girl into the district.

No sooner do we get her in there, than the house sergeant looks at her, and like I said he was an old-timer and a nasty old coot, he said, "Holy Christ!"

And he identifies this woman — it was Judy Gardner, who was a famous semi-stripper in those days at a bar known as "The Wedge," at Broad and Ridge Avenue.

Well, she was soaked right on through.

He said, "What the hell happened?"

We told him the story.

Thomas M. Grubb & Allan "Lucky" Cole

And he's lookin' at her and he says, "Christ sake," he says, "Can she talk, or anything?"

I said, "No," I said, "That's why I brought her in to you, Sarge. I don't know who she is."

He knew who she was, and where she lived.

Then, y'know, he peeped into her eyes, lifting 'em up, and her pupils were well dilated.

He said, "Holy Christ, she's high."

Awright? She's usin' narcotics, probably heroin. And like I say, she was well known at this time, she was one of the original strippers.

And he said, "Whattya wanna do with her?"

I said, "I don't know, Sergeant. What do you suggest?"

He said, "Well, just leave her here, put her back in a cell, and just let her dry out."

They got a coupla blankets and threw 'em over her. By the end of our shift — we came into the district, before, actually, the end of the shift — the sergeant had her pretty well straightened — she was more coherent.

He said, "Go talk to her," and stuff. So we talked to her.

She told us her name, who she was. And she didn't say she used drugs, naturally. But the sergeant suggested that we drive her home. Well, this didn't mean that much to me. And she learned our names and so forth, and we did drive her home.

Lucky, I made a friend that night. We didn't pinch her. Not only me, but Johnny also. She became a valuable source to us later on, much later in my career, maybe not so much to Johnny because he stayed into the uniform in the districts. Just by doing her this favor, not arresting her for use of narcotics and so forth.

That was an odd instance, picking up a celebrity, so to speak, and taking care of her. That was one experience.

Then there was something a little more serious that happened. Again, it was on the twelve to eight shift. We get a call of a burglar-prowler, prowler-burglar, whatever it was, in this toy warehouse which had gotten hit frequently.

So we went up there, and we went in. It was a big, old warehouse. And bein's it happened so often, nobody really paid a whole lot of attention to it — figured it was kids in there, or something.

Well, we went in, and Lucky, let me tell you, it's the strangest thing, when you walk into a place and you're pretty sure somebody's in there, or it could be several people in there.

But you can't see them, and you've always got the feeling that they're looking right at you.

Johnny and I kinda split up, and we went in.

Johnny's walkin' down one side of the place, off the wall, and I kinda go down the other side. And it's a high place, stacked with boxes of stuff. And we're lookin' and lookin', and we got our flashlights out.

Here's another thing that helped me. Mike had told me, "Never hold that light directly in front of you, kid. Whenever you're using your light, hold it down some."

Well, I did that. That was one of the things I remembered — what Mike had told me, my teacher, my mentor.

And I'm going down, and naturally we had our weapons in our hands. 'Cause you never know, in a place. Well, we're about halfway through it, and evidently I spooked one of these people that was in there.

Next thing I know, I hear "BANG!"

No sooner than I heard the bang, it felt like somebody pushed me. I staggered for a second, and like — like — something burned me. And I didn't know what the hell it was.

You gotta remember, in my time we didn't wear bulletproof vests. We didn't have bulletproof vests.

I never saw who fired the shot. I never even saw the flash of the gun. Obviously, he was to the side of me.

I went down on the knee, and I stayed down. The light went outtta my hand. And of course, Johnny started comin' over toward me. Well, then I discovered — I knew I was hit, but I didn't know how bad I was hit. And all's I felt was this burn in my chest.

I said, "Holy Christ, Johnny, I think I'm shot."

And he's lookin', he's pullin' my coat open and stuff, and I'm bleedin' a little bit at the chest.

He said, "Look, Tom, look."

Thomas M. Grubb & Allan "Lucky" Cole

And he's puttin' his light on my badge.

Well, whatever came out of that man's gun hit my badge, dented my badge, then ricocheted right across my chest. Leavin' a trough there where it ripped the skin open, and I was bleedin' from that.

I never told your Aunt Cassie about this, 'cause that would only upset her and there wasn't really any reason to tell her. I knew I wasn't hurt that bad.

So, y'know, Johnny kinda helped me up, and we kinda backed outta the place then, not knowing where the hell these people were that were in there. And he brought me back out to the car.

We called for assistance, and other cars came up and stuff, but nobody was caught.

I'm lookin' at my chest, I'm tryin' to look, and I can't see, all's I see is blood.

Johnny said, "C'mon, Tom, go over t'the hospital."

My sergeant was there, and immediately he said, "C'mon. Get t'the hospital."

Well, this guy musta fired a .22, Lucky, 'cause I think if it was any bigger, it would'a penetrated. But the badge was all scraped up, dammit, and whatever was left of the projectile just ripped across my chest, ripped the shirt and everything.

And I got like a two-inch gash across my chest.

In the hospital they lay me out, y'know, and they're lookin' to sew and stuff, but it was just like a trough of flesh torn out. And they didn't even sew it.

What they did was clean it up, y'know, put a bandage on it, say, "Come back, couple'a days," and this bullshit and that.

Well, I was sore, but not that bad, really. Only thing it did was, it ruined my badge and it ruined my goddam shirt.

That was really the first time I got hurt on the job. And it was scary. It was really scary to know that somebody can pop you and you don't even know who. Or where it came from.

Of course Johnny was upset over it and all, but I never even missed a day's work, Lucky. There was no big deal made out about this, 'cause I saw nobody, I didn't know if it was a man or woman who did this, and I didn't discharge my weapon. So there were no real reports to make.

Thomas M. Grubb & Allan "Lucky" Cole

It kind of just slid by. There wasn't a big deal made out of it.

That was the first time, like I said, I got hurt and really got frightened on the job. Actually, the only thing I got out of it was a nice, two-inch scar right in the center of my chest.

God forbid this person was standin' in front of me, I'd 've been dead. 'Cause it hit me smack dab in the middle of the kill zone, when you're firin' a weapon. And if it would've been straight ahead, I would've been gone.

No need to say, I was a hell of a lot more careful after that.

Things went along normally, like they usually do. Half the week on the wagon, half the week in the car.

After the first incident in Hahnemann Hospital they knew me, and after this incident they knew me a lot better.

And they kinda cater to you a little bit, and you got special treatment, got to know a lot of nurses and so forth, and that wasn't too bad, at that.

It's a funny thing, the police department, Lucky. Anything that happens, within a week, Christ's sake, it seems like everybody in the department knows about it. Specially the adjoining districts.

And whenever you'd have occasion to go to another district on an assignment, they would talk to you, "How you doin?" and this and that, and, "Christ, you're lucky," and all this B.S.

Well, it kinda got old hat after a while. A lotta guys tellin' me how lucky I am, and other guys tellin' me, "You're an ass, for goin' in there." It's just the way things are. You can't do anything in the police department — good or bad — that everybody doesn't know it.

Thomas M. Grubb & Allan "Lucky" Cole

CHAPTER ELEVEN
The Rule of Three

I GUESS THE next best pinch I made was — again, Johnny and I were workin' together on the wagon. And, you know I know something about cars.

Well, we're ridin' along, again early in the morning, three, four o'clock in the morning, and we spot this car going up into the black area of the district.

I noticed that it was really saggin' in the back. And normally this isn't right, unless you've got a whole load of people in the car, but there was only one guy in this car.

So, 'member what I told you about car stops? You gotta be careful, and this was out of the ordinary. As far as I can recall, it was a big car, a Buick or a Cadillac or something.

I told Johnny, "C'mon, we're gonna stop this car."

Johnny says, "Yeah, I see."

So we pulled it over. And the guy stops, nice, nice. And I'm up talkin' to him, and go through the routine — license, owner's card — and he was cordial, a black man.

I asked him, "Would you mind openin' your trunk? I think something's wrong with your wiring. Your back tail light's blinking on and off, like you're making a turn."

He said, "Oh, no," he said, "That's nothing," he said. "I'll fix it when I get back."

Now mind you, this is three, four o'clock in the morning.

I said, "Well," I said, "I can't let you drive this car the way it is."

That was my excuse.

He said, "Well, uh," y'know, he started hemmin' and hawin'.

I said, "If you don't wanna cooperate," I said, "you'll have to come with us, into the district."

"Well," he said, "Look," he said, "I don't wanna have to do that."

So he opened the trunk, o.k.? And in the trunk there's four of these five-gallon cans. Shiny, aluminum. I knew immediately what I had.

I had a runner. This is a bootlegger carryin' the pure alcohol in the back of his car.

So I talked to him. I told him, "Look," I said, you know, "You're under arrest."

And he started his, "Well, can't we talk about this?" and this and that.

I knew what he was tryin' to do. He was tryin' to buy us off. Well, he offered us a coupla hundred dollars.

"Well," I said, "Geez," I said, "That's nice," I said, "but you're under arrest."

We locked the car up, put him in the wagon, take him into the district. Tell the sergeant what we got. Sergeant sends one of the guys that's in the operations room with us. We got the keys to the car.

We drove the car into the district, and he gave us his authority to open the trunk, so we didn't need a warrant. And we got him in there, and we got the four cans of grain alcohol.

That was a big pinch.

The sergeant was tickled to death, and made some remarks, "Geez, didn't this guy wanta talk to you?"

I said, "Yes, Sergeant. He offered us X amount of dollars."

And the sergeant's just lookin' at us, like, y'know.

I said, "Well, whatta we do with this stuff?"

He said, "Well, we'll lock it up in a cell."

I said, "Great, Sergeant," I said, "Make up a property receipt."

Well, this kinda shocked him. See, whenever you bring in evidence, you gotta make up a property receipt. And I wanted this because I knew, sure as hell, some of that alcohol would disappear.

It was worth about five hundred dollars a can.

So, reluctantly, the sergeant made up a property receipt and I took a copy.

The next morning we took the guy out of his cell — we had hearings in our district at that time — and he was arrested for transporting illegal liquor.

It wasn't a big pinch, but at the time, bein' rookies, it was sizable for us. So that was another good pinch we made that nobody could steal from us, 'cause we were the only ones involved.

84

That kinda made us look good in front of the captain, too, because this is twelve to eight at night. And we stopped him.

The captain brought us in the following morning after the hearing and he wanted to know, "Why did you stop this car?"

And I told him. He looked at me, and you've gotta remember, on these other tapes I described Abe Gold to you. Belligerent, nasty, cursing; but would never actually harm you in a way that you'd be suspended. And so I thought he was a good man. Johnny hated his guts.

But anyway, he congratulated us and gave us a day off, which was a big, big deal at that time. And we had our day off.

Of course, when word got out about this pinch, some of the old-timers told us, "Jesus Christ, you guys are really stupid."

Meaning that we should have taken the money off of this guy and just let him go on his way. But I couldn't do that. I never did it and I never would do it.

Lucky, there's an old sayin', that things happen in threes in the police department. Well, sure as hell it's damn near true.

We're working four to twelve, which, by the way, was my favorite shift to work. This time, we're in the car, we're workin' the upper end of the district, and I guess it's, oh, maybe seven o'clock at night, we're ridin' up there, and we're passin' some of the stores.

As we're approaching, we see this guy run outta this store. And while we still are lookin' at him, here comes another guy out, hollerin', "Stop, thief!"

We pull up, and Johnny jumps outta the car, I pull up ahead of the first guy, and he doesn't know which way to run.

So we snatch him up. Here, he's got a gun. He went in and held up this store. Now, he doesn't pull the gun when we get him. Actually, Johnny had to tackle him and knock him down.

But we got him, and we got ourselves a gun. That's a gun pinch. That was a big deal.

And we got the store owner. And he robbed the owner and he had a few bucks on him, y'know. And we transport both of them into the district.

Thomas M. Grubb & Allan "Lucky" Cole

Well, same sergeant's there — he worked our shift. He's lookin' at us and he says, "Well, red ass," he says, "you're havin' yourself a good month, ain'tcha?"

Again, we — the next morning — we stand this guy up in front of the magistrate, and he's charged with various offenses, possession of a gun and all this nonsense.

And again, the captain calls us in, and he said, "Hey," he said, "You got a gun."

I said, "Yes, sir."

He said, "O.K., you've got yourself another day off."

It was more or less a rule that any time you made a gun pinch, even if you found somebody walkin' along the street with a gun and you got him, you got a day off. So that was an incentive to do a little more police work than average guys used to do.

It also set us in pretty good with the captain, because we're pilin' up felony arrests. Which is good. We stopped a holdup, caught the guy, got his gun. That's pretty good police work.

As a matter of fact, for that we got a commendation also, which was not that big a deal, but it was my first.

It wasn't much longer after that — see, we worked in cycles. We worked seven days on each shift. And again, it was on the twelve to eight shift, we're workin' the wagon down in Center City.

I guess it was — I forget the name of the street, but there were a lot of restaurants on the street. And they were closing up. And we're just rollin' along.

And we see a scuffle, it looked like, up this alley. Well, that's not too uncommon after the bars close and everything. You get the drunks punchin' each other out, and all this nonsense. And we go up and here, it's a black guy strong-arming another black guy.

And he stabbed him. As a matter of fact, he stabbed him several times, but we didn't know it till we got up there. We threw the light on him, and the bastard tried to run, but in those days I could run pretty good, too.

I'm closin' on him, and I told him, I said, "Stop, or I'm gonna shoot."

Well, that stopped him. And we snatched him. He's got the knife. He dropped it, y'know. We picked it up.

And here, the guy he stabbed is in pretty bad shape.

So again, we did something you rarely do. We called the sergeant — we couldn't leave one guy and take the other guy to the hospital, both, so a car came down.

The sergeant came down, another car came down, and we told him what happened. He takes the guy, the attacker, takes him in the patrol car.

We pick up the other guy and we're takin' him to the hospital. Again, to the Hahnemann Hospital. That was the hospital in our district. We leave him there. We learn the guy's gonna live, but he's in bad shape.

We stand this guy up, next morning, and by Christ, the captain's there. Well, this was a rarity for the captain to be there at the hearings.

Again he came up, and, y'know, you can feel when a man's tellin' you're doin' good work. And we were on his right side, let me tell you. He couldn't do enough for us. We got two days off. Which again, was unbelievable. Two days. He let us go right after the hearing.

He said, "You're relieved of duty today," he said, "And I don't want to see you tomorrow, either."

So that was really good, on twelve to eight. I did not like the twelve to eight shift.

But that was our three pinches in a row, within two months. And that was kind of exceptional.

Thomas M. Grubb & Allan "Lucky" Cole

CHAPTER TWELVE
Plainclothes And Hot Cars

ON FOUR-TO-TWELVE — that's why I liked the shift — you're always busy. One thing or another, mostly domestics, arguments, fights, this thing and that. And we used to get a full share of them there. Some with the low lifes, some with the better people.

The big shots used to live in The Parkway House or 2601, and they were wealthy people. But they had their problems too, and we used to have to go over and take care of them, settle their problems.

You did it in a little different manner. You had to step a little carefully there, because they were wheels. Christ, the managing director of the city lived there, and we had a problem with him at one time.

You were very busy on four to twelve. That's why I liked it, because your night just flew by. It went by so fast you didn't realize it.

Like I was sayin', at this time we got a pretty good reputation in the district, Johnny and I; being young, aggressive, and this nonsense and that. All we were doin' was our job and keepin' our eyes open.

Frank Rizzo was then the captain of 12th and Pine. Frank Rizzo, who later became the Commissioner and the Mayor, as you know. One day I'm in there, workin' day work — and it hadda be near the end of the week, Wednesday or Thursday or something — and the sergeant calls me in.

He said, "Hey, red ass," he said, "You're to report, tomorrow night, down to 12th and Pine. See the captain."

Well, this was odd. I really didn't know what was going on.

The sergeant said, "I think he wants you to work clothes for him."

When they say that, they mean plainclothes. This was a kick, it was the first time I ever did it.

So, next night — now they didn't ask for Johnny, just one of us, that was the funny part. So the next night, or Friday night, I got all dressed, and I'm gonna work plainclothes for the captain.

Now mind you, all the big nightclubs and everything were in Center City. And that's what I figured I'm gonna work, 'cause the 12th and Pine District is right in the middle of Center City, there. I figured I'm gonna go in clubs and have me a good time and maybe make an arrest, or not. Just to see what's going on.

Lucky, that was a big, big, big mistake. Honest to God. I came in all dressed and everything and I met their plainclothes men, and they just needed help, that was what it was. We're supposed to go out and hit a place that's a speakeasy. That's where they sell the white liquor and so forth and so on.

Well, Chrissake, these two guys knew what they were doin', but I didn't know, and we're gonna go hit this place. And of course, we use one of their cars. And we get up to somewhere up in one of those guts in the black area.

The first thing this guy tells me, he says, "You take the alley, Tom," he says. "We're gonna hit the front and anybody comes out, you snatch him."

Now Lucky, I'm all dressed, mind you. I mean, shined shoes, topcoat, the whole bit. Boy, I gotta go up this alley and it's nothin' but water and slop and trash and everything else.

I didn't care for that too much, and wouldn't you know it, they hit the joint, and these people came out the back. I thought they were gonna knock the goddam fences down.

Not one, two or three, but maybe five come runnin' out. And I'm in the middle of 'em. And I'm tryin' to grab one, and I grab this big bastard, and down I go, and all the slop and shit with my camel hair topcoat on. And I stink, and I'm filthy dirty, but I got this guy.

The funniest thing was, it's not a big pinch. It's just for Frequenting an Illegal House, o.k.? Well, that was my plainclothes thing. That was my job that night. Needless to say, I wasn't too keen on those kinda jobs. But it was my introduction to plainclothes.

The following week, we go back on the regular duty. And again, it was like, I don't know what shift I was workin', but I get called in. Tell me again, "Report down to Captain Rizzo." And again, he asked me to work plainclothes.

Well, with the first experience I wasn't too keen on it, but you never, ever, turn down an assignment. Y'know, you get on the shit list, and that's it.

Thomas M. Grubb & Allan "Lucky" Cole

It was a Saturday night. I went out with these guys and this time I was a little wiser. I wore some old clothes, figuring I'm gonna get stuck with the same kinda shit again.

So we go up, and we hit a house, and again, I'm in the back, and the other two fellas go in the front, o.k.? Well again, bastard comes runnin' out, and I snatch him.

This time I got him good. I got him when he's comin' out the gate, 'cause I didn't know how many others would be comin' out. And I got him and I bring him back in, and I notice he's got blood all over him.

So we get back into the house, and this was one of the experiences where I learned about people. We get back in, and there's a woman in there. She's all fulla blood.

And she's yellin' and carryin' on. She's cut across the breast and down the back, and I'm wonderin', "Holy Christ," — looked like a butcher's shop. Blood all over the place.

Got her, one of the guys called for a wagon, had her taken to the hospital. And while they were waitin' we got the story.

It seems that her husband — now mind you, her husband comes in and he's loaded and he's got his friend with him. And this is the guy that I caught, the guy that did the cuttin'.

Well, they're drunk, and it seems like this guy wanted to put the boots to this other man's wife.

And the other man said, "Go ahead," you know, "You like it, you try it."

The woman didn't go for it, she's resistant, and this other bastard starts poundin' on her and starts cuttin' her.

We had a good pinch in the end, y'know; assault, attempt to kill, and everything else.

And that was it, that night. We only did the one job, because it lasted so long.

It was just the idea. How could one man bring in another man to have intercourse with his wife? And, y'know, this kinda just threw me back a ways, but it's just the kind of people you deal with.

All this is a learning process, because I don't even have two years in the business by this time. But you're learning all these different things, and this is how you learn not to trust people. No

Thomas M. Grubb & Allan "Lucky" Cole

matter what they seem like, you always keep that doubt in your mind and you're safe.

Or you're almost safe.

The only trouble with that is, though, you don't trust these people but, Lucky, some times it kind of goes over into your private life when you're dealing with other people that you know.

And always in the back of your mind, you've got the suspicion of, you know, what will they do, what could they do, and it's a very uncomfortable feeling.

Even though you don't like it, it's always in the back of your mind. And you're safer with that feeling, because anything that happens, you kind of half expect it.

I'm going to tell you about this one domestic problem that we handled. It's funny, we knew the man that was involved in it. They both happened to be black — the man and the man's wife. And it was just around the street from the district.

This man used to work in the garage across the street, where sometimes you had these minor accidents, scrapin' a wall or something. And we always used to take the police vehicles to this guy to fix 'em.

He'd bang out the dent and repaint it. All those cars in those days had dents all over them. They were old cars. And like I say, I knew him.

We went to the house, it was right across the street from the garage on Callowhill Street, and a stone's throw from the district.

It was on a weekend, I guess a Friday or Saturday night, and he had been drinking. And, I don't know, he got into a hassle with his wife and, y'know, it's just a common thing.

We talked to him and everything, calmed him down and calmed the woman down, and then it was, "Gimme some sugar, honey," and it's the kiss, y'know, and the pat on the butt, and all this stuff and that.

And maybe we were in there, half hour. Everything looked serene. It really looked like they were gettin' along.

We told him, "C'mon, you come outside with us and cool off a while," and all this and stuff, and I said, "and then you go back and you make nice, nice."

91

Well that worked, Luck. We did take him out and talk to him for a while.

He says, "I think I'll sleep over in the garage tonight," he said, "Just to let things cool down."

I said, "That's great."

But anyway, next morning, I should say the next afternoon — I think we were workin' four to twelve then — we come in and, y'know, you're standin' around for roll call. By then we're kinda old timers, we've got almost two years in the business.

And guys are talkin'. They say, "Hey, did you hear about," I'll just say Herbie.

"What? What happened to Herbie?"

He said, "Nothin'. He blew his wife's head off last night."

Well, Holy Christ, y'know. You're thinkin' about this, it seemed that he went back in and tried to make nice, nice, and she wasn't ready for nice, nice. And they got hasslin' again, he grabbed a shotgun and blew the top of her head off.

Blew it right off — the top of her head.

You kind of think about this. Christ, we had this guy, everything seemed nice and, bang, he kills her. Well, we're on record for havin' a call there, but we adjusted the call and this shootin' didn't happen till much later on.

And you can't go searchin' people's apartments and stuff for anything when you're in there. And it just looked like an ordinary domestic quarrel.

But it just goes to show, you can never be sure of what the hell's gonna go on when you leave. 'Cause you can't lock people up for that shit. So we learned a lesson there, too.

Lucky, there's a few things that happened, I tell you, that were funny.

This particular night we're doin' four to twelve, and we're drivin' up the parkway in the car, in the patrol car. This was when we're working the upper end of the district, as we call it — it's the upper or lower end. The lower end we worked with the wagon.

We're up in the "good" area, 2601 and Parkway House. And we get a radio call. They used to come out, and the recorder takes it down on the log. It was a stolen car.

Well, this car just happens to go by us at that time. And Johnny grabs the license tag, and we had a hot sheet in the car. That's a list of all stolen vehicles.

And he tells me, "Tom, here's a hot one."

I said, "Well, we'll just grab it," y'know, no big deal.

Well, we do. We snatch this car. And it was a funny situation. The man that owned the car was actually driving it. And we stop him.

Now a stolen car, you don't know again who you're getting, what they've done. So we go in and this time I take the hand, put it down on my weapon, approach the car, got the holster unsnapped.

And we're talkin' to the guy, and here, he was a funeral director from South Philly. And he had a brand new car.

So we told him, "Hands on the wheel," and this bullshit and that, and told him, "O.K., want the registration," want this, want that.

Now we know it's listed as stolen. And he's got the registration and whatnot. So this is a little baffling.

I told him, "Get out of the car, please."

The man's fairly well dressed, he had a suit, tie, shirt and so forth.

He said, "This is my car."

I said, "It is?"

And the papers checked, the owner's card and stuff, but then again, the guy coulda left them in the car when it got stolen.

So we got him outside, and he's gettin' a little upset over this. So I tell him, "Look," y'know, "We're gonna take you into the district."

When you get a stolen car, what you do, you take the occupant in your vehicle, you lock up the car, take the keys, either get another car up there to drive it in or leave it there until you go to the district and get somebody to drive it in.

Well, that's what we did. We called for another car. Another car came up with two guys, and one of the guys drove the car into the district.

It was funny. We're in the district and we think we've got a hot car. And here the guy starts tellin' his story. How one of the workers had taken the car during the day and he reported it stolen, but he

93

neglected, when the guy came back with the car, to call and say that the car's been recovered.

Well, we've got him in there for a couple of hours before we straighten this mess out. And he's startin' to get hot and he's rantin' and ravin'. So Johnny, Johnny got most of the brunt of the stuff, he was with him.

He told the guy, he said, "You keep it up," he said, "I'm lockin' you up."

Which he could have.

But the sergeant said, "Nah, nah, don't arrest him."

And we let the guy go.

It was just a very, very funny coincidence, how that happened. We let the guy go and it was a stolen car, but not reported recovered, and he was driving it. So that passed by, that was just another experience, how weird things can happen.

It was later, months later, we were in the same area, only this time Johnny's drivin', o.k.? And sure as hell, we spot another hot car comin' up the Parkway.

And we check the tag as it goes by. And it's hot. And he's movin'.

So Johnny's drivin', I tell him, "Go ahead, Johnny, get it."

Johnny takes off after the guy. Well, on the Parkway there's railroad tracks that run underneath. And around these conduits, I guess you wanta call them, there's a stone wall, maybe three feet high. And this guy's drivin' in and out of them, and on the Parkway's where all the cars park for the hotels.

This guy's whizzin' in and out and Johnny's goin' after him. Well, we chase this guy ten, fifteen minutes. And we're swingin' around and he cuts in past one of these parked cars, and here's the conduit wall.

Johnny swung in after him, but too wide, and Johnny hits the friggin' wall.

We didn't have seat belts in cars at that time. When he hit the wall, his nose hit the steerin' wheel, and I went through the windshield. Thank God I had my hat on.

I'm half knocked out and the car's all mangled up and we're hangin' over the edge of this goddam conduit. We knocked part of

94

the wall down. And if you went over this wall, Luck, you fell down about 40 feet. Well, that woulda been a real mess.

So Johnny wakes up, and I get up.

And he's askin' me, "You awright, you awright, you awright?"

I told him, "I'm all right, but I'm gonna kill you."

He's lookin' at me, and blood's all comin' down, ripped my head open.

And he said the funniest thing. Now the motor's lyin' up against my leg, y'know, it was pushed back into the car.

He says to me, "Tom," he says, "Do you think we can pass the car on to the next shift?"

And I lost it then.

I told him, "You son of a bitch, I'm gonna kill you."

Knowing that — he knew me pretty good — he got outta the car and started runnin' on the Parkway. I can't get outta the car, the motor's against my leg, and it's burnin' my leg. And I'm bleedin' all over.

Finally I get out of the car. And he's makin' it down the Parkway.

And here, another patrol car's comin' up with this other cop, Jerry Rivers, who was a friend of ours.

Jerry's lookin' at Johnny, and he stopped, he said, "What's the matter, what's the matter?"

Johnny says, "The car, the car."

Jerry says, "C'mon, get in here."

He didn't know what happened. And Jerry gets Johnny into his car, and he drives back to where I'm at in the car.

And the car's a mess. I mean there's no front to it, the motor's sittin' almost up against the driver's seat.

He's lookin' at me, and you've gotta understand the expression on this guy's face. He had those big, buggy eyes, and they were buggin' out.

And he's sayin' to Johnny, "What happened?"

Johnny, he's tellin' him, "He's gonna kill me."

And Jerry, he doesn't know what the hell happened.

Jerry saw that I was bleedin', so he figured, "Hey, let's get you over to the hospital."

Thomas M. Grubb & Allan "Lucky" Cole

But in the meantime he called A.I.D., which is the Accident Investigation Division, told 'em of the accident, and that we were goin' to the hospital.

He got me over to the hospital, and they put about 20 stitches in my head.

This A.I.D. cop comes in, and, matter of fact I was still on the table when he talked to me, and he's tellin' me, "Hey, Grubb, don't worry about nothin'. I punctured the front tire." He said, "And you lost control."

Actually the guy was doin' me a favor, and was doin' Johnny the bigger favor, 'cause he was the driver. So I just thanked him and, y'know, that was pretty much the way it was. He wrote up his report of a blowout and we didn't get in any problems after that.

Thomas M. Grubb & Allan "Lucky" Cole

CHAPTER THIRTEEN
Fellow Officers

NOW I WANT to describe some of the other guys that were in my squad. Like I said, I worked with two squads. I was in Number Two Squad, and we used to split the week up.

I worked with Number One Squad and then Number Seven Squad. This way you got to know most of the guys in the district.

I just want to explain some of the characters that were in one of the squads I worked with. You know my partner, Johnny. He was my partner when I was workin' double. But then there were other guys in the squad that stood out.

Rudie — his real name was Rudenski, Pete Rudenski. Pete was funny. Actually, I knew Pete before I went in the police department. I played football with him at South Catholic High School. Pete used to wear pants that were up to his ankles.

And this was comical when you saw him, he wasn't that big a guy. And his hat was about half a size too small and used to sit right on the top of his head. Pete never said too much, but he knew his job. He was in the department a couple of years before me.

He worked with an Italian fella named Campanella. Well, Campanella never shut his mouth, and Pete never opened his mouth. Anything that Pete did he kept to himself, as well as Campanella. Campanella was one of the kinda guys that could talk and talk and talk and say nothing.

And boy, did they hate for you to come up on their sector, even by accident. They used to work A Sector, which was 92 Car.

Then we had old Louie Green and Sam Gallucio on 94 Car. These were the two philosophers in the squad. Both were older men and really nice guys.

If you ever had any kind of little problems you would talk to them, and they'd kinda help you over the hump because of their experience. They had, oh, maybe fifteen years in the department at the time I came in.

Next to them were Dewey and Spilotro who worked 96 Car. This was day and night. Dewey was the big hog, a big drinker, and not too reliable. I told you a little about him my first night in the business.

Spilotro was a much shorter man, maybe five foot nine, stocky build. Very pleasant fella, easy to get along with. He had none of the traits of Dewey. He knew his job and he would do his job and more or less take care of Dewey.

Then you went to the back end of the district where Johnny and I used to usually ride 97 Car. This was one of the bigger sectors in the district and had a variety of peoples from very wealthy to very poor. All ethnic groups, black and white, a real combination of everything.

Then beside us — that was E Sector — then you had the remaining sector, which was F Sector, 98 Car, which was manned by Jack McGuire and Jonesy. I don't remember Jonesy's first name, but he was the only black fella in our squad on a car at that time.

It was a funny thing, when I used to be boxin', when I was a kid, I met his son, who was also a boxer. And that was one of the few guys that beat me in the ring. This was when we were boxin' in the Golden Gloves.

We often talked about that, but Jonesy was a gentleman. And he never bragged, he just — when we talked, he was just, "Oh, yeah, I seen that fight, and it was a good one."

Then we had the two wagon crews.

There was Sid Bioff and Dave Wisniewski. Again, another team of men that were opposites, yet the same. Sid was Italian, Dave Wisniewski was a big Polish guy. Real good guys to work with, and would always be the first to help you out if you got in a jam.

The other team on the other wagon was Valente and Wills. These were two white guys. They weren't that great, but they were two of the officers that you hadda work with. Each one in his own mind thought he was the best thing that ever came down the pike.

I'm gonna make you up a little diagram of the district, roughly, so you can understand what I'm talkin' about, and also one of the roll room, Lucky. This'll give you a bearing on how the guys used to come and leave the districts.

Thomas M. Grubb & Allan "Lucky" Cole

Remember what I told you about the district before, is that we ran from Broad Street down to the Schuylkill River, North to Poplar Street, South to Chestnut Street.

There was a golden rule, when you rode a patrol car. You remained only in your sector, unless you got a radio call to go off your sector, or if another car was a one-man car, you might go over to look out for him if he got a job.

And that way you would just kind of cover the other guy's butt.

I'll try to describe some of the areas that we worked in.

From 17th Street back to maybe 21st Street — Green, Mount Vernon and Wallace Street — was a pretty trashy area. This is where they had the big apartment houses which were very run down. And they would not only sell apartments by the week or the month, but by the day.

And these were for the unfortunates, and this was where you had the really mixed population from the redneck whites to the poor blacks. With Puerto Ricans sprinkled in.

Also, this was the area where you had the most problems with your rapes, your assaults, your disturbances in the house and various other problems that might arise.

From 20th Street back towards the Schuykill River, this was the better area, due to the fact that the Parkway runs through there, where you had several large hotels where the wealthy lived. So this way you dealt with the wealthy people and the more sociable people as well as the low-life people.

You had very few problems in these locations, except for maybe a guy that was keepin' some chippy in one of the apartments, where they'd have a falling out and you'd have to go there to settle the matter. We did this often.

South of Spring Garden Street was the Center City area, which ran from Spring Garden South to Chestnut Street. These were the various business locations, and some hotels where you had influential people living. Also, on the lower end of this area you had the various big apartment houses and business establishments.

Like I told you, Johnny and I kind of had the best of both worlds, because we worked half a week in the northern part of the district and half the week in the southern part of the district.

Thomas M. Grubb & Allan "Lucky" Cole

It comes to mind, two of the funny experiences while workin' with Johnny.

One day we got a call, it was maybe we were workin' four to twelve, and it was just, it was in the summertime, and it was about, oh, maybe six o'clock in the evening.

We get a call up to this one building, up at 24th Street, up near Parrish. It was a nice home, occupied by several young women that used to work in the area. We got up there, we got a call of a disturbance in the house. Well, this was nothing unusual.

We got up there and here, we get in the door, and here's this one woman.

She's almost hysterical, yelling, "It's upstairs, in the bedroom, it's upstairs!"

And, what the hell, we didn't know, we were tryin' to find out what was upstairs.

She says, "It's upstairs and it's in the window!"

Well, we figured there's a guy comin' in the window, or goin' out. So we get up there and we get in this bedroom, after we gotta force the door in. And I'm lookin' around, and I don't see a goddam thing in the room.

And this woman comes up and she's hysterical.

She says, "There it is, at the window, it's at the window!"

I'm looking at the window and here, there's all blinds and curtains up there.

Then, all of a sudden a bat flies out from under the curtains and it's flyin' around the room.

This woman's hysterical and she's hollerin' to Johnny, "Shoot it, shoot it, shoot it!"

Johnny, you gotta know him, he's there and he pulls the gun out and he's gonna shoot the goddam bat.

I told him, "Johnny, don't do that," and, "after all, y'know, it's a bat."

The woman runs outta the room, closes the door. So I'm lookin' around for something to swat the bat with. Well, this was really comical.

Thomas M. Grubb & Allan "Lucky" Cole

Johnny's got a broom, and he's runnin' around the room, swingin' at the bat. I just got something like a sheet or a pillowcase or something. I figured I'd throw it over the bat.

After about twenty minutes, we do get the bat. And Johnny didn't have to shoot it.

It was just a comical thing that occurred. And with all these women yellin' and everything, Christ, you'd think it was a riot or a murder going on in the house. And that concluded that little episode. And we killed the bat, naturally.

There was a second experience. This was in, oh, broad daylight, in the summertime. We're workin' the wagon. And we get a call of a disturbance in this military uniform manufacturer's office.

We get down there, we go in, don't see any problem, and the guy approaches.

He says, "Quick, it's up on the roof!"

So we go up on the roof and I'm askin' him, "What the hell is it? What's the matter?"

He said, "There, in the chimney."

We walk over to the chimney, and sure as hell, you wouldn't believe it — now this is at the edge of Center City, down by the Parkway. In the chimney is this animal.

And I look down there. Man, it's snarlin' and clawin', but it seems to be stuck in the chimney. Johnny is over talkin' to the man.

I look down there and I say, "I ain't gettin' that son-of-a-bitch."

Johnny's over talkin' to the guy, so I nonchalantly walked over, I said, "Hey, Johnny," I said, "Go over to the chimney, there," I said, "Reach down there, will ya? Pull that the hell out."

Johnny didn't even ask what it was.

Well, he walked over and he started to reach his hand down into the chimney. And here's this raccoon, and it is snarlin' and it's clawin', but it can't get up.

Right away the guy starts hollerin', "Shoot it, shoot it!"

Johnny got the gun out, and I said, "Stop, don't shoot! What the hell you gonna shoot for? The bullet's gonna go down the chimney and God knows where it's gonna go."

After that we decide, "Let's call the Morris Refuge." They're the ones that pick up the dogs on the street and so forth.

Well, it takes about 15 minutes for them to get there. And the guys come up on the roof, y'know, and this one guy from Morris Refuge goes over to the chimney.

And he's reachin' down with this big glove on, and the goddam thing grabs the glove and it got his finger in the glove.

He pulls it up and then he starts yellin', "Shoot it, shoot it, shoot it!"

Well, it was a joke. Here comes the raccoon up, it's on the roof now, runnin' around.

This Refuge guy's hollerin', "Shoot it," the guy from the store's hollerin', "Shoot it."

And we aren't shootin' up there, 'cause God knows, that bullet's gonna go right through that animal, and God knows where it would land.

Eventually they get a cage up there, and a noose, and everything else. By this time, Johnny and I just stepped back into the area of the roof where it wasn't runnin'.

And they got it. But what was the point of shooting? Everybody, when they couldn't get it, they hollered, "Shoot it," and nobody was goin' to do any shootin' up there.

It may not sound funny now, but it sure as hell was funny when it happened.

Luck, like I say, you pass your day, around three-quarters of the time you're just bored to death, ridin' around, but every now and then you get somethin' that gets the adrenaline running.

Almost every tour of duty, you would have to take care of an accident. It would come out on the radio as a disturbance on the highway. Ninety-nine times out of a hundred it is an auto accident, but it could be a riot, also.

There was just one accident that stands out in my mind. About an oddity that I just couldn't understand at that moment.

We had this accident down on Arch Street, two cars, it was rather nasty. They really wrapped each other up pretty good. And by the time we got there, one guy I see is sitting on the curb. The other guy is still in the car.

We helped the fireman to extract the one guy from the car, and he's banged up pretty good, can't talk to him. But I see the guy sitting on the sidewalk, and he looked o.k.

So we sent the one guy on to the hospital with the rescue squad, and then Johnny and I stepped over to the man on the curb. And he had no visual signs of injuries.

And y'know, we talked to him — "What happened?"

Get some information, and the oddest thing was, while we're talkin' to the man, he just keels over, figure he's passed out.

He's dead. Just fell over, dead.

So naturally, we got the wagon, he goes to the hospital too. And it was just so odd. Here's the one guy, all banged up, bleedin' all over, and we learn in the hospital, he's o.k.

But the other man that doesn't even appear to be injured, after the accident he went over and sat on the curb, then fell over with a heart attack. We didn't learn that until afterwards at the hospital.

It was just an odd thing, and we learned a lesson. Just because somebody looks all right doesn't mean they're all right.

Lucky, also, in our patrolling around, on Spring Garden Street there used to be this — well there were several, actually — large three-story apartment houses.

In this one apartment house you had a number of girls from upstate who worked at the Bell Telephone Company. And they used to come to the city, get their job, and they'd get their apartment up there.

Also in the apartment were a number of nurses that worked at the Hahnemann Hospital, who we knew from going to the hospital, the Emergency Ward and so forth. We got to know some of them, and this was a location where we used to get a lot of stops.

The girls from Bell Telephone Company, when they would work say the four to twelve shift, the telephone company used to give them taxi fare to ride home to their apartment house. This was a constant thing, and you were liable to have two girls or three girls workin' the same shift coming home in a cab.

A lot of the officers knew this, and there was some fraternization goin' on. And you'd meet them and you'd see them

103

coming in at a certain time in the morning and so forth, you'd get to know these people.

Actually, these girls were flattered because the cops were stoppin' over saying, "Good night," or "Good morning," or whatever. They were quite friendly to a number of the officers. And this also included the nurses from the hospital who we knew.

Bein' a happily married man, I never partook of the favors that were offered by some of these young ladies. Some of the guys dated them and so forth, and they were a nice bunch of people.

The reason I mention this is, oh, it was one night, or I should say one morning, perhaps two o'clock in the morning, we get a radio call to go over to this particular apartment house.

And we go in, it was very quiet, and we met one of the girls, who was very hysterical. And she was sayin' something's wrong with this young lady up on the third floor.

We went up there and we didn't know what was wrong with her, she was just screaming and this and that. So we went up and we could hear her from outside the door.

She's yellin' all kinds of funny things, "I'm gonna jump, I'm gonna jump," and whatever.

And we're wonderin', "What the hell's she yellin' about?"

With the permission of the young lady that we spoke with, we broke into the room. Well, it was more or less a large apartment, there.

And here, when we break in, here's this young girl, stark naked. And she's runnin' toward the back of the apartment.

We go in, and we're kinda shocked, first thing, and we're tellin' her to, "Stop!" Y'know, "What's wrong? Talk to us."

And she runs to this back window. And this is the third floor. And the window's open, and she gets in the window frame, she's kinda crouched down.

We're just goin', "Wait, we're not doin' anything to you," y'know, and she's really off her rocker.

And out she goes.

Y'know, that was it. She just went out the window.

And Christ, it was terrible, Luck.

Naturally we got the flashlights, we run down, and she's in this sort of a back yard. And they must have had clotheslines out there with the props up, that's the wooden poles.

Well, she landed right on a pole.

Lucky, it went right through her. Right through her lower chest and stomach, and she was impaled on the pole.

When we saw that, naturally the first thing we did was go out to the car, radio for a wagon, radio for the detective division to come up.

We learned, after the first hangin' we had, don't touch the body, just leave it there.

We don't know if she's dead or alive, but from the appearance of her she was dead.

After this occurred we talked to the young lady she was rooming with, and it seems that this girl used to come home with the same taxi driver every night. And we learned that there was a thing going on between her and the taxi driver.

I don't know what the reason was, that he was not gonna see her again or some b.s.

This made her very despondent, and that's why she killed herself.

Thomas M. Grubb & Allan "Lucky" Cole

CHAPTER FOURTEEN
Ladies, Lightning and Lowlifes

WHEN WE WERE just traveling around, I was always very sociable, liked to talk to people. And at the various restaurants that we went into for our coffee and so forth, you talked to the people in there. And a lot of them were street people and you learned a lot of things, especially when they got to trust you.

One particular waitress on Fairmount Avenue, she hit the numbers one time and the guy didn't pay off. And she was really bitter.

So like I say, we used to stop in there, particularly on four to twelve, maybe to have dinner or grab a sandwich. And we got to know her, and she told us all the goddam number writers in the district.

Told us where the pickup men were and where the banks were. And she just left it up to us. She just wanted to hurt somebody, and these are the ways you got information from people which could be beneficial to you then or later on in your career.

We also learned about the junkies in the district. Who they were, who they used to buy from. This is just the street junkies buyin' the nickel bags, few at a time or whatever. We learned a few places where they used to shoot up and so forth. And you got to know some of the junkies.

Also, you got to know some of the racket guys in the district. Sometimes that's not good for a district cop to go interfering in their business, because that will get you in a jam for various reasons.

But you just filed all this away in your memory log for later dates.

We also had quite a few bootleggers in our district, o.k.? And there were also some stills there. You know what a still is, Lucky — that's where they make the homemade whiskey, the white lightning.

How did we learn about these things? From people on the street.

You grab a guy, he's got maybe a half a pint of white whiskey. You don't arrest him, he's nothing. But you talk to him and you learn from him where he got the stuff from. You give him a break. You don't pinch him, you just file the information away for a later date.

You grab a junkie on the street with a bag. So what do you do with him? You ride him around the area like he's giving you information. You've got him in the patrol car. And then he'll be so frightened that the other junkies will see him and figure him for a rat.

This is something I learned.

And he would tell you where he bought his stuff. Y'know, off a street pusher. But again, that's your source of information. Everything works on information you can gather out on the street.

The easiest thing was with the prostitutes. We had a number of bars in the district, and I told you about the one particular lady who was a star in her own right.

You get information from doing them favors in a way that, if you catch them wrong, you don't arrest 'em. You give 'em a break, figuring, "You owe me."

At a later time you will get information from them, maybe make a good arrest instead of just a nonsense arrest. 'Cause as you know, a prostitute, they're picked up, they're locked up, they spend a night in jail and usually are released the next morning. It's not a big deal.

Also, in the district there's two officers who are plainclothes men. They go around the district and they're supposed to be — they're more or less the vice guys, it's their job to lock up the number writers and the prostitutes and the dope users.

That's what they're supposed to do. It's not so much the uniform guy's job to do. They're the captain's men. They work strictly for the captain, they don't have any patrol duties of any kind.

So if you wanted to, if you liked the guys or whatnot, you would give them a tip on where to grab something, such a junkie who's carryin' a couple of bags or whatever, or a user. Well, we did this a couple of times.

We gave these two plainclothes men in the district the information, and they went out and they arrested this prostitute who was a user of heroin.

But as we later learned, these two creeps got this girl, she was an attractive woman, and they used her, and then they arrested her on top of that.

Well that's a funny thing. Those prostitutes don't like that, you know, they don't want to be used if you're going to arrest 'em.

Thomas M. Grubb & Allan "Lucky" Cole

Lo and behold, maybe three or four weeks after this thing occurred, we saw this prostitute, we knew her from the area. And we're in havin' a cup of coffee when she came over to us.

And she mentioned these guys' names, and she coulda got them into a lot of trouble, but they did arrest her, you know, at that time. And she told us what happened.

That cured us of giving any information to these two plainclothes men. They were real creeps. After that, we kept the information to ourselves or we made the arrest.

Well, Lucky, after bein' around a while you learn things and, yes, we did make some whiskey arrests. We had this one guy that we used to catch frequently with a half a pint or whatnot and we never really arrested him. But we did learn from him where he used to get the stuff, o.k.?

Now mind you, we're two officers in a patrol car. So you don't sneak up on people very easily, right?

We went in to the captain, and I had a talk with him, after I got permission from my sergeant to talk to the captain.

Now there's two reasons for that. One is called the chain of command. You don't go to your captain unless you go through your sergeant first.

The second is, you don't know if the sergeant has some dealings with these whiskey makers or not. So, y'know, you kind of clear yourself first.

We talk to Abe Gold, and we told him what we suspected. We told him the location and everything. Now you know, whiskey comes under the A.T.F., the Alcohol, Tobacco and Firearms Division, o.k.?

So we told him, and he said, "O.K., just sit on it," and he got some clearance from somebody.

After a while he called us in and we sat down and talked and he says, "How did you get this place?"

And I told him.

He said, "Well, that's just fine," he says, "We want the kettle."

Now the kettle is what they make the whiskey in.

He said, "How do you know?"

Thomas M. Grubb & Allan "Lucky" Cole

I said, "Well, up in the area of Francisville," I said, "you can smell it, Captain."

We had tracked it down early one morning. They always cook like, after midnight to maybe five or six in the morning. We're down at the corner of this street by a playground, and you could smell the fumes coming up from the culvert. We knew that was the area, we knew the guy gave us an address, right?

This particular night the captain says, "O.K., we're gonna hit it."

He made arrangements with these guys from the A.T.F. or whatever. And we went up and here, it's just a house, three story house. So we go in and there's a coupla people in there — man, woman, coupla guys — and we told 'em it's a raid.

Well, Lucky, this is the first time I've ever really seen a still in operation. First of all, you couldn't see a thing. We went into the house and we searched it room by room by room. We couldn't find a goddam thing.

So then we're in the cellar, and it's just like a big, old basement. Can't tell nothin'. But there is the smell there. A faint smell.

We start walkin' around the basement, and all of a sudden you start to feel like different feelings in your feet, from the concrete. Underneath there they had the wood. And under the wood, like a pit, a large pit, was the kettle. And the other stuff was fermenting under there, in the barrels, right?

Well, we know we got it. But we couldn't find the lines. See, they gotta have copper lines running up to make the stuff good. The more they cook it, the better it gets.

We found this one line that went out, and it was really great. The suckers had the line running up the walls, up into the chimney, and out the chimney. The drainage they had running right into the sewer line.

And you couldn't see a thing just by looking at it, but when we really got down there and tore things apart, we found it.

That was a big feather in our caps, and the captain grabbed a big still. And of course, we were the two officers who discovered it, and that made us look good to him.

Actually we got a commendation for it, — y'know, for the investigation and all that stuff by "Your Uniformed Forces." So that

Thomas M. Grubb & Allan "Lucky" Cole

sat us pretty good with the captain and it sat us great with our sergeant. He got a vice pinch and we're all happy.

Lucky, while workin' in the district where you're at every day, hours and hours at a time, you can make a lot of friends. But you can also make a lot of enemies. And I guess we made our share of both. Some were pretty nice people, some were nasty-asses, believe me.

I remember one time this prostitute that used to frequent one of the bars that we knew, I didn't know if it was her boyfriend, I later learned it was her boyfriend, he used to pimp her.

Evidently she was holdin' back on some of the money that she earned, and this guy really tuned her up. I mean, he put her in the hospital.

And from the other girls on the street, we learned about that. And then this girl came back to work, she was a waitress, really.

We talked to her and you could see she was split up in the mouth and still bumped up. At first she wouldn't say much of anything. And then she told us what happened.

Well, in our travels one afternoon we spot this guy, and we pulled over, he was in his car. We talked to him, and we more or less told him, y'know, how we felt. And we knew this girl wasn't gonna prosecute him.

So what we did is more or less put the fear of God into him. And that was it for that time.

Not too long afterwards it happened again — this was in her apartment. And we got a call and we went there.

Well, he was beatin' the hell outta this girl.

And that's when we got into him. And we straightened him out pretty good, took him to the hospital, then jail.

This son-of-a-bitch never forgot us.

These are the kind of people that you don't turn your back on when you see them. I think he got a year out of that. He had a weapon, and so forth. These are the kind of enemies that you make.

They don't forget you.

But on the other hand, this young lady was more than grateful, because he didn't come back to her for a long time, at least not while we were in that district. And she became a valuable source of information for us.

Thomas M. Grubb & Allan "Lucky" Cole

In all the time I worked the districts, Luck, there were other things that came up that were totally unexpected, like one Sunday morning, I'm working day work.

I was in the district, I don't know if I brought the coffee in to them or what, but we're standing at the window talking to the house sergeant when this middle-aged black woman came in. And she walked up to the window, and naturally we stepped aside.

And she put a pistol up on the counter. It looked like a Civil War pistol, one of those cap and ball things. And this kind of shocked us.

She said, "You'd better go to my apartment," she said. "You're gonna find somethin' there."

We took the woman's name, and the house sergeant, he said, "Go ahead, you guys get over there, see what the hell's goin' on."

Well, Johnny and I left the district. The woman was detained there, naturally, she wasn't going anywhere. And we went over to this apartment on Wallace Street. And the door was open. We went up, went in and looked around, went up to the bedroom.

Sure as hell, we saw in the bedroom, here's these two people in the bed. The man is on top of the woman, and he is shot six times. And the bullets passed through him and went into the woman.

That was one bloody mess. I mean, there's still blood runnin' off the bed down onto the floor. She shot the hell outta them.

This was her husband, and I guess one of the husband's girlfriends or something. And she caught them. And she blew them both away.

We radio from the car for the coroner's office, for the detectives and so forth.

We waited there till they came, we told them the story. Then we went back into the district, and by that time a couple of detectives had come over to the district.

This woman said, "I just caught him, and I fixed his ass good," she said, "And I fixed that bitch, too."

And that was it. That was her whole story.

And she just — you couldn't believe it, Luck. She shot him in the ass, she shot him in the back, in the head, and, like, the bullets'

111

Thomas M. Grubb & Allan "Lucky" Cole

went through him into the woman. And they were both cold dead in the bed.

But seein' stuff like this never really bothered me. I guess I became callused lookin' at those things most people don't see.

There was just one thing that used to get me that I could not stand, and I used to shake when I saw it, and that was kids.

Kids getting hurt. Kids being abused. And you do see a lot of that in the districts.

There was another occasion when we got a call to a house where the man was allegedly abusing the wife and carrying on and everything. And, you know, you can't get to these places in a minute or two, Luck.

When we got there, the landlady took us up to their apartment. And we got in there, but we didn't see anything. The place was a mess. But we didn't see anybody there. So we start to look around.

And we opened up a closet, and here's the woman hung, and two kids.

Hung. In the closet.

And he is hung, in the next room, in the closet.

Adults, it wasn't that bad, but the kids, it was terrible.

You know, just to see kids, hung up.

These are some of the things that I would never tell Cass when I got home. I only told her the good things or the funny things that might have happened on the job. I felt there was no need to make two people feel bad about something.

There was one occasion when I really lost it.

We were riding on Mount Vernon Street. I remember this very well. It was a place they called "The Ranch."

This was where, really, the poorest of the poor and the low-lifes lived. There was everything in these places. And they used to rent the rooms by the day.

And we're riding by these, and you've gotta visualize, like, two sets of steps leading up maybe, eight, ten feet off the ground and eight or ten off the next level. And up to these houses sitting up on, like, a hill.

We go up and there's some people — we got a call up there, a hospital case. And we get up there, and here's this little white boy.

112

He's on the pavement, and one of the women has some kind of a rag or something — a towel — on his head. And the kid's about, oh, maybe five years old, four years old.

So naturally, right away we snatched the kid, put him in the car, take him over to Hahnemann Hospital. Well, at that time, I didn't know it, but you've gotta have a parent there to treat the kid.

This kid's head was layin' open at his forehead at least the width of his head. And I mean, he was pourin' blood.

Just a little tyke.

And I was kind of hot.

The doctor told me, "We can't treat him till you find the parent."

Well, I said, "O.K."

We stormed outta the goddam hospital, and they've got the kid there lyin' on a gurney.

We go back up to this place and we can't find the parent. And we're lookin' all around and I go back to the hospital and the same bullshit. This is when I grabbed the doctor.

I shouldn't have done it, I was wrong all the way, but I told him, "Do something for this child before he dies."

And I mean, this kid's head was laid open.

Well, they still wouldn't do anything. They kind of put towels on it, compresses, to try and stop the bleeding.

We went out and we checked this area around real good, and we found this bitch. She was in a bar, half drunk, guys hangin' on her, y'know, real tramp. We dragged her out of the bar to the goddam hospital. She's half drunk.

The doctor in the hospital says, "How do I know this is his mother?"

Well, that really set me off, and I said a few choice words to him. And he was a pretty young guy.

They did treat the kid — she signed the paper. That was the whole thing, to get a signature from her.

That's when I learned there were people in the world who didn't give a goddam about their child or anything else.

They didn't care about themselves. How could they care about anyone else?

Thomas M. Grubb & Allan "Lucky" Cole

Well, that was another experience. It was bad. Real bad for me, because I couldn't stand anything happenin' to a kid.

It was around that time, we were out just patrolling, and in the next sector to us there was an automobile accident. And, you know, several people in the car. And we didn't pay too much attention to that, because another car got the assignment.

But then we got a hospital case, to go down to the hospital, the Hahnemann, and remove a body. This was one of the few times it happened during the day. And we went over to the morgue, and we delivered the body like we should.

And I told you that that morgue attendant at that time was a real creep.

He says, "Hey, you guys got to see this. This is an accident this morning."

We go over to the cooler, and he pulls down the sheet. And here's a little kid there. Like six years old, seven years old.

Little, frail thing. Dead.

He says, "That was that accident, up on Green Street."

Well, that ruined my day. I couldn't get that kid out of my mind for months. It's just some things stay with you, you just can't get 'em out, because every night, I come home and look at my children.

And just think, "Could that be your kid?"

Especially with that doctor that wouldn't treat the other kid.

I'm thinkin' of your Aunt Cass bringin' one of our kids to the hospital or a doctor and they tell her, "I ain't treatin' the child."

It just stuck with me. It stuck with me to this day.

I could never handle kids getting hurt. I used to lose it, y'know, with parents that beat their kids and stuff like that. I just couldn't handle that and, well, everybody seemed to know it.

Right around that time, a young lady called the district and wanted to talk to me or Johnny. And it was the girl — Judy Gardner — that we picked up in the street, in the pourin' rain. The stripper.

Like I said before, she was a junkie, but she wasn't the average street junkie. She was a prominent person at that time.

We met, she came over to the district. We talked, and she told us of a holdup that was going to occur. And, you know, when you hear these things, you've gotta take them with a grain of salt, because you're not sure.

She laid it all out, and she told us about these two guys that had done other jobs. They were strongarm men, yet they would also do stickups.

We considered it, we listened to it, and knew that we had given her a big break, not disgracing her by arresting her, y'know — woulda gone in the papers and so forth.

We lay out one night, and this was going down later than our shift, so we changed partially out of the uniform. And we lay outside this bar where we knew the stickup was gonna be.

Well, we just waited there. And we're laying outside, and sure as hell, I guess it's just before closing time, these two guys come outta the bar, and we had a description of them, and they had stuck up the bar.

When they came out they didn't expect anything, they didn't see any police or anything else. And it wasn't too difficult getting them. They practically walked into us.

We're sittin' right there in the car, and nonchalantly we get out as they're goin' to their car. No sooner did they get in the car when I got 'em on one side and Johnny got 'em on the other.

They were armed, but with the guns against their heads they weren't gonna make any kind of moves. We got 'em outta the car, and we disarmed 'em.

Like I said, in those days there were no handcuffs, so it was just, "You sit there and I'm gonna put the gun against your head and if you move you're gonna get shot."

We got 'em into the district, and old Francis McFall, he booked 'em, we turned the guns over to him, called the detectives. Then we transported 'em down to 12th and Pine, which was detective headquarters.

And again, the detectives gave us some nonsense about, "Hey, you shoulda called us."

Well, bullshit. You did it to us once on a rape. This is our pinch. We'll walk 'em through it with you.

We gave 'em the statements, not naming how we came about this information, because you don't have to tell 'em that. They gotta do that on their own.

But we got 'em comin' outta the bar, we got the bar owner over there, and we had all the receipts these guys had grabbed from the bar. And that was a big feather in our caps.

Thomas M. Grubb & Allan "Lucky" Cole

CHAPTER FIFTEEN
Socializing

HI, LUCKY, UNCLE Tom. I don't know if you're getting tired of these tapes yet, or not. You gotta tell me, kid.

I'll tell you a few of the strange things that happened to us, you know, while socializing. There were other fellas from the other squad that became friends — Carey, Cooper, Dawson, and a few others that we were pretty tight with.

As a matter of fact, there was one occasion that comes to mind when this guy Willsy — he was a partygoer, he liked to party — he got together a picnic that we were going to go on.

And it hadda be, oh, at least ten couples. And we put a few bucks up which he collected, y'know, to get some beer and sandwiches and whatnot.

Well, came the time of the picnic, we were all supposed to meet at his home, which was in the far Northeast at that time.

And us being from South Philly, it was a ride to get up there. In the course of going up it starts to rain, and I mean it's raining buckets.

So we get to his house, and everybody arrived. And the funniest thing was, Willsy never showed up at his home.

We met with his wife and we talked to her, very nice young lady who kinda pulled me aside and said, "Tom, he never came home last night."

In other words, he got paid, it was the day after payday we were having the picnic, and he never arrived home. So there were a lot of things that his wife couldn't purchase that were supposed to be set up for the picnic.

As it turned out, we had a picnic in his house, and I mean, y'know, I told you we threw a few bucks together. Well, we did it again.

And his wife went out and bought stuff, and we gave her some money to buy the sandwich meats and the breads and the rolls and so forth. And we went over and got a few more cases of beer and sodas for the kids.

Actually, it turned out pretty nice, and I guess it was sometime late in the afternoon when Bobby Wills shows up. And naturally, he's drunk as a skunk. And he blew his pay and whatever — he didn't have it.

So before we left — now he had a couple of kids also — so before we left Johnny suggested we all put a few bucks in.

Like I said, it was right after payday, so we all kicked up ten bucks and gave it to Mrs. Wills so she could buy food for the week for their children.

I guess it turned out all right, but if we wouldn't have been there, that poor woman would have had no food in the house.

And that's the kinda guy Willsy was, he was a real creep.

Much later on, I guess it was, oh, several years later, I found out that nut got drunk one night, was up on the Tacony-Palmyra bridge, don't know what the hell he was doin' up there.

But he either fell or jumped off, and landed on Delaware Avenue, killing himself.

It was a shame, because the kids hadda grow up without a father, but maybe they were better off. I know the young lady certainly was better off.

I'll tell you a few other things that happened in the district.

One night we were reporting in for twelve to eight — you know, last out — and Johnny and I were workin' together on the car. But before we hit the street, the sergeant comes over — this was Fred Cooper, our sergeant.

And he asks us both, "Hey fellas," he said, "I need you to do me a favor."

Naturally we said, "Sure, Sarge, anything."

He said, "I wanna ask one of you fellas to take the windows till this other cop, Art Valente, comes on duty."

He was already like, half hour late.

I'll remind you what the windows were. This was a beat on Chestnut Street where some of the larger stores are located, jewelry stores, so forth. And we used to have a beat man there, and his detail was from eleven thirty to seven thirty in the morning.

At that time I told the sergeant, "Look, Sarge, I'll take it."

He says, "Soon as Valente comes in," he said, "I'll have Johnny drive him down and relieve you, and you go back on your car."

Thomas M. Grubb & Allan "Lucky" Cole

We agreed to this, and Johnny dropped me off at the windows, and I started walking the beat down there. Well, it was like one o'clock, one thirty, and no Art Valente, no Johnny, no nothing.

And then it started to get much later, and next thing I know, oh, maybe it's four o'clock, four thirty in the morning, I see the sergeant's car pulling up.

He calls me over, he said, "Tom, I wanna tell you something."

I said, "Sure, Sarge."

He says, "You're gonna have to take the beat to the end of the tour of duty."

I said, "Hey, no big deal," I said, "What happened?"

I thought maybe somebody got hurt, or, y'know, you don't know what happens on things like this.

He told me, "Valente got himself jammed up."

I said, "Sarge, how? How's this?"

He said, "Well, the bastard came in," he said, "he was three-quarters, half drunk at that time. So he went on the car with Johnny, and then, no sooner did they pull away, than they get a call up to a house on Mount Vernon Street where there's a party."

Your job is to go down and call off the party, quiet the people down and what have you, just talk some sense into them. It seems that they went into the house and Valente, being half hit in the ass, decides that he's gonna stay at the party.

Some Spanish girl winked at him, and like I told you, he was the kinda guy that was after almost anything in skirts. Thought he was Don Juan.

Well anyway, he's at the party, and Johnny tells him, "C'mon, we've gotta leave."

He won't leave.

Tells Johnny, "Oh, go 'head, I'll be out. Gimme a half hour. I'm gonna make it with this girl."

So Johnny, bein' the easy-goin' kinda guy that he was, he goes out, and he starts patrollin' by himself. Well, this is a real "no-no" in the police department.

Anyway, while he's patrolling in this half hour, he gets a call. And he goes and answers some trivial call, whatever it was, another little disturbance which he quieted down.

Thomas M. Grubb & Allan "Lucky" Cole

He goes back to the party where he dropped Valente off. Valente is now pretty much drunk. He won't come out.

Now when something like this happens, the main thing you should do, the right thing you should do, if you can't get him out, you call the sergeant. It's his responsibility to get the guy out or whatever.

Johnny doesn't do this, he keeps patrolling around.

Maybe another three-quarters of an hour later, all hell breaks loose. It's like a riot. Radio calls are going on, and several of the district cars, includin' Johnny's, get called up to this house where Valente was.

They're fighting in there, there's supposed to have been a gunshot, everything's going on.

They take everybody out, and here's Valente, drunk. Lost part of his uniform — hat, blouse coat, so forth — and the sergeant's there.

Well, he brings 'im into the district. The captain hears about it.

Comes the morning. The sergeant comes down, picks me up, because I've got no way to get back to the district. Takes me back to the district, and this is when he's tellin' me all of this, what's goin' on.

While I'm in the district, I find out that papers are gonna be made up on Valente and Johnny and the sergeant for neglect of duty.

When papers are made up on you it's for disciplinary action, and when this occurs there's a suspension in your future.

And this is what we used to call "going up the golden stairs." When you were gonna get suspended you had to go down to headquarters and get in front of the inspectors and all, and they suspend you.

Well, things went along in the district, and then they had to go down for their hearing. And when they went to this hearing, the most peculiar thing happened.

Art Valente gets one week's suspension, Johnny Bennett gets two week's suspension, and the sergeant gets suspended for two weeks.

The actual cause of all the trouble, he gets off with a week. I never truly found out what the hell went on at that hearing, but it just struck me funny that the instigator of the whole problem gets off with only one week's suspension.

Well then, here it is, the sergeant, who's really a good guy, he got sucked into this for failure to control his men.

Johnny, I talked to him, and I was very upset with him, y'know, why he let this go on, knowin' it was wrong. But Johnny, the way he was, he was just too damn easy in some things.

I told him, "You shoulda punched him in the goddam mouth and dragged him out."

I knew better, 'cause Johnny wasn't the kind of person to do that.

As far as Valente, we just couldn't see eye to eye after that. And I talked to him once, and that was to tell him if he ever got near me or tried to jam me up, I was gonna break his jaw.

Several of the guys heard that, and they knew just how Valente stood with me. That was mainly because I felt sorry for Johnny, bein' the kinda guy he was, too easy.

I'll never forget, the good Sergeant Fred Cooper, he came up to me after they were all suspended.

And he told me, he said, "Tom," he says, "you can't look at it that way."

He says, "It's Johnny's fault, too," he said, "but Christ's sake," he said, "how a guy could do that to somebody in the squad, it's just unbelievable."

Valente was on the sergeant's shit list also, but that didn't seem to matter. Somewhere, somehow, Valente had a lot of, well, contacts outside, politically. He had a good rabbi who took care of him.

Time went on, y'know, you kind of forget about things, you're back doin' your regular job.

Like I said before, but I've got to try to explain this to you — this job, it was so boring, particularly when you had to work by yourself, and that was quite often.

You know, you had an assigned partner, but for one reason or another, he's assigned to another detail or he's put on another car by himself due to guys' being off or sick.

121

And to me, I found this to be the toughest part of the job. The sheer boredom of riding around for hours and hours, particularly on the twelve to eight tour of duty.

You just, you start getting inside your own head, wondering, you know, what could happen, what might happen.

After some of the situations I was in you begin to wonder, look, are you gonna chicken out if somethin' really happens when you've gotta go in on a job by yourself.

You've got nobody to watch your back if nobody backs you up, you know, with another car.

And it kinda gets to you after a while.

Outside of that, you start to let your mind wander while you're patrolling around by yourself, particularly in the winter or rainy nights.

And you just don't seem to want to care about a whole lotta stuff, and you begin to wonder, is this the job for you? You know, knowing that this is gonna be it for a lot of years, at least twenty, maybe more.

You begin to wonder if this is the right thing, knowin' you've got a family to support, and a family you want to come home to every night. And sometimes there's guys that don't come home at night, or wind up in the hospital before their shift's over.

All too often you second-guess yourself, and then you get through this period and these kinds of nights.

You try to break up these nights by — my procedure was to get a cup of coffee every couple of hours. We had the all-night luncheonettes and whatnot open, and this would break it up for me and kind of get your mind at ease while you're having a cup of coffee. I guess I did this all the time I was in uniform.

I guess it was because of this boredom and loneliness while working a one-man car on that twelve-to-eight shift — I detested that shift. I hated the seven days I had to work it. Couldn't wait to get off it.

It was always a good feeling when you checked off the shift and you went home to your family. Like I said, we had the three children then, it was a different world.

122

You left everything from the previous eight hours outside when you came home. You started acting like a human being and living like a human being for eight hours.

I could always remember your Aunt Cass, she would say when I'd come home, "You have a good night, hon?"

And if nothing comical happened, I'd always tell her, "Yeah, good night, babe. Nothing happened, no problems."

I'm gonna tell you something funny, Lucky. When I was in — before I went in the police department, I used to stop over at, oh, a coupla saloons in the area.

Primarily on a Saturday afternoon, where I would go down and have a few beers and shoot darts and pal around with guys that I went to school with, from grammar school right through high school.

All friends, boyhood friends, neighborhood friends. And they all knew me, and I knew all of them.

It was the funniest thing, when I did go in the department, I didn't stop going to the bars for a while. Like, on a Saturday afternoon if we were off, we'd go down and talk to the friends that we knew all our lives.

It was comical, because a lot of these bars, like any bar, they take the numbers. There's always a guy takin' the numbers or horses or whatnot.

And this one particular bar, Dean's, Twenty-Ninth and Tasker, I used to go around there.

It was funny, Luck, you walk in and you hear some of the guys takin' the action, and you knew who they were. They lived in the neighborhood.

And after, oh, I'm in there not three minutes, everything would go quiet.

I guess — I used to wonder to myself, "Now, why the hell are they doin' that?"

And then after a while I got to know that it was outta respect. They knew I was a cop, they weren't gonna do this stuff in front of me, and that kinda makes a fool outta you.

But then I realized, "Christ, I'm interferin' with some of these guys' livelihoods."

They really weren't hurting anybody, they were just taking bets.

123

So after a very short while I stopped going around, and that was it. I'd see the guys on the street and it was different, y'know, hello and goodbye.

I don't know if you remember your Grandpop Guinan that well, Lucky, but Grandpop, he was from the neighborhood all his life. And he used to like to play a few numbers.

There was one particular gentleman used to come up and down the street, I used to see him. He was a great friend of Grandpop's, name was Timmons.

Man's dead and buried now. But Timmons was the local number writer. Grandmom Guinan used to play numbers with him, and Grandpop.

After I became a cop, he never stopped at the house. And when he would see me on the street, like either coming home or just going out or something, I might have the uniform on. He used to cross the street or walk backwards, go back up the block and not come by us.

It wasn't until, I guess it was Grandpop that told me, "Mr. Timmons is scared to death of you, Tom."

And — you know, that I would arrest him. And that was silly.

I told Frank, I said, "Frank, that is the silliest idea — let that man do his business and I would never, in a hundred years, bother him."

Because he was an older man, and he was makin' a few dollars.

But that's some of the funny things that happen, when you become a cop, in the neighborhood.

Cass and I used to often laugh about Mr. Timmons, 'cause we'd be sitting out on the porch with the children or something, and he would go by and he'd say, "Hello, Mr. Grubb," and "Hello, Mrs. Grubb."

Before that it was always Cass and Tom, because he knew us, we knew his family.

I used to just laugh, y'know, you couldn't directly go to him and say, "I'm not gonna bother you," 'cause you couldn't do those things. But Cass and I used to laugh about it, many, many times.

Here's another favorite one of our stories:

Thomas M. Grubb & Allan "Lucky" Cole

Now, this is, oh, it was on a weekend. And, you know, your Aunt Cass, when she was young, she used to like to go out and go to a dance, or something like that, and I wasn't that much of a dancer.

She used to bug me sometimes, 'cause my fun was to go to a movie or take the kids to dinner and stuff like that.

This particular night, Johnny's wife and my wife were friends, she had told Cass, "Hey, look, there's a big party down at the 48th Ward."

This was a social club down at 20th and Snyder. I knew it, I knew people that went there often.

Well anyway, your Aunt Cass bugs me, "This Saturday night we'll go with Johnny and Dee and we'll have a nice time," and so forth.

So I said, "Sure, Cass, we'll go down."

Well, we did go down, and we got all dressed to go there, it was a nice place. And we're sitting in the club, and I'm havin' a few beers, and Cass, you know your Aunt Cass never drank.

And Johnny and his wife's dancin', I danced with Cass, and Johnny danced with Cass, and, y'know, one of those things.

We're down there maybe an hour and a half, and Cass comes over to me and she said, "Tom," she said, "I think there's going to be trouble."

I said, "Hon, what are you talkin' about trouble?" I said, "It's a nice time, nobody's causin' any trouble."

Johnny's dancing with her, next minute I know, and he comes over to me, like, dancing by, and he tells me, "Are you with me, Tom?"

I said, "Certainly I'm with you. Who the hell do you think came with you?"

The next thing I know, he walks over to this guy, grabs him, and doesn't punch him, but throws him. And the guy goes down on the floor, and it's right by our table. And the guy gets up, naturally he goes after Johnny, and so do all his pals.

Well, all hell started to break loose in the place.

I can't leave him out there with all these guys, so I go out and I'm gettin' into to it with him, y'know, helpin' Johnny.

And it was really a brawl, let me tell you.

125

I figure, here, I'm a cop, and I'm brawlin' in the club.

I said, "I'm gonna get fired." That's what I told Cass, I said, "What the hell's goin' on?"

And it was, y'know, just like you see in the movies — punch, down, bam, slam, throwin' guys all over the place.

So I grabbed your Aunt Cass, and I told her, "C'mon, we're gettin' outta here."

And I grabbed goofy Johnny, and he's still fightin', and I told him, "You better get the hell outta here."

I got Cass by the hand, and I'm pullin' her toward the door. And this was down like, on a cellar level, and we walk up the steps to get outta the place.

And we're gettin' up, and we get on the street, and the doorman, I told him, "I haven't been here tonight, you understand?"

He said, "Yeah, Grubb, I understand. You ain't here."

When I get outside, it was in the wintertime, and I said, "My topcoat!"

I had just bought this new topcoat, and you checked them downstairs.

I said, "I'm goin' back and get my coat."

And Cass says, "You're crazy."

So I went back down. And they're brawlin' up the steps and down the steps and all over the place. I went to the checkroom after bouncin' a few guys and gettin' pushed and shoved, and I got my coat.

And then we left the club.

Lucky, you don't know how many times your Aunt Cass has mentioned this to me, and we've gotten a laugh about it.

Thank God, nothin' happened to Cass, and I don't know what happened to Johnny and Dee that night, but the next time I saw them they were all right.

I just told him, "You crazy bastard, don't ever, ever, get me into the middle of a jam again."

Like he always did, he says, "Yo, Tom," you know, "one of those things."

Thomas M. Grubb & Allan "Lucky" Cole

Not knowing it then, but this would be the last time that we ever did any kind of brawling, in the street or in a club or anywhere else, together.

I don't want you to get the wrong idea, Lucky. I was never a person to go out and look for a fight or get in trouble. And if I could talk my way out of anything, I would do that.

I always thought it was better and more brainy to do that than wind up fightin' somebody, and wind up — even if you kicked them to hell, you would wind up with a fat lip or something.

This was always my theory, and, God, it lasted me all my life. And I think I made out a lot better believing that way.

Luck, I'm gonna take you back to the funniest incident that I recall, and this was when I was a real rookie, just after I left the training by Iron Mike.

Johnny and I were on a car, and we were down in Center City, ah, either 19th or 20th and Market, that gets the feed-off from all the Parkway traffic. And it was either a Friday or Saturday evening, maybe, oh, seven, eight o'clock.

I mean, traffic was tied up so badly that you couldn't move. And the funniest thing, we get a radio call, and whoever it was on the radio from Central Radio wanted to know what was the problem, what were traffic conditions, why was everything all tied up.

I stood up on the roof of the car and I looked, and all you could see was headlights for miles. And what the hell am I going to say to this guy.

So he asks again, "What are conditions?"

I responded on the radio, "There's just too many goddam cars."

Well, that wasn't the right answer, even though it was the truth. The next day I had to write out a memo, why I'd used that profanity on the radio. And at this time, Lucky, there was only one radio band for all police cars in the city.

Every now and then guys in the district would say, "Hey, what's conditions?"

The guys'd say, "There's too many goddam people," or "too many cars."

Thomas M. Grubb & Allan "Lucky" Cole

They all knew that I said it, because when you respond on the radio, the dispatcher calls your car number, you respond with your car number, and they know in the district who's assigned to what cars.

So that was a big boo-boo in the beginning, I guess the first year I was in the department. But it was a good memory.

CHAPTER SIXTEEN
Fellow Officers

SHORTLY AFTER THIS — there had been a lot of holdups at State Stores — they initiated this program where they would put an officer in the State (liquor) Store with a shotgun. And he would kind of hide in the back in case a stick-up did occur.

This is an introduction to the fella I told you about on the phone, Willie Reed. Willie Reed was a very black, ugly kind of a guy. He had these big lumps on his face, and he was only a little whippet, he's about five foot seven, and he couldn't have weighed more than 130 pounds.

And he was the typical hip-hop type of guy. Always bouncin' around. Always funny. Comical, very comical. And he would keep you laughin'.

On this particular day they put Willie Reed in this State Store on our sector, up on Fairmount Avenue. Well, Willie was a drinker.

And he was the kind of guy, I'll tell you the truth, he's in the district for months before I knew he was a drunk, because one day he came in sober. And he was a completely different guy. And that's the only way we knew that he was a drunk.

But anyway, they put Willie in the State Store, and he's in the back where all the stock is, and he's got a peephole where he can look out to the front in case anybody came in and attempted a stickup.

The procedure was, an officer would be in there at all times, business hours, and the shotgun. They used to carry three shells of .00 buck in the shotgun.

Now I know you know .00 buck is, it's like eight 38's in one casing. And the officer that was being relieved would unload the shotgun, and he would hand the shells to his relief, and the gun.

He did this with Willie, and of course, Willie's bullshittin' around as he always did; the guy that was relieved, he left. And when Willie went to load the shotgun, he put the shells in. And, you know, it's a pump shotgun.

Well, Willie got the shells in, but he forgot that he had his finger on the trigger at the last shell and when he shoved the pump back up, BA-BOOM.

It went off.

Needless to say, he blew away half the stock in the goddam stockroom. And of course we gotta report a shooting at the State Store.

That was in our sector, and Johnny and I went up, and we went in, and here's Willie in there with the shotgun with one discharged shell.

And the whiskey was actually runnin' down the floor.

We took Willie into the district, and he had to make out a report of what happened. That was the first real incident with Willie Reed.

I never really knew what the hell he put on his report, but somehow he lied himself out of the problem that he had. Defective shell, or some nonsense like that.

I guess Willie Reed was one of the most interesting characters I met in the police department.

Actually I liked him very much, because he was a funny, funny guy. And he used to keep things very light. They never put Willie in a vehicle. Willie always walked a beat. I guess they couldn't trust him in a car.

We got to learn something about Willie. Willie was fairly new in the police department, and all the time he was in, he worked undercover narcotics. And really, Willie Reed looked like a narcotic user. He looked like a junkie. And he could act the part, I mean, it was just like a natural thing for him.

Willie Reed used to always have a sayin', like he used to have trouble with his home life, I guess.

He'd say like, "When I was out all night," and stuff like this, he'd say, "I come home," he'd say, "and when I hit the door, my old lady get on me."

And he'd say, "Deb, baby, you got to lissen, now," he'd say, "I be workin' on a big case that's gonna break inna paper any day, now."

He'd say, "And if she kept it up on me," he'd say, he used to tell her, "Honey, I'm gonna fix my tie, pat my sky, put my foot in the

Thomas M. Grubb & Allan "Lucky" Cole

path and be on my merry way." He'd say, "And most of the time, she'd calm down."

He used to say that so much that you just memorized it from him, because that was his line. And he was always havin' problems at home. 'Cause he'd disappear for a couple of days.

Sometimes he wouldn't even come on duty. And the sergeant would cover for him as much as he could, and then he would have to send somebody out to find Willie. He was a character, let me tell you, Luck. I could never forget that man.

I'll tell you what I learned about him later on when I got to be a detective. I learned, and this is some years later, that Willie was fired from the police department. You heard all different reasons.

I met Willie later on, and Willie was a stone junkie. I mean, it was pathetic.

And shortly after I heard he died.

But he was the kinda guy, he could lighten things up, any kind of a situation. He was comical. He could make light of it and he just had that way about him. And I couldn't help but like the guy — no matter what the hell he did. I hadda like him.

Boy, he used to get jammed up in so many different ways. And like I say, I don't know why he got fired, but the word was, he became a junkie and he got caught at it. And that was Willie Reed.

Goin' back to the stuff I told you, I know I've already put it on the tapes, Lucky — the things we used to do to Johnny Bennett. And the guys knew it, they knew we were the closest of friends.

Like, when we'd come in before roll call, Johnny'd take his hat off and lay it down. And one time I took his hat and I turned his frontispiece upside down. That's like a badge that you carry on the front of your cap.

The captain used to hold a lot of the roll calls. And he'd walk up and down the ranks, y'know, and examine the men's uniforms, and then he looked at Johnny with the frontispiece upside down on his hat.

He said, "What the hell's the matter with you? Didn't anybody dress you today?" And that would be it, he'd tell him, "Fix that hat."

A Cop's Life

Then there was another time, oh, maybe a week or two later, this other fella used to have these little tiny flags, like on a toothpick. And I got the flag of Israel, and again, I stuffed it into Johnny's hat.

And we got the sergeant up there.

He says, "O.K., fall in."

Johnny throws the hat on and again, the captain holds the inspection.

And Holy Christ, when he came down to Johnny and he saw the flags of Israel in his hat — our captain was Jewish — he looked at Johnny, he said, "Who the hell are you s'posed to be, Skoopie the Messenger Boy?"

Johnny and I used to have a routine. Like I told you before, a lot of times what you'd do, like, particularly in the winter months, you'd be out patrollin', and you'd see these derelicts lyin' on the benches in the park, or somethin'. And I mean, it would be freezin' cold.

So I used to say, "C'mon, Johnny. Let's take this guy into the district."

And really, we'd arrest 'em for DK, which was Drunk and Disorderly, but you're actually savin' the poor man's life, because he'd freeze to death out there.

When we used to get these drunks, y'know, half of them you hadda wake up, and they'd say, "What? What's the matter? Whattya arrestin' me for?"

And Johnny used to say, "For violation of the Felton Sibley Act."

Well you know, Felton Sibley was a paint company. But these drunks would say, "I didn't do that," and y'know, you made a little humor out of it.

You never hurt these guys, you just took them in to get 'em outta the cold. And every winter month you used to fill up the drunk tank with them, and you actually were protecting 'em, if nothing else.

Because in the morning they'd get in front of the magistrate, and the magistrate would just tell 'em to "Sweep up the floor and get outta here." And that's what they would do.

Also, down in Center City, there was a tailor's shop, and it had the funniest name. It was "Escobar and Bayha."

Thomas M. Grubb & Allan "Lucky" Cole

When we would arrest people for various minor things they'd ask, "What's your name?"

Johnny would say, "That's Escobar and I'm Bayha."

And the guy would look at you like, "What the hell is that?"

And they never remembered the names.

We used to play little things like that. We got along real well together. We just, after almost two years, we knew each other's moves and we had no big problems, lemme tell you. It was a pleasure workin' with this guy.

Sometimes we used to go up in the park, like if we were workin' twelve to eight. Durin' the day we'd get up there and we'd have a ball game. And we'd play maybe another district, or something.

Well this particular day, this one fella, Ed Gates, nice guy, he worked with us, our squad. Ed was a fair ballplayer — wasn't good, but he's fair. And anyway, he gets a hit, and he tries to stretch it into a double, and he slides.

And lo and behold, he breaks his goddam leg, right?

That was something, now. We don't know what the hell to do. And we took 'im to the hospital and we found out his leg was broken.

Now he did this off duty and we're figurin' out what the hell to do. So, Ed, we take him home, and he's hurtin', we got him some pain pills.

What we did, when we were comin' in for duty, we got him out of his house and we practically carried him to our car, and we drove to the district.

We dressed him in a uniform, the whole bit. And while we were goin' up the steps, comin' in to the district — there were two flights of double steps, y'know — we laid him down on the steps.

Johnny ran in.

He told the house sergeant, "Holy Christ, Ed Gates just fell on the steps and I think his leg is broken."

Well, that was a good deal, because you're injured on duty. That means you don't lose any time and you get paid. We got away with that and Ed was out for, oh, I don't know, a month or so. And, y'know, just takin' care of the other guy.

133

Thomas M. Grubb & Allan "Lucky" Cole

So that worked out all right for us, and I thought that was rather comical. And Ed thanked us for all the time we were in the district, you know.

I'm gonna tell you about another domestic squabble we handled that scared the hell outta me, and it was Johnny that scared me.

We go into this place, I don't know if it's Mount Vernon or Wallace Street, and normally I used to handle the guys, and Johnny would talk to the ladies.

This time we went in, and they were battlin' away, y'know, the yellin' and the throwin' of stuff, and so forth. And this was a two-room apartment, like a parlor setup in the front and then the kitchen in the next room.

I was talkin' to the woman, and she was slapped up and all. Like I told you before, the normal thing you do is separate them, that's the first step you take. And Johnny's in the parlor area, out of my sight, with this guy.

I'm talkin' to the woman, tryin' to calm her down, lettin' her yell and spill her guts out and tell me how bad this guy is and everything. Just let her get everything out.

I get her calmed down, and my back is more or less toward this parlor, living room, whatever you want to call it. And when I turn around, there's this guy standin' there.

The first thing I see, he's got a .45 in his hands.

Well Lucky, let me tell you, I got scared. A .45, when you look at it, down the barrel, the hole looks like it's about three inches wide. And I just looked at 'im, and I couldn't say much. And I wouldn't go for my gun, I figured this son-of-a-bitch is gonna shoot me.

I tried to tell him, "Now look, everything is fine. Your wife is o.k., she's not angry with you," and this and that.

The next thing I know, here comes Johnny walkin' around him. And I couldn't understand this. The first thoughts that had gone through my head were — this guy's got the gun, hit Johnny on the head, he's out cold in the other room. I know he didn't shoot him, 'cause I'da heard it.

And here, I am standin' there lookin' at this guy with this .45 in his hand, and Johnny standin' beside him, laughin'.

I thought, "What the hell's goin' on?"

134

I didn't know what to do. And Johnny walks around him. And then I run to the guy and I grab his hand.

And the gun he's holdin' is one of these play guns, but it's shaped just like a .45-caliber automatic. Like the G.I. Joe guns they used to have.

Let me tell you, good thing I had tight bowels that night, I would'a shit myself.

I got Johnny, and I told him, I said, "You are outta your friggin' mind," I said. "I coulda killed that man."

He said, "Ah, I didn't think so, Tom," he said. "We're even."

He played the trick on me but scared me, because I used to do that shit to him. Actually, I started to laugh afterwards, but I was really frightened. And he got even with me on that turn.

But, y'know, it was later I laughed, not then.

Another incident that happened, we were workin' twelve to eight. And, I dunno, Johnny was workin' another car that night, we were shorthanded.

My way was, I would come out of the district, and I'd go to this little restaurant, a little coffee joint actually, up on 19th Street just below Ridge Avenue. It was only, you could reach around practically, to Ridge Avenue.

I'd sit in there and I'd have a cup of coffee. And I used to make a routine, every two hours I'd stop and get coffee somewhere. It would keep you awake, and it would give you something to look forward to, so you wouldn't be that tired.

On this particular night, I go into this place. We knew each other well, the proprietor and myself. And I just sat down and he poured the coffee out and we're b.s.'in'. And this guy comes runnin' in.

He says, "Hey, there's a hold-up around the corner."

Naturally the guy looks at me, and I jump up, I said, "What?"

He says, "Guy's holdin' up the cab around the corner."

So I go out, and I'm lookin', and here, I could see the cab. And I run up to the corner.

No sooner I get to the corner than BAM, BAM, BAM, BAM.

Friggin' bullets are bouncin' off the wall, and I'm behind the wall. And I pull the gun. I can't see anybody in the cab. I know

135

they're in there. And the guy's in the back, he's shootin' out the window.

Well, I let loose, Lucky. I empty my gun. I used to only carry five rounds in my revolver. And we had this friggin' ammunition that they used to issue to us, and it was a low-grain bullet. And it looked like a wad-cutter that you use on the practice range.

And I let go all five.

I blew the windows outta the cab. While I was shootin', I was runnin' towards the cab. I figure that guy isn't gonna stick his head up now.

I got up to the cab and the window was out, y'know, and the back door. And here he is, he's crouched down there, and I reached in, and I smashed his skull with the gun. He went down, and that was it, I dragged him outta the cab.

The guy in the store had called for an assist officer with the shooting. And I'm draggin' this big ape back to the restaurant, really. And all the cars are pullin' up and everything.

Well, sergeant right away, "You awright?" and this shit and that, and I said, "Yeah, I'm o.k."

Y'know, I never hit that guy. The bullets didn't even penetrate the cab. They went through the window but they didn't hit him, because he's down below the door. And the bullets — no holes in the doors, just dents.

But it was enough to keep him down there, so I hit him in the head.

The adrenaline was running so much after the first shot that I really didn't care. I wasn't scared. I knew what I hadda do. And afterwards, after it's all over, I got him outta the car and everything, and the other guys are there.

Then Lucky, believe it or not, even though I didn't hit this guy, I mean with a bullet, I got the shakes.

Then you realize, "Holy Christ, another coupla inches, he coulda killed you."

I went back into the restaurant and sat down.

The sergeant came in with me and y'know, "You awright," and everything, and this and that. And it was just the way it all occurred,

Thomas M. Grubb & Allan "Lucky" Cole

so quickly, it was only a matter of minutes. I had the shakes for a while.

I got more coffee, and then the next step, the sergeant took me, he says, "Come on, get your car back."

I took the car back to the district, and the sergeant, we went back into his room, and he had a bottle.

Said, "Take a coupla pulls on this. You awright? Make sure you're awright before you get back on the street."

Well, I hadda make up some papers for firin' the gun. I made up my Incident Report. And the house sergeant used to make up the Arrest Report — you just tell him what happened, he'd type it all out for you.

I guess I was in the district maybe two hours after that. And I thought, "Awright," but you know, it's a funny thing.

The sergeant said, "Park your car," says, "Ride with me the rest of the tour."

And that's what I did. And we take care of each other. And anybody knows when there's shooting involved that, I don't care if you kill somebody or if you never even kill them at all, you get shaky.

That was an incident that I'll always remember.

Shortly after that, Luck, was when I requested a transfer to the Special Investigation Squad — my captain, he was the first one to o.k. it.

"I hate to lose you," and all this, he said, "but it's time, — if you get a break, take it."

So I put in for it, but it wasn't granted right away. Things didn't work that fast, then. And I told Johnny what I was doing.

I told him, "C'mon, why don't you do it, too."

But he wouldn't do it. He wouldn't put in for a transfer.

So things went along just the way they were for the previous two years.

And we used to buddy up with Dave Dutton. I told you who Dave Dutton was. He was the black officer used to be down at the abandoned car lot. That was his duty station. Sometimes he filled in as turnkey, but not too often.

Thomas M. Grubb & Allan "Lucky" Cole

I remember we spent a lot of time with Dave down around, ah, let's say the holidays, like New Year's. We worked New Year's. And we'd get down t'the lot with Dave, and he'd always have something to drink down there, which was his normal thing.

And Christmastime, he used to decorate the shack that he had down there, and he'd have Christmas lights on it and everything. And actually, we'd have a party.

It was just odd, the location where we were. But the good times that we had, just workin' uniform, when you have good guys to work with. I enjoyed every minute of it, I'll tell you the truth.

We used to invite maybe another guy or two down that we were very close with, because, y'know, it's breakin' every regulation in the police department. But we enjoyed it, and Dave Dutton was a wonderful guy.

And actually it came time, my transfer came through, and it was the funniest thing.

Dave Dutton said, "Hey, Tom," he said, "You ain't gonna leave us down here now, are you?" He said, "What in the hell is Johnny gonna do widdout you?"

It was funny. This was around the holiday time when they finally — you know, the transfer was approved by the powers that be.

I told Johnny, "This is my last week down here. I'll be reportin' to a squad later."

I tried again to get him to come with me, but he wouldn't move. I don't know, Johnny was a bright guy, but for some reason he liked the district work. It seemed to fit him better than being in plain clothes on a special squad.

But all the time I spent in that district, I learned a lot of things. I learned how to be a policeman.

Like I told you before, you cultivated informers, that's the best way to put it. By getting an informer, you catch a guy a little off base, maybe with a couple of sticks of marijuana, and you give him a break.

You tell him, "You owe me," and by God, you used to collect later on. Or you caught a guy with a couple of pints of white whiskey. Things like that.

Thomas M. Grubb & Allan "Lucky" Cole

And you give 'em breaks. You catch a prostitute and, y'know, you get propositioned, but you don't arrest her. And you tell her, "You owe me."

Lucky, believe me, these things came back and paid me tenfold later on in my career.

But all the things that you do, if you just treat people the way they treat you, you can go a long way in the police department.

Before I left the district — I gotta tell you this. You meet a lotta good guys and you make some close friends, but believe me, there's some guys you don't want to be within ten feet of.

They were just bad numbers. You knew that, if you hung around with them long enough, or happened to work with them, they'd get you in trouble. They were always a little too shady to be around.

You got to know these characters, 'cause like I told you, often you may have a vehicle of your own, like you're assigned to a car. But at times you fill in, or they'll fill in with you, or something of that nature.

And you've got to watch them, all of the time. Not only the drunks, the drunks were harmless. They'd only hurt themselves, really.

But they could get you jammed up.

Here's a thing about the police department: Your reputation precedes you, be it good or bad. You can't escape your rep that you get in the police department. And most guys have a reputation for bein' good guys, others bad.

You learn those things, and you shy away from the bad ones.

I had occasions to have pretty nasty things occur, because I got a reputation for bein' a tough guy strictly because of that gang situation, y'know. As quiet as you want to keep it, word gets out.

And then other guys hear about it because they've got the same problems that you solved, but you're the one that didn't have the problems anymore. And people talk, and so forth.

Well Lucky, it came down to, oh, I guess the day before I was getting transferred. And I came in the district to work my last day, and the next day I was reporting to my new assignment, which was the Special Investigation Squad.

Thomas M. Grubb & Allan "Lucky" Cole

This was the choice thing at that time in the police department. It only consisted of forty men and you worked the entire city. And you worked on everything but numbers. Y'know, whatever things you turned up, you worked on, and that was it.

I was surprised by some of the guys, the close guys, when the tour of duty was over, I think it was day work.

They told me, y'know, "Don't leave."

And the sergeant and a few of the guys, we went over to a bar very close to the district, and we had a little party. It was nice to know that you left on a good footing, and left some good friends that you would see again in the near future.

Thomas M. Grubb & Allan "Lucky" Cole

Part Two - Detective

CHAPTER SEVENTEEN
Special Investigations

THIS IS HOW I got transferred up to the squad.

My big day came after I received the transfer orders, and I got all duded up. I wore my suit, shirt and tie, made sure the shoes were polished.

I wanted to make a good impression on the captain I was going to report to.

Well, I went up to this unit. It was an old police station, and our squad was on the second floor. I went into this building, second floor, into a large room. At the far end of the room were a couple of offices. I saw a clerk sitting at the desk in this roll room, and I told him who I was.

He said, "Oh, yeah. I got your transfer orders right here."

He just looked at me kinda odd, and he introduced himself. He was Tim Doyle.

I introduced myself, y'know, and the formalities — "Glad to have you with us, Tom."

I was there rather early, actually, before the eight-to-four shift came in. He directed me back to the captain. This was Captain Cecil Lonergan. And he showed me his office.

I went up to the door and I knocked on the door.

Told me, "Come in."

I came in. Here's this bald-headed old man sittin' at a desk. Didn't even look up, Luck.

Just told me, "Sit down."

I sat.

He introduced himself, and he's lookin' at me.

After a couple of seconds he said, "What are you dressed up for?"

Not knowing what to say, I said, "Well, Captain," I said, "this is the way I thought I was to report."

He said, "Oh, no. No, no."

He said, "Before I go any further, first thing I want you to do is go home and get changed," he said. "You'll see what the other guys look like when they come in." He said, "Try to make yourself look inconspicuous," and so forth and so on.

I said, "Certainly, Captain."

He said, "By the way," he said, "I want you to sit outside," he said, "I'll talk to you later."

So I took a seat outside and waited. I'm sittin' there and I'm kinda shootin' the breeze with the clerk, Tim Doyle, and all of a sudden this black fella comes out of the other office that was back there.

He was rather a big guy, dark skin, roundish face, he's about six one, six two, maybe, coupla hundred pounds. Very formal.

He walked over to me, he looked at me — "Who're you?"

Well, I didn't know who he was. He coulda been a sergeant, lieutenant, or what. So I told him who I was.

And he said, "You're new here, right?"

I said, "Yes, sir."

So with that, he just told me, he said, "Well, you just do what the captain told you."

I said, "He just told me to sit here."

At this point he walks into the captain's office. And, — I should say, he did talk to me a little bit more, where I came from, what I did, and so forth, and so on. And then he went into the captain's office.

I'm sittin' there talkin' to Doyle, and I guess about, oh, twenty minutes later, this guy comes out. He had mentioned his name — James. He called me into the captain's office.

He said, "Sit down," and so forth and so on. And he had my record in front of him.

He said, "Look," he said, "I'm James Ryan. I handle all the undercover officers."

Now, I didn't know how many officers there were, or who they were, or anything else. And I'm just listening to him.

I said, "Yes, sir."

I still didn't know his rank.

He said he spoke to the captain. He said he could use me, if I was willing. And I didn't know anything about undercover work, I was a uniform cop, what'd I know?

143

The captain says, "Look," he said, "If you work with him," he said, "it's a good deal."

I said, "Whatever you say, Captain," bein' a youngster and not knowin' too much.

Captain says, "Awright, I'm gonna assign you to James Ryan."

Well, that was the beginning.

Thomas M. Grubb & Allan "Lucky" Cole

CHAPTER EIGHTEEN
Undercover

AT THIS TIME Ryan told me, "Come with me."

I went out with him and went into his office. Ryan went on to explain that he only had one other white guy working undercover. Never mentioned his name.

He said that he had some things in mind that he wanted done, but the other guy was busy in another section of the city. And he wanted me to do some undercover work at a factory.

He explained to me that they were going to try to apprehend all the number writers and number backers, or bagmen, as they used to call them, in this place. He asked me what section of the city I lived in, and so forth and so on.

After that he said, "Well, look," he said, "I'm going to explain to you where I want you to go and what I want you to do."

He said, "It's all arranged," he said, "but before I tell you," he said, "I want you to get outta here and do what the captain told you."

I agreed, I said, "O.K.," and that was it.

I went home and got changed. Put on some dungarees and so forth.

I came back and Doyle said, "Go in and see Ryan."

So I went in and saw Ryan. And then's when he told me he's gonna put me in a factory, and he's already arranged to have a job for me there. I was going to be a sweeper.

Now a sweeper's a kinda guy, he gets all over the factory, and, y'know, you get to meet anybody that's workin' in there, different floors and so forth.

So I went to this factory, and I went in and saw the personnel officer, and right away he put me to work.

Now Lucky, I really never even explained this to your Aunt Cass, because she just thought I was going to work every day and that was it.

I went into this place, I worked there, oh, three, four months, can't remember exactly. But in that period of time you get to know guys, sweepin' around — "Hello, how are you," and all this nonsense.

And you get to see the number writers.

They're passin' around, different floors and stuff. And actually, most of them were in maintenance, and there was another guy that was a sweeper. He was like me, he just swept up the place and kinda kept it clean.

I got to talkin' to him, b.s., after a while, oh, I guess I was there two or three weeks. And then, y'know, you see the guys playin' numbers. So I started to play numbers.

And all you do, is you learn the guy's name, or you learn as much about him as you can, and you don't write it down then, you just memorize it.

At the end of the day, when your shift's done, you get outta the place and you make your notations. Joe Blow, sweeper, first floor, something, he's the number writer. So that's what you did.

Then you went on with your job, and over a period of time, I got to know quite a few of the guys in there.

Now, this was not in South Philly. It was in the East section of the city, quite a distance away from South Philly. So nobody knew me, and I was just another worker in the place.

After three months or so, I got to know all the number writers in the place. And I played numbers with 'em. I'd play a coupla bucks a day. Now I really couldn't afford it, but I'll tell you what used to go on.

I'd play the numbers — in those days they used to give you little receipts and stuff — not all of 'em, but some of 'em. Each night I would write down who I played with and even numbers if I could recall them.

I never hit anything, but the writers used to take the whole number and also they would take leads — you know what a lead is, each number at a time. And they would come out and they would flash fingers — like, if it was a one, they'd put one finger up, a four, four.

And everybody knew it without too much conversation.

Well, I got to know them all. And then I used to watch. At the end of the day, they used to turn the totals in to one guy who was a mechanic. And this mechanic used to take the receipts. Each day, he would get 'em.

I tried to follow him, oh, I don't know, three or four times. But the guy was pretty shifty, y'know, and you can see a car after you each day. It's pretty hard.

I used to lose him down near the waterfront and the trainyards and all that stuff. And finally, I started to change cars. You know, my brother was a car dealer, I used to borrow a different car from him every month.

I finally followed this fella, this guy, the pickup man, down to an area where he gave the stuff to the backer.

The backer used to take the stuff to the bank or whatever. He was the bigshot. And I got his license tag number, make of car, and all that stuff.

I guess I used to report to Ryan maybe once a month. I only had to report to him once a month and tell him what I did. And I would give him the information — who I talked to, who I played the numbers with, and what I had learned.

Near the end of the third month, beginning of the fourth month, I had the place pretty well scammed for all the guys that were takin' action in there.

This is when I learned what Ryan was doing. He used to meet me down by Pat's Steakhouse at Ninth and Wharton, because there was a cemetery, oh, a square block between Wharton and Federal.

And we would meet on the other side of the cemetery. I would tell James just what I did, and I'd give him my notes, right? And that's the information I passed on to him.

At this time I said, "Look, I think I got everybody in the place, here."

He said, "Fine," he said, "What I'm gonna do," he said, "I'm gonna get warrants out for each one of these guys."

With the information I gave him on the car and the license tag, they had traced the tag, they got the owner, and they knew who the pickup man was and where he dropped the stuff off.

I guess it was a week or so later, I meet Ryan up at headquarters. Now he didn't come into headquarters too much, 'cause he didn't want other people to know him. And actually, he didn't want anybody in headquarters to know who the undercover guys were.

Thomas M. Grubb & Allan "Lucky" Cole

Only one that knew it was Doyle, and that was an assumption, simply because he knew I talked to Ryan. And of course, the captain knew it, and that was it.

After Ryan got the warrants, he told me where he was going to meet me, and this was down at the place where I was doin' this undercover work. It was a big factory. And he met me there, there were a coupla police cars there from this particular district where the stuff was gonna go down.

And the cops came in. Each cop went to a different floor, and we went with the warrants. Well, there was hell to pay, because I served the warrants. I pointed out the guys, 'cause they didn't know them.

And walk up to 'em, give 'em the warrant, arrest 'em.

Then, after that, I was pulled outta the place, for my own good, really. And we went up to headquarters and we listed it all out. And he told me that I'd hafta appear in court against each one of these guys.

That lasted a few months before we got into court, and of course, it was no real big deal. It was only the lottery, the numbers game, you know. But the point was, they had their orders.

So we pinched the guys, and some walked, and some got out in a few weeks or a month or didn't go to jail at all.

Ryan said, "I don't want you to come in to work anymore." He said, "I'll call you or I'll get in touch with you."

So I told him, "O.K."

I realized then that Ryan didn't hold any rank. He was just a detective like me. And actually, he just ran this particular phase of this operation.

After that I got friendly with Ryan, because he thought I did a pretty good job. And it was a simple job, there wasn't really much to it, just to, y'know, wrap up these number people.

And thereafter he started to school me, never at headquarters. We would always meet at a location, and he used to talk to me about the narcotics and what to look for and this and that.

I had basic knowledge, but my knowledge was from the street — when you got information about this guy or that guy you scooped 'em up, like I told you in the other tapes.

Thomas M. Grubb & Allan "Lucky" Cole

Well, James enlightened me as to what to look for, and he said he was going to use me in a certain area where there were white junkies.

I told him, "That's o.k.," y'know, "whatever," because I was gettin' interested in it by then.

He taught me how, if he'd give you a suspect, he would usually have photographs. Now, he taught me how to order the photographs.

All he needed was the name, and we used to fill out slips very privately and send 'em down to Identification Records, and they would ship us back envelopes of photographs of junkies that'd been arrested, suspected junkies, and what have you.

This was the good part of workin' undercover. He would tell me certain places that he'd want me to frequent. Just to hang out, y'know, talk the talk, act the act. And just to kind of be a sharpie, that's all. And I did do this and this was a hell of an experience, believe me.

I was pointed out to one particular bar. It was in Center City, and I went down there. I used to stop there like, for a couple of hours every night or every other night. And then I'd go over to another place and just hang out.

The hardest part was to keep a register of what money I spent, because I used to get reimbursed. You didn't have money to piss away when you were a cop.

I did this when I was workin' on the numbers in the factory also, because you play a coupla bucks a day, and I'd want my money back.

But when I used to go in the bars it was the same thing. And you buy drinks, maybe you buy somebody a drink, and these bars were all whites.

You got to know the people in there, you made it a point to talk to the bartender, not too much, you know, inquiring, but you got to watch the people that came in. And after maybe, oh, three, four weeks, you got to see most of the same people again and again.

You talked to them frequently, like the bartender'd tell 'em, "This's a friend of mine," y'know, "Tom," and this b.s. and that.

You never gave your right names. And you got to know some of the guys as well as some of the girls.

149

Thomas M. Grubb & Allan "Lucky" Cole

After bein' introduced to quite a few of them, they'd ask you, "Hey look, want a smoke?" or this or that, and they'd give you a marijuana cigarette.

This used to be the trickiest part for me, because I never smoked that stuff, and I never wanted to get used to it. But I learned who could get the stuff and who used to carry a few cigarettes or whatever.

Then I learned the ones that were usin' heroin. Heroin was the drug of the time. Now, you gotta remember this was all the beatniks, I guess I should say, and they were easygoing, and they weren't, I don't know if you want to say, too smart or not, but they used to talk freely.

There were occasions when I got invited to a party and I used to get frightened, because, you know, you get there and you don't know what the hell's gonna happen.

Some of them were smokin' marijuana and some of them'd be usin' heroin. And I learned at that time heroin could be used in a helluva lotta ways, particularly with the women.

I got in with them, and I learned a lot. And eventually I got taken to some of these parties.

Well, the first time I ever smoked a marijuana cigarette, it was not the swallowin' the goddam smoke, like they used to make the big thing of inhaling.

I would take it, and I'd puff it, and those things burn out quick, so you had to really fake it. You didn't get too much of the smoke in, but some used to get in.

And to tell you the truth, most of the time it would just give me a goddam headache and make me sick.

But the thing was, you acted the part so you were accepted. And I got away with a few of them, and I learned who the people were. And then I started to go to different guys and buy some of the marijuana cigarettes.

Say, "Look, I got some friends," y'know, and this bull and that, and just con them.

They had seen me around for a coupla months now, and it was no big deal. And with the women it was easier. At that time I had black hair, I wasn't too bad lookin', and, y'know, they'd all want to make a friend.

So then I got to know who was usin' the heroin, who was usin' the marijuana, who was usin' the pills, and it made things easier and you talked the lingo. That was the hardest thing for me to really learn — their way of talking. But Lucky, it really, it wasn't that difficult.

And after goin' to one or two of the parties is when I really got screwed up. I was at this party, and at the party — y'know, there were a lot of people there.

They weren't just street people, they were people from the middle class, and some from wealthy, wealthy families. Because you're talkin' to this one and that one, and they tell you 'bout the other ones, and so forth.

Actually, you could see by their dress that — y'know, they wore some good clothes. Naturally, at that time I was dressin' up also, 'cause you couldn't go in lookin' like a bum.

I never carried a weapon, Lucky, because it was too easy to see, too easy to detect. And it was just a putting together of information.

This particular night I went to this party, and it was one girl that stood out, blond haired girl, very attractive.

I learned that her father was one of the bigger wholesalers of produce — fruits, vegetables, and so forth — down at the food distribution center. At that time it was down in South Philly, it was on Front Street.

I learned her boyfriend's name, and he used to be around with her a lot. But his family wasn't as prominent as the young lady's.

But anyway, I gathered all my information, like I told you, about the numbers thing. And she invited me to this party. And it was in a very, very nice area, one of the hotels.

I went, not knowing really what to expect, but you gotta just fake it half the time. Went up and had a few drinks and talked and stuff.

And then they started with the goddam injections of the heroin. Well, this was scary. This was really scary, 'cause you see them there cookin' the shit and the spoons and the little silver trays and whatnot. And injecting themselves, or somebody else would do it for them.

Thomas M. Grubb & Allan "Lucky" Cole

Now it was really pathetic, because you saw straight lookin' people doin' this shit, and you wonder, "My God almighty," y'know, how bad are they, how far are they strung out, and this and that.

At this particular party was the first time I really spotted the supplier. He used to bring the shit in and the girls or whoever, one guy maybe, would buy it. And I spotted both of them.

I got the names through conversation — "Oh, Billy Boy can give us all we want. You can get this, you can get that,"

And that was about the size of it.

Well, this one time at this party, the ones I was really friendly with, they were injecting, and naturally I got invited to take a shot.

This was really scary for me, Luck, and what I used to do, what I learned to do from Ryan, is to just take a straight pin — now, not go into your vein, but somewhere near it — and just stick yourself, so it would make a mark.

Maybe a little scab, from the puncture of the pin. And I used to do it on my hand, right between my thumb and forefinger.

That wasn't uncommon, because some of these girls used to shoot under their breasts. They would shoot in their privates. They would shoot in between their toes.

Anywhere where it didn't show too much, 'cause as soon as you spotted tracks — you know what a track is, I'm sure you do. They're burn marks from the heroin, and they leave, just like a railroad track, on the veins on the arm, or on the back of the leg, or wherever.

I figured let's try the hand, that seemed to be good enough, and, matter of fact, this was suggested to me by Ryan.

Said, "If you ever get in a situation, this is what you do."

So that was good information, and I used it this particular night.

When you're shootin' between the thumb and forefinger, there are veins in there. But see, everybody wasn't a mainliner.

There's what they call skinpopping. That's when you just shoot it under the skin and not into the vein. And when you do this, it takes a longer time for it to circulate to your bloodstream, so you get the high.

Well, I did this, I took the needle. And some of them actually had homemade syringes, some had real syringes, the ones that could buy them.

152

I took the goddam thing, and I only put it in the skin and out. In one side of the skin and out, not into my hand, and I squeezed it, naturally, and the shit ran down my finger and under my hand, and that was it.

And, oh, I was really accepted then.

Like I say, this went on for a while.

Also during this period of time, if I didn't mention it, I used to buy stuff from the different ones. It wasn't from the main guy all the time, but I had made a couple of buys from him, nickel-dime bags and so forth.

Which I'd tell him, "Hey man, this is for later, me and my girlfriend," or somethin' like that.

But some of the other ones, from time to time I purchased the marijuana cigarettes and a nickel bag, or whatever. And I had them all down on paper. I knew who I was dealing with.

One particular place where we used to meet and go, it was in Center City, it was a bar. And in this bar came a lot of the women performers from the Troc. If you don't remember that, that was the only burlesque house in Philadelphia at the time. And I met a lot of the performers down there, because now I was a steady in the place.

I met people like Blaze Starr, Candy — Candy Barr I think her name was. She did about sixty years in prison for shootin' a guy, her manager or somebody. And a lot of the other performers. I met Cheez 'n Crackers Hagan. He wasn't a junkie. At least he never used anything to my knowledge.

You got friendly with them, you talked with them and this and that. And sometimes they would ask you, y'know, where's this or that, where's this, or where can I pick this up at.

The real one that I knew that was a junkie was this Candy Barr. She was a pretty little blond-haired girl. And like I say, later on she went to prison for murderin' a guy.

Well, after a while I was really gettin' sick of this shit, because I was never a big drinker, and I got to thinkin', "Goddam it, here I'm," y'know, "victimizing people," so to speak. And I'm going to arrest them eventually.

I used to meet with Ryan, like I told you, every three weeks or so, or whenever he would leave a message for me to meet him, I

153

would meet him. And I would give him these things — this person, that person, a purchase, a buy or whatever.

Any of the stuff I got, I used to turn in to Ryan, with the slip, so he could verify it on the warrant, whatever you got. Maybe you got a bag of heroin, or maybe you got marijuana in a certain amount from this individual or that one.

After this was done, I didn't want to play with it anymore.

After doin' all this, turnin' all this stuff in, like I said, the warrants were gotten, and it was my job to appear in court and verify the buys and persons I bought from.

And it's a bitch to stand up there and look at a person who considered you a friend, and tell what happened.

Now this went along with men as well as women. And it wasn't, it didn't make you feel very comfortable and I kinda felt funny about it. But it had to be done and I did it.

But I did speak to Ryan, I told him, "That's it for me," I said, "I think I'm burnt down here, and I don't want to, you know, do this any more."

At this time I didn't know if that was the end of me in the squad or not, but I did tell him. And he told the captain, of course, and that was it up to that point.

You see, Lucky, not that you're afraid of anything, but when you testify against these people, like I say, they're all kinda characters, a lot of nice people, what you would consider nice. You would talk to them every day on the street if you didn't know them.

And they remember you, God, did they remember you. And I just used to get a bad feeling about this.

Cass didn't know too much about this stuff, because in this squad you had no hours. And I would go out, sometimes I would go out, ten o'clock at night, twelve, sometimes eight in the morning.

You just came and went as you wanted, particularly in this situation where I was working. Nobody knew what you were doing, because you didn't sign in or anything of that nature. The only one that knew what you were doing was this guy Ryan, and he used to report to the captain.

No need to say, you made enemies doin' this, Lucky.

Thomas M. Grubb & Allan "Lucky" Cole

CHAPTER NINETEEN
Special Investigations

DURING THIS WHOLE undercover thing I officially remained in the squad. Afterward, I went — actually — into the squad. And nobody really knew what I was doing, because no one ever mentioned anything.

The only thing they knew — perhaps later on when I went down to court to testify, you're liable to have seen one of your guys down there on another case or something. But it was pretty hush-hush.

There was one situation while we were on this narcotics stuff, that one of the men, young man, got arrested. He was, he was a heavy user.

And I met his wife. Beautiful girl. And I don't know what he did, he went to Lexington, I think, for the cure. He didn't do jail time or anything.

Later on I had occasion to get this guy, and I got him really dirty. I got him carryin' a few bags and everything else. So that meant jail time for him.

I took him into headquarters, and I talked to him — you know, he knew me. That was the worst thing, he knew me, who I was.

While we were in headquarters, he says, "Look," he said, "You gotta do me a favor."

'Cause he knew he was gone.

He said, "I want you to go get my wife."

This kind of threw me back. Now, they were in their twenties, maybe give or take a coupla years, and I looked at him, I said, "Yeah?"

He said, "Yeah, I want you to go arrest my wife."

He told me where his stash was in their apartment. And she was a big user, and he told me where she shot up, y'know, what part of her body and so forth.

I told him, "O.K."

He said, "Please do this for me."

I said, "Now, tell me something," I said, "Why are you asking me this?"

He said, "Well, detective," he said, "if my wife, if you don't get her," he said, "she has no money to go out and buy the stuff."

And he said, "You know what's going to happen."

Well, I did know, from the junkies I dealt with. When a girl is hooked and she's got no bread, the two things she's gonna do is become a shoplifter, which is the better half, or she's gotta become a prostitute.

And this guy — evidently he loved his wife and whatnot, they're only married a few years. And he had turned her on to the drugs.

He said, "Look," he said, "I don't want her out in the street, hustlin'."

And that was it.

So I told him, "I'll get her."

Well, I got a warrant on the information he gave me, and I took another guy with me, from the squad. And we went up and we served the warrant, o.k.?

We went right to where they kept the stash. She used to keep it, they had this, like, brass bed, one of these nice brass beds.

And the top of it, one of the knobs used to come off, and they had it stuffed. She used to keep her works down in there, and the stuff, the heroin.

When we did clean it out, we found maybe half-a-dozen dime bags, which was sizable.

We arrested her — on a warrant now, mind you — and he had told me where she shot up, but I couldn't strip the girl, that's a boo-boo, you know that. And I took her into the district.

In the district I called for a policewoman, and the policewoman came, and she stripped her and searched her. And then they found where she was shootin' up.

And she was shootin' up like, near the vaginal area, and y'know, that was just her thing. But anyway, I did arrest her.

I never told her about her husband's turning her in. I figured they could talk among themselves eventually and maybe she'd find out, but I didn't think it was right to tell her that.

She did ask, "How did you know about all this and that?"

I said, "Just on information."

This girl, she later went to trial. And her husband was already in Lexington. And this was her first pinch, her first arrest. Even with the possession of stuff, she got a pretty good break.

She was — you know, they've got a choice of going to jail or going to Lexington, Kentucky, for the cure.

Naturally, she picked the cure. And that was that.

I didn't see her again for six months.

Well, Lucky, after I got out of all that, I was assigned, naturally, to the squad, but I still didn't have a partner.

So I went back into the squad, just like a new guy going in, and none of them really knew me. And at this time I'm into the squad, God, for months, six months — more, seven months.

And I get this guy, Sal DeLuca, as a partner. Well, I didn't know Sal DeLuca and Sal DeLuca didn't know me. And it's a funny thing, you know, when you work with some men you get to know them very, very well.

Sal wasn't a bad guy, which, after quite a while I got to learn about him. I learned that Sal had worked South Philly. He worked in another district downtown.

Of course, Sal was an Italian. Sal was a funny, funny guy. He always had a cigar in his mouth.

We worked together and, you know, two cops gettin' stuck together like that, you talk a lot. I never told him anything about the undercover work, and as far as he knew, I got transferred into the squad the same time he did.

Like I told you in the beginning, nobody gets into these squads without a rabbi. A rabbi meaning somebody political that can help you get a transfer and a unit. Sal and I worked together pretty good. Sal was from West Philly.

Sal was kind of a hotshot, and he used to use the procedure of ordering photographs of anybody that'd been arrested for use of narcotics. And they used to come in, oh God, he'd order 'em by the dozen.

It was funny, that.

He'd say, "Hey, Tom, look what I got," and he would show me these photographs, and Christ, many of them I knew that I had arrested already.

157

But I never said anything to him about this. You know, it's best to keep your mouth shut about certain things, and just let nature take its course.

During the first month that Sal and I worked together, I got to see the other guys that were in the squad. And then I could see that, oh, I guess it was like, two-thirds white and the other third was black.

And there were some real characters in this squad, believe me.

One fella stands out, really, in my mind. That was a guy named Capasso. Steve was from South Philly, and Steve was the biggest bullshitter you ever wanted to listen to.

Steve always had The Big Bust comin' down, and he would always like to have a coupla other teams from the squad to help him in the arrest.

Sal used to eat this up. He thought that this was the greatest, 'cause he's new in the squad, he hasn't made any arrests or whatnot, yet.

On the other side, the black fellas, there was a guy named Freddie Morrison. Freddie was a sharpie, there's no doubt about that. Freddie always used to have big information on busts that we should make.

Freddie wasn't bad, but he was quite a b.s.'er also. And Freddie was the kind of guy you had to watch with three eyes, if you had three.

I also got to learn a little more about the squad and the different men in it.

There were two men that evidently were the captain's boys, and they used to make some good arrests.

I used to say, "Gee, these guys are well informed."

Now, none of them knew that I had worked undercover, and nobody ever said anything.

I don't know if the captain ever did or not, but later on I found out that the captain used to pass information on to these particular two guys, and they used to come up with some substantial arrests. And it would look good on the books.

Thomas M. Grubb & Allan "Lucky" Cole

Well, goin' back to Sal. Like I said, Sal worked the South Philly district, and I learned that Sal used to be a clerk, a police clerk, before he became a police officer.

Sal was a helluva typist. That I liked. God, I liked that so much. Because this is when we start making our own reports, our arrest reports, our follow-up reports, and so forth.

Let me tell you, I am not a typist, I never was. I used to use the four-finger system, and what I used to call it was the biblical system — seek and ye shall find. I could never type like this guy.

I found that we made a pretty good combination after a while.

But Sal's theory was, he used to take the photographs that he used to get from I.D. and Central Records, and, y'know, you had the photographs, you had the pictures and everything.

And Sal used to, we worked primarily South Philly — South Street, actually, which is the North of South Philadelphia, and it's primarily black. Well, Sal's theory was, always get on the books. And that wasn't a bad theory, 'cause it used to keep the captain happy, and he'd stay off your case.

We all used our own cars in that situation. We used to use Sal's old Plymouth a lot. And I mean, it was an old junker. But nobody knew it, and we used to patrol like, South Street, Bainbridge Street, all in around there. And then we'd be gettin' up to my area — Center City, which I knew.

Thomas M. Grubb & Allan "Lucky" Cole

CHAPTER TWENTY
Junkies

WE'D GO ALONG and Sal would spot a junkie, he'd have the picture in there, and the guy would be a user. I mean, these are all users that he had. None of them were guys that really purchased any amount of narcotics or anything. But still and all, that was an arrest.

So we would spot a user, and naturally, we'd pull up and we'd get him. And we would put him in the car, and Sal used to have this attitude that he had to be the tough guy. I'd be easy, like "good cop, bad cop." And then we used to just to take the poor guy that we picked up, take him into the district.

And when you examined him, you examined his arms and his legs and whatnot, sometimes had him strip. But most men would shoot in their arms, and we'd see he'd have a track, but, y'know, when a guy's used drugs recently, there's a scab or something that looks fresh on their arms.

Well anyway, we would talk to the guy and bullshit him, and then we would arrest him, put him in a cell. And then he would be sent down to Central Holding, where a doctor would look at him.

And he would determine if it was a recent use or not. Well, with this decision we would get whether the guy was negative or positive. Positive was a good arrest, he used drugs recently. Negative, cut 'im loose. And that's what they used to do, cut the guy loose.

Well, this went on, oh God, for a long time, and Sal had all these photographs and everything. And we picked up a lot of users. You know, patrollin' those areas, you couldn't miss, because unfortunately, this was the poor black area, and a lot of them used drugs down there.

But we could never get a supplier. That was the big thing to get.

We used to run so many of those guys through the doctor, and every now and then you'd come up with a positive.

A lot of times these junkies were no dummies, either. If they used recently, what they'd do is take a fingernail and scratch over where they shot in and break the skin. Or take a lit cigarette and burn the needle hole.

And you couldn't decide whether they actually were using recently, or if it was an old thing, or whatnot. And it was a toss-up whether you got a positive or a negative result from the doctor.

Sal and I did that for a while, and of course, while you're workin' with a guy you get to know him pretty good. And I learned that Sal was a fanatic for horses. He loved to play the horses.

Sal was quite a conversationalist. We used to go down to his district where he had worked, and he was quite friendly with the lieutenant and the captain, because he used to be the captain's clerk.

He knew a lot of the guys down there, and there were a lot of good guys. And I got to know them, and some of them used to tell me, "You gotta watch Sal. Sal is a b.s.'er," and this stuff and that. And you take all that with a grain of salt.

Now, they didn't know me, but you try to be friendly with guys, and they take you as they find you.

With Sal's ability as a typist, and his integrity and ambition, it kinda got to me and I liked the guy. And after a few months, I trusted him. We got together pretty good. From time to time we'd go out to his home and have lunch, because our time was our time.

You could just do anything you wanted, as long as you didn't touch the numbers. I told you that in the beginning. This squad would not touch numbers.

I never told Sal that I worked undercover, or that when I worked undercover it was primarily identifying numbers guys in the first place, and then identifying narcotics users.

It was later on that while patrolling around, in which we did a lot of riding to different areas, I would see somebody that I had arrested while undercover, and I knew that they had a habit.

I would tell Sal, "Hey, look. Pull over, let's grab this one."

When we grabbed the one that I wanted, y'know, we'd pinch him, and then we'd take him into the district and we'd talk to him.

Usually I'd talk to him first and I'd say, "Don't you say anything unless I ask you." And then I'd tell him, "Look, give me somebody. Give me somebody I don't know."

What the guy would do is say, "Look, give me a break. Give me a break."

Thomas M. Grubb & Allan "Lucky" Cole

I'd say, "Yeah, give me a break. I'll give you a break, but you tell me who you're buyin' from."

This was tough, because nobody, no junkie wants to tell you their source, 'cause you arrest their source, then they gotta find another one to get their junk.

Sometimes you got lucky, sometimes you didn't. Some guys would suffer the pinch. The only time they would definitely suffer the pinch is if they were negative, but if they were positive — had used drugs recently — they knew they were going. That was a good three to six months automatically.

Every now and then I would get somebody who would tell me their source. And I would keep that to myself.

And later, I'd tell Sal, "Hey, Sal, we're gonna go here, we're gonna go there, at a specific time," when I was told the guy would be holding.

He could be holding maybe three bags, maybe thirty bags.

But the point was, these guys never kept the stuff on their person. What they would do was, they would stash them in different places, and I mean some odd places.

Under bushes, in cracks in the wall, under a car. You never knew where the hell they were gonna stash their stuff, but it was always close to where they were.

When I got to Sal, I would tell him, "Look, we're gonna grab this guy, and here's where we're gonna go."

And he was amazed that I would know this shit. And we would make a good arrest. We would make maybe a three, four, six bag arrest. It all depended what the guy was holdin'.

Well, of course, when we went to court it was a good arrest. We got a distributor, a pusher. And that always looked good on the onionskins.

The onionskins were what came out every morning at headquarters. When you made an arrest durin' the night, it was reported to headquarters.

The captain insisted that every arrest that we made — anybody in the squad would make — would be reported, and he would get a copy of it every morning.

Thomas M. Grubb & Allan "Lucky" Cole

When he used to get these copies, he would see you made a pinch. He used to like to see the positive pinches, and a possession pinch more than anything.

If he saw you doin' that, he would keep off your case, he wouldn't bother you. He used get on the cases of the guys that weren't showin' pinches.

Really, he left us alone pretty well, because we would always make at least one pinch a day. Even if it was negative, it would be a pinch, and it would show in the onionskins that he would get.

It didn't take too long before I got a firm dislike for the captain.

We did have an excellent sergeant, Joe Ricca. Ricca was a helluva guy. Ricca didn't bother you at all.

You know, he'd give you advice if he could, but most of the guys up there besides myself were — I was the youngest guy there, as far as the police department was concerned.

I only had like three years in, and the other guys, Christ, had ten, fifteen, twenty years. Y'know, they had been around a lot, different divisions, different squads, and what have you. Some actually had 25 years in the business.

But I found that the sergeant treated you all the same, he was a good cat.

And every now and then we would go out on a raid. And the raid would be something like, Steve Capasso would have a big deal going on. And he would get the squad together, and maybe get ten guys.

He used to pull me, the youngest guy, and nine other guys. Some black, some white, y'know, whatever. Whoever wasn't doing anything, or whoever felt like workin'.

We would go and hit a place. And sometimes we found stuff, sometimes we didn't. The place was usually occupied by users, but like I told you, a user was the low end of the totem pole.

When we hit a place, we hadda search it. And I mean, we used to ticket the search. And Christ, you would find, if you were lucky, drugs in some of the worst places you would ever wanna look.

I went into some places where you would take a picture off the wall, and under the picture was brown, on the wallpaper or the paint

Thomas M. Grubb & Allan "Lucky" Cole

or whatever, and then all of a sudden the brown would scatter because it was all roaches.

I mean, they were some of the most filthy places you could ever think of. And you hadda go in there and search 'em.

And Holy Christ, it was terrible, let me tell you, Lucky. When you came out, you'd have to practically get undressed to make sure you were clean.

The big thing was, when you hit a place, even if you found one bag in there, somebody had to admit to a possession, or you took the owner of the house, or the occupant of the house, whoever's renting it.

And it could be a woman, a man, or whoever. But you made some arrest there, if somebody wouldn't admit to the stuff.

You also sent everybody that was in there down to the police surgeon to be examined, to see if they're negative or positive for drugs. And of course, you got some positive, some negative.

Steve usually had pretty good information when he took the guys out to hit a place. I don't know if he got it from Lonnie or he got it on his own, because we never asked.

You see, in this squad everybody worked on their own. So everybody had pretty much leeway. Narcotics was primary, but anything else — burglaries, robberies, rape — you name it, you could pinch them.

Like I told you, Sal DeLuca liked to work the main drags of the poor black areas — upper South Philadelphia, Bainbridge Street, South Street and so forth.

There were a lot of junkies down that area, and we used to patrol there every day. And without fail, we'd pick up one or two or what have you.

This particular day we picked up one guy. And he had tracks up and down his arms, like railroad tracks. So we stick him in Sal's car, and Sal's gonna take him into the district, and I told Sal, "Hey, wait a minute. Let's drive him around a while."

Well, man, the guy didn't like this at all, but I knew from experience that this was the thing to do. I learned this when I was in uniform. And we start drivin' him up and down South Street.

This guy was havin' a fit, he was lyin' on the floor of the car. So I got in the back seat of the car and was holdin' him up.

I told him, "You look out the window, you s.o.b., and, y'know, let the people see you."

Before we went three blocks like that, that was it. He was gonna talk to us.

So we drove him into the district. We used to go to a Center City district.

And we get him in there, we tell him, "O.K., talk to me."

And they never wanted to talk.

But we'd tell 'em, "Look, if you don't talk to me, you're gone, and we're gonna take you back out again."

They were always afraid of somebody seein' them in the car, that they were a rat.

So we used to make an agreement, "Look, I'm gonna let you go, but you gotta give me three. Give me one before I let you go.'

And he'd tell us something. It might be a location — a house — or describe a guy — give us his name, description. And we'd keep him in the cell while we went out and got this guy he told us about, or woman, whatever the case may be.

We'd go out, and sometimes you made a possession pinch, and we used to usually make a good pinch.

Then we'd come back, and before we put the one in the cell we had just arrested, we'd go back and we'd let the other guy go.

And tell him, "You owe me."

This was the deal, this was the way we did it all the years I was in the squad. And we did well like this, we made a lot of good pinches.

Now the thing was, if you went out — like, if we'd say we're gonna work days, we'd go in, check in, eight o'clock in the morning. We'd get out, hit the street, maybe make one pinch, y'know, it was a junkie, you knew that by your records and what have you.

Even if he was negative, you would make that pinch and it would go on record, you'd book him and so forth, knowing that the onionskins were gonna go to headquarters in the morning. And the captain went over them, and he'd see you made a pinch.

165

Well, after you did that, maybe that could be like, ten o'clock in the morning, you had the rest of the day off. You didn't have to do anything unless you wanted to.

I mean, it wasn't officially a day off, but you could show you made an arrest that day and that you were active.

We often did this, because Sal would want to go to the track or what have you, and I'd go home. And it worked out pretty good that way.

From time to time — Sal was a connoisseur of wine — and often, we'd make that daily pinch, maybe two, and then we would head over to Jersey. And we would head over to the vineyards, to the wine companies, and we'd sample the wines over there and maybe purchase some.

Then we got an in where you would get meats, where the butchers who would butcher the farmer's cattle and so forth, we'd go over there and buy our meats.

Also, in the egg country, like Vineland, we would purchase our eggs, and I mean, by the crates. Because, y'know, he'd take half, I'd take half, and we used to distribute 'em among our families. And you got the things for, God, a third of the cost that you would pay in the city.

So a lot of things like that, personal things, worked out great. Long as you could show that you were takin' police action that day.

166

CHAPTER TWENTY–ONE
Special Investigations (III)

AFTER WORKING A WHILE with Sal, we got to be pretty tight. Although I liked Sal, I could never get the feeling that I had workin' with my first partner in uniform, Johnny Bennett. I guess it's because Johnny and I had so many things in common.

Johnny was married. Sal was single. Sal didn't have a family. Also, Johnny and I, we used to share a lot of things, like the baseball games and socializin' together, his wife and Cass. And it just wasn't the same, although Sal was a good guy.

Like I told you, Sal was a crackerjack typist, which I benefited from. Every arrest we made, we made up our own reports, which were quite lengthy.

It worked out that I'd do the dictating and Sal would do the typing. And he could actually type as fast as I could talk.

I'm not sure if I described Sal DeLuca to you or not, Lucky, but Sal was about five foot nine and about 150, 60 pounds, straight black hair, and going bald.

This he hated. Sal would wear a hat a lot. You couldn't mistake DeLuca, he always smoked a cigar, wore that hat, and used to always walk fast.

The thing was, he reminded me of Joe Penner, if you remember — "You wanna buy a duck?" That's the way Sal walked, slightly bent over and really hustlin', with the cigar stickin' out of his face.

Although we worked pretty well together, we never socialized together. Sal's idea of a good time was to sneak off to the racetrack, 'cause he was a horse degenerate. And he loved to talk horses, and that just wasn't my thing.

The thing I liked best about Sal was, you could trust him. He wasn't the kind of guy who was always walkin' around with his hand out lookin' for a payoff from anybody. This made working with him a lot easier.

Sal was a digger. He always wanted to make the big pinch, but for some reason he was gullible when it came to some of the other guys in the squad.

We had this character, Steve Capasso, who was also from downtown in our neighborhood. Steve was an Italian guy, and he looked like he came from the Mafia, instead of bein' a cop.

Steve always had the big bust goin' down. He was gonna confiscate all kinds of junk or this or that, and he used to suck Sal into a lot of things that I went along with at first.

After a while I had to have a talk with Sal and tell him, "Hey, wise up, Steve 's nothin' but a b.s.'er — bullshitter."

There were occasions, like I told you, when one team would need to help another team or several teams. And this guy Steve used to come in and spread the word that he had this big thing goin' down, and he needed the help of maybe two or four more guys.

Well, soon as DeLuca would hear this, he would be the first to volunteer us. I went along with it for a few times.

This one particular time we met, like at Broad and Washington Avenue, at four o'clock in the morning. Steve told us about this big shipment that was coming in, and that he was going to hit it and he needed us for backup.

Sal and I went down there, four o'clock in the morning, and two other cops came as well, from the squad. We got there maybe quarter of four, and it was in the dead of winter.

And it was cold. Now, we laid out there, quarter of four to four o'clock, then four fifteen, four thirty. No Capasso.

So I look at Sal, and I ask him, "What the hell's goin' on, Sal?"

"I don't know, I don't know."

We waited till near five o'clock, and that was it for me.

I told him, "I'm goin', you can stay if you want to."

Well, that was the first time Steve pulled his bullshit on us.

Then, it was a couple months later, Steve had this other big bust that he wanted, and again he asked for help. Sal, again, always wanted to be in on the big bust, and I hadda go along with it. He was my partner.

I told him, "Sal, you know Steve is just a bullshitter, and it ain't gonna happen."

But this time Steve was so sure, and Sal was so convinced that I said, "O.K.," and we go.

And again, we went up into North Philadelphia this time, and this was in a rather nasty part of the city. And we're layin' down by the docks, and Steve says that this shipment is coming in, and we're gonna grab the guys and everything.

We waited around for him, and finally he did show up. This was the best part. He showed up — again this was three-four o'clock in the morning — and I figured, "Hey, maybe the guy does have something."

Well, we're sittin' there, waitin' and waitin', and a car pulls up and I figure, "This's gotta be it, and Steve 's gonna make this deal."

He goes to the car, and of course we're all right there, watchin' him, ready to jump out and help him if needed. We had a prearranged signal.

But Steve's standin' there b.s.'in' with these guys in the car, then the car pulls away. Naturally, when it pulled away we waited to see what was gonna happen.

He came over and he talked to us, says, "Aahh," y'know, "it ain't gonna happen," he says, "They chickened out. They didn't have enough stuff," and all this and that.

That just about cured me of going on Steve's jobs. Of course it was difficult to explain to Sal, that he's just usin' us, he's bullshittin' us, figurin' that the captain's gonna hear about these big busts, and he's really workin' out there in the street. Actually, these things were all in his mind.

I told you the squad was about one-third black guys, and I got along pretty good with them. And there's this one particular guy I told you about, Freddie Morrison.

We used to call him "Bogey." Freddie was a little guy, real sharp, spoke well, and knew the streets very well.

And from checkin' the arrest sheets, we saw Freddie made good arrests.

One night Freddie comes in, he says, "Hey look, Grubb," he says, "you doin' anything tonight?"

Naturally there's no big deals going on, so I said, "No, Bogey, what's on your mind?"

He said, "You and Sal want to help me out on a pinch?" He said, "Just the three of us," he said, "that's all we need."

Thomas M. Grubb & Allan "Lucky" Cole

I asked him, I said, "Whaddya got goin' down, Freddie?"

He told me about this tractor-trailer of stolen stuff that he was going to see that evening. He was going to make a deal with these black guys that had stolen this rig.

Well, first off it was a Peterbilt tractor-trailer that he described, which in itself was worth, oh, $100,000.00, even in those times.

And it was supposed to be loaded with hot stuff that they clipped — they hijacked the trailer, actually. And he was gonna make a deal with these guys.

The deal was that he was gonna come up in a rental, and he was gonna take so much of this load off their hands, and, y'know, he was supposed to get rid of it.

Now it wasn't gonna be the whole load, 'cause it's a tractor-trailer and he's got, like, a twelve-foot box rental. And everything looked great.

I said, "Good, Bogey," I said, "we'll give you a hand with this."

I guess it was, oh, maybe six o'clock in the morning, we get up to around Castor and Tioga, there's a lot of trailer companies up there, where they park the rigs and so forth.

Sure'er than hell, Freddie pulls up with this rental. And he pulls over to this certain tractor-trailer. He had the number and we knew the make of it, it was described to us, and it was hot.

And Freddie gets out front with these guys, two black guys. Now what we're lookin' for, is if there's anybody else beside these two guys. And lo and behold, Freddie starts makin' the deal with them, and then he gives us the signal.

And we close in on these two guys, weapons out, 'cause you don't know what the hell they're gonna come up with.

Well anyway, we make the pinch. And we got these guys, and what they've got in the trailer is a load of these portable radios and televisions and all this stuff.

We got them, we got the vehicle. And naturally I've got them on the ground, and Sal called the wagon up, called for assistance.

It was like a circus up there. All the wagons from the district came in. We had to call the major crimes unit, we let them in on it, really. And it turned out to be a good arrest.

Thomas M. Grubb & Allan "Lucky" Cole

Right away, in my book Bogey was o.k., because he knew what he was doing, he had his shit all together, knew exactly where they were gonna be and what he was gonna do when he met them.

We actually got a commendation for that arrest. The captain was well pleased with it, and only three of us were in on the pinch, which made it even better.

Course the captain took the credit for it, said he was informed of the whole thing, which he wasn't, he learned about it later.

After this pinch, I guess we kind of got on the A List with the old man, and he even spoke to us once in a while, you know. And that was something rare, because he didn't give a damn about anybody.

The captain had two teams of men — Rudenski, LaTorre and Swann and Terry Cooke and a guy named Reagan — who he used to feed information to.

Now, it's not hard to make a good pinch when somebody tells you where to go and where the stuff is, you know. You just go there, make the pinch, you got your warrant, and that was easy.

These guys always used to make the top of the arrest sheets. And they were the examples he used to always use, like, when we would have our meetings — "Hey, do you know that this team made the big pinch, or that team made the big pinch."

This was why it was hard to get on his good side. The old bastard never gave us any information at all.

I later learned that this guy, Terry Cooke, was his rat. Anything that went on in the squad quickly got back to the captain.

On this particular occasion, maybe half the squad, when we came in, were notified to stand by. And we went out on this pinch, on a raid, you might say.

It was in South Philly, down around Fitzwater Street. And we hit this house where there was supposed to be a lot of junk.

In the process of searching the place, the sergeant, who was a hell of a nice guy, Joe Ricca, was sort of limping around. And when you search a place, Lucky, you're up on things, crawlin' around in ceilings and down in basements and everything else.

Nick came up to a couple of us and he said, "Hey, look fellas. I hurt my leg today," he said, "You saw me slip and fall in here."

171

Well, whattya gonna do, y'know, the guy's a good guy. You cover for your friends in the department.

Cooke happened to overhear this and see the sergeant. And the fact is that later on, after we had made these arrests, we took a few people outta the house, we got a half a kilo of heroin. So the arrest was good.

But the thing was, Ricca went to the hospital from there, and he had fractured a bone in his ankle earlier in the day, not on this particular job.

Cooke got in to the captain, we learned later, and he told the captain that the sergeant did not get hurt on the job.

Well, that was enough for me and a few of the other guys that learned about it, 'cause you just couldn't trust this bastard anymore.

The sergeant was out for about a month or so, and when he came back, he got transferred out to another district. We lost one helluva supervisor and a good friend.

In comes a Sergeant Foyle, who we later learned had worked with Lonnie in the Burglary and Robbery Unit for years. So we knew that they were asshole buddies and you couldn't say too much in front of this guy.

Thomas M. Grubb & Allan "Lucky" Cole

CHAPTER TWENTY–TWO
The Raid

It was just about this time that they started the citywide raids. Now this used to happen every six months or so. These were real beauties. This happened to be the first time I went on one of these citywide raids.

We used to come in to work — if you were workin' durin' the day, when you came in to check off they told you, "Stick around."

And the guys that came in, like at the second shift, who worked eight o'clock at night, or twelve, whatever the shift would be, they would wait. Nobody would know why. The first time I never knew why.

We stayed in headquarters, nobody could touch the phones, nobody could call out, nothin'. And at three o'clock all the cars would pull up, and we would get loaded into the cars — all the teams — and we'd go out to Convention Hall.

Well, we get out to Convention Hall, and at this time everybody knows, "O.K., it's a raid." These were the other guys that were older than me and knew more about it.

When you went in the Convention Hall, the Police Commissioner was there and some of the high brass. And what would happen was, they would call up your team.

Like I said, Sal and I were a team. There were some teams that consisted of three guys, but never less than two, never more than three.

You were called up, the commissioner, standin' there with the captain, would hand you an envelope. And in this envelope, he would tell you, "There's four warrants, there's four photographs. Go out and arrest these people."

Luck, I'll explain to you how these raids are put together. The undercover guys go out and make buys or know people that might have been pushin' a little bit, or at least using.

And they're the ones that swear out the warrants on these different individuals. Then the squad goes out and busts all of them.

We'd have to make these arrests within three hours, because they all had to be arraigned down at City Hall at seven in the morning. Well, you never knew what you got.

You got your envelope, you went out to the vehicle you were assigned to, and usually it was a coupla highway guys would drive you around, just to have a uniform with you when you hit these doors. Now mind you, this is four, four-thirty in the morning.

My first ones were up in Germantown, and Lucky, this was the one section of the city I really did not know that well. I was like, just staggerin' around, lookin' for the places we had to go to.

The first thing I did is, when we got these highway guys I asked 'em, "Which one'a you guys know Germantown?"

Fortunately, one of the guys knew.

He said, "I know it." Says, "I've worked Germantown."

I said, "Great. You ride with me."

And Sal went with the other guy.

Well, we get up to Germantown and we start rappin' on doors, and it's a funny thing. You only have a limited amount of time, and you hope that the person you're lookin' for is in the house at that time. Or apartment, whatever it might be.

Usually you had to knock the door down, because nobody answers the door at four o'clock in the morning. Not in that neighborhood.

We made our pinches, we searched the place, and you might find a little marijuana, maybe a little heroin. And that was the big thing in those days, the heroin.

So we stopped, oh, I guess we made our three stops. And we were real lucky, 'cause we got the people we wanted, we found a little stuff in each place, so they were good pinches.

On the fourth pinch, we hit this door — now it's gettin' close to the magic hour where you got to get the hell down to City Hall with these prisoners.

We hit this door, and we grab a guy, look at our picture that we've got of the guy, show him the warrant, we search the place, nothing. Haven't got a damn thing in this place.

Thomas M. Grubb & Allan "Lucky" Cole

We get the wagon, as usual, and we throw this guy in the wagon. And he's swearin' to God he isn't the guy that we got the warrant on.

I look at the picture, I look at the guy, I said, "It's gotta be him."

Well, that was the funniest part about it, Lucky. We arrested this guy. And we took him down — now he was a junkie. Don't get me wrong. He had the tracks on 'im, the whole bit. And we ship him down to central cell room, o.k.?

And then we gotta go down ourselves. And we're down there, it's like, seven o'clock in the morning, and there's a funny thing.

We're down at the hearings — actually, at the arraignments. And we come up second with our group. And the first three, right away, certified for court.

And the fourth guy, I swear to God, we took this picture out and showed it to the D.A., A.D.A., and he looked at it, and the guy said, "It ain't me. It ain't me."

And they went, and they said, "Something's wrong, here."

Usually they just shanghaied these guys, they railroaded them.

But the A.D.A. just said, "Wait. We'll wait. I want to get a fingerprint check on this guy."

Sure as shit, it was not the same guy. So what we just did was book him for use. He wasn't positive. We knew he was negative, because the scars were old on his arms. But that's the way we got off the hook with that.

It was unique in the way it happened — the guy swearin' it ain't him, we've got the picture of him, and you know, you look at a picture, you look at a person — same one. Description fit, the whole bit.

But it was not him. His fingerprints did not match the fingerprints on file.

So he got a bye. He just got held overnight while the doctor took a look at him, and when they pronounced him negative, well, then they walk.

That was the first raid I went on, Luck.

Thomas M. Grubb & Allan "Lucky" Cole

CHAPTER TWENTY–THREE
Junkies (II)

THERE'S ALSO ANOTHER phenomenon that occurs after a raid — all the junkies and pushers kind of go underground. And you don't see much of anything happening on the street, simply because they figure anybody that's grabbin' 'em is undercover, or they're gonna put a warrant on 'em, and that's a bad thing.

When we used to go out after that, we didn't see too many junkies on the street. They would be up in some shootin' gallery or someplace new where they're hangin' out that was not known to us at that time.

So, for the next couple of months you didn't make many pinches. When you saw a junkie on the street you grabbed him, but he was never holdin' anything. And you could never get much out of them, simply because they knew if they said anything, they'd be on the shit list.

Like I told you before, we would just ease around the different areas, the ones we knew. And if we spotted a junkie we'd pick him up, just to get on the arrest sheets, even if he wasn't positive. And run 'im through the system, and it would show up as an arrest, and that's what the captain wanted.

We were really scroungin' around for quite a while, and this one particular afternoon, it was late in the afternoon, we see this one guy. And Sal recognized him as a junkie, and we grabbed him.

And the man had a quart bottle of beer with him. And we didn't think too much of that, and bein' reasonable fellas, he said, "Hey, man, lemme finish my beer."

He said, "I know you're gonna arrest me," and all this and that, and he didn't give us any problems.

So what the hell, we put him in the car, and I'm sittin' in the back with him, and Sal's drivin'. And we used to run 'em up to headquarters, because there wasn't too much doin' then. Normally, we'd just run 'em into a district. But with this guy, we were halfway up to headquarters when we grabbed him.

And he's sittin' in the car, and he's swiggin' his bottle of beer, and it was in the summertime. And the funniest thing happened.

Sal's playin' the radio, and there's a song on there, and believe it or not, I remember it was "I'm Gonna Sit Right Down and Write Myself a Letter."

And this guy that we got in the back, he's singin' somethin' entirely different.

And we're goin' along, and we're listenin' to the radio, and this guy's singin', and I ask him, "Man, what the hell's the matter with you? You hear a different drummer?"

He says, "Hey, man, I makes my own kinda music."

By then he's finished his bottle of beer. And something occurred to me, first time I even thought of it, I said, "This bastard's got his stuff in the beer."

I told Sal to pull over.

By then the beer was gone, and I get this guy outta the car. I had searched him once, and I went over him again, top to bottom. And he's high as a kite.

I said, "That's a bitch. This is something I never came across before."

So we take him in to headquarters, and we book him, and we send him right down to the doctor. Now, you know the doctors can't draw blood on a prisoner without their consent.

This guy wouldn't give his consent to draw blood, but they took a urine test on him, and he came up positive as hell.

What he had done is, when he got his heroin, he put it in the bottle. Maybe he saw us comin', I don't know, but he dropped his bag into the goddam bottle, dissolved the stuff, and was drinkin' it slowly.

It takes a while to get into your bloodstream, but it was into his.

From then on, nobody would drink a goddam soda after I got 'em, nothin' at all.

I just wanted to show you, you can never trust a junkie, and you can never believe a junkie. And that is the God's truth. Not unless you got 'em strung up and hangin'.

Well, we went along with the minor arrests, I guess up to the next, well, raid, as they call it. The same deal, out to Convention Hall, get your envelope, and go out and arrest these people on the warrants.

177

Thomas M. Grubb & Allan "Lucky" Cole

Nothin' serious ever happened, except on one occasion. We go in, and we want this particular guy, and it happened to be the first house that we hit on this raid. This was in West Philadelphia, this time.

Like I said, Sal wasn't a big guy, and we had two uniform highway patrol men with us. But after we went in, we hadda hit the door, and we grabbed this guy, he's lyin' on, like a cot in the room when we went in, call it a living room if you want. And, y'know, you go right to him, make sure he's got nothin'.

But while we're in there, out from a side room comes this broad, stark naked.

Well, everybody got distracted for a minute, and this guy made it right to the window, out the goddam window in his underwear.

The highway guy jumps out after him. Now I've gotta give that guy credit, he went down, oh, maybe fifteen feet. And the highway guy's chasin' him.

I said, "No sense all of us runnin' out there."

I said to Sal, "Sal, get in the goddam car, we'll go around the corner, see what happens."

Well the funniest thing was, out in West Philly, you know that, there's all the old alleys. We swing around, I guess maybe two blocks, and we're goin' down, the other highway car's behind us.

And lo and behold, we swing around this corner, and here's this guy motorin', I mean, he is runnin' like hell. And I get out and I go after him, and I'm closer to him than the guy that's chasin' him.

Well, I've gotta tackle this son of a bitch in the middle of the street, and there's no traffic those hours, but we sure as hell got scraped up good. And here I am, wrasslin' with this guy in the middle of the street, he's in his underwear and me in my finery.

The other highway cop finally comes up, and he puts a knot on his head, you know, the stick — BANG. And that kinda ended that.

That started our raids off with a bang. And the other events of that night were just nothing, you know, normal thing — bust 'em, make an arrest, take 'em out.

The fun came when we made the arraignment. This guy's still in his shorts, and we line 'em up, and I'm in there, and I've got some bruises from when we went down in the street and everything.

178

Thomas M. Grubb & Allan "Lucky" Cole

The judge holds the guy for court, the guy turns around to me and says, "Hey, man," he said, "Who the hell taught you to run so fast?"

And it was kinda funny for the guy to say that, 'cause that's all he did say.

With that I had to laugh like hell at him, I said, "Hey, man, you think you're the only one that can run?"

And that was the end of that.

As I said, Lucky, after the raids things really dry up on the streets, so you're lookin' for anything you can turn. I started to go out at night simply because there was nobody on the streets durin' the day.

What I did is, I went back to my old stampin' grounds in the Ninth District. And I met up with some of the people that I had known for a long time, and some of the people that had given me information in the past.

We'd talk, spend an hour, and try to learn something there. It paid off after a while. One of the people that I had given a break to informed us of a place a lot of narcotic users frequented.

This guy was a musician and they smoked a lotta pot and all this and that. And he told me of this place.

He said, "I don't know what you'll get in there," he said, "but if you go through it," he said, "you're gonna wind up with a lotta weed."

In those days weed, marijuana, mary jane, that was all your marijuana stuff, all your terminologies.

So we went up to this place, I got ahold of Sal, and he set it up for us pretty good, this informer. And we went in, it was white, the place, and I did my thing that I was kinda used to doin' by then, and we were accepted.

'Cause I used some names, and so forth, and sure as hell, they were all smokin' their marijuana, it came out, and I got Sal to kinda ease outta the place.

And Sal called for a wagon.

Sal got the wagon, and we kinda cleared out the place. I guess we arrested maybe eight or nine people. And we didn't have a warrant, all you could take is what you could see.

179

Thomas M. Grubb & Allan "Lucky" Cole

So what we did is run everybody into the district except the person that was running the apartment. And then I had Sal go up to a magistrate that he knew and get a warrant. I didn't leave the place, I stayed right there with the one guy.

In three-quarters of an hour or so, Sal was back with the warrant. Then we could search the place. Well, we did find quite a bit of marijuana, 'bout, oh, I guess a shoebox full.

That was a good pinch, and we laid that mostly on the one that rented the apartment, although we had the others for smoking and so forth. That was a good night's work, and a good pinch.

Thomas M. Grubb & Allan "Lucky" Cole

CHAPTER TWENTY–FOUR
Murder

A few days later, it was in the morning, the whole squad was called in. And there was a rather brutal murder up in West Oak Lane. A woman was beaten to death, and it was in a prominent area.

Our job was to go out and canvass the whole area, shake down everything, see what evidence you could find, talk to everybody that you could talk to.

We went through a whole apartment house out there, which was a big apartment house, maybe two, three hundred rooms in it, and tried to learn something about what occurred.

Well, everybody was working solo, just went around talking to people, tried to compare your notes at the end of the day in headquarters. Really, there wasn't a whole lot that came up.

This was the Elmo Smith case.

Now what I did do on this was, when we got up there, it's all like country living up in the East Falls, there. It seemed that the girl that got killed was attempting to get in her car, or had just gotten out of her car. We all had to beat the woods, looking for him or evidence.

From what we learned, she was bludgeoned to death with a heavy instrument, y'know, the old blunt instrument deal.

And we worked on that.

Lo and behold, later on this white guy, Elmo Smith, was arrested by two guys from our squad. Obviously, Lonnie had gotten the information and passed it on to them. It was just the two of them that made the actual arrest.

Well, Elmo Smith was the last guy in Pennsylvania to go to the electric chair. That's why I mentioned this, Lucky.

CHAPTER TWENTY–FIVE
The Marathon

AFTER THIS, WE went back to our normal cruisin' around for junkies or whatever else we could learn.

And on this particular day, it was early in the afternoon, oh, maybe one o'clock, we see this character out in West Philadelphia, and we recognized him, we had pinched him before. And we caught him dirty at that time.

So naturally we grab him, and we put him in the car and we're talkin' to him, and sure as hell he's dirty again. Remember, they usually shoot up in the arm, and you'll see a fresh prick mark on the arm, like a little scab.

Well, this bastard, after we got 'im, right away he takes his fingernail and he scratches the scab, y'know, cuts himself with his nail. That's a dead giveaway, you know he's dirty.

So we got him, we take him in to the district, and we talk to him, and we tell him, "You're gone, you've had it."

And he's cryin' and beggin' for a break, and this shit and that.

We tell him, "You want a break, give us something. Give us something good. At least a possession. You're not gonna walk unless we've got something good."

Now what we used to do is hold them in the cell room of a district until we went out and checked out whatever information they would give us. Well, this guy, he gives us a name, gives us a guy, gives us an address.

He said, "He's holdin', he's got a lot of stuff, he's holdin'."

We said, "O.K., you just relax."

We go out, we got this name, good description, and in our picture file we've got a picture of this guy that he mentions. So we go over to this apartment in West Philly.

We go in — now we gotta knock at the door, we've got no warrant or anything — but we knocked, and fortunately, he's in there. So we talk to this guy.

Sittin' right on the goddam table is his works. Now he just musta shot up, and he's still got two bags of heroin, two nickel bags. So we got him real good.

What we do is, we take him to a district, but not the one where we've got the other guy, another district in West Philadelphia.

We sit him down, and we're talkin' to him, "We got you — possession. You know this is your fourth fall, you're doin' time."

And he doesn't want to do time.

We told him, "Give us something. Give me something."

So he tells us about a burglary. And this burglary took place out in Yeadon. Matter of fact, just on your way to your Aunt Sissy's house is this gunshop. And he's tellin' us about these guys that ripped off this gunshop.

Now the funniest thing was, we later learned that one of the guys he was tellin' us about, that ripped off this gunshop, was a guy we had arrested once or twice before.

We go out lookin' for this so-called burglar of the gunshop, and luck was running with us. We pull up to this place, and we go in, and there's a woman in there, an older woman. And it's her son.

We spoke to the woman, said, "Just want to talk to him," and so forth, so on.

She said, "He down by the playgrounds."

We go down to the playgrounds, and here he is, shootin' hoops up there, so we latch on to him. We take him into the district, and we start grillin' this guy. 'Cause there's guns involved, and it sounds like a pretty good arrest.

After quite a while he finally breaks down, and he tells us that they did the job. He tells us the other guy he did it with.

He said, "But he's in jail already."

That was good, and we talked to him more, and we find out that this sucker has already sold these guns, like he gave 'em to three or four different people. But there were so many guns missing, that he had to have a stash somewhere.

So what we did is, we take him with us.

Now it's in the evening, and we're goin' around to the places where he claims he sold these guns to people. And at each place we went we brought him with us, so the guy knew we weren't bullshittin'.

Thomas M. Grubb & Allan "Lucky" Cole

We had him handcuffed, he wasn't goin' anywhere, and we'd go right to the door, and we'd just tell the man in there, "Look, I want the gun, and that will be it. We're not going to arrest you."

After a while, y'know, of, "Oh, not me, I didn't do this, I didn't do that," I'd say, "Well, in that case, we're gonna take everybody in the house, we'll get a warrant and search the joint."

Before you know it, the gun would show up.

We told the guy, "We're not gonna pinch you."

So that was the first gun we got back.

We made, oh, two or three more stops, and at each place we got a gun. I think we got like four that night.

Now it's going into the early hours of the morning, and when you're hot on a roll you don't stop. And we've got this poor bastard with us, and he's dyin' and cryin', and he's hungry, and he's gotta go to the bathroom, and all this and that.

The thing was, there were so many guns taken that we knew there hadda be a stash somewhere. He gave us the ones he sold the weapons to, but he would not come up with that stash.

He finally comes up with another kid that he sold a gun to, or gave to him to hold, or one of these deals. Now we're pretty tired, and we get out to this place, and it's out in the real sticky part of West Philadelphia.

Like I say, we've got no warrant, so we can't go breakin' down doors. We figure the best thing to do is wait for this guy to come out, figurin' that nobody'd contacted him or nothin', 'cause we got the man with us.

So we got up on his roof, where we could see the back and the front of this house, and Sal's at one end and I'm at the other end of the roof.

And lo and behold, this guy comes out the back way of the house. Well, we've gotta get down off of this roof, and we can snatch this guy anyway, 'cause he doesn't expect anybody. And he's holdin' the gun on 'im when we get 'im.

Now this guy, we don't tell him we're gonna let him go, 'cause he's carryin' the gun. We pinch him, stash him in the district. Now we've got two guys in the district, and we've got the real mouthpiece with us, the informer.

I tell him, "We want the rest of the guns," and he's swearin' to God there's no more guns.

We played around with him all day, all night, now it's gettin' to be early in the morning.

So I'd just had enough of this guy, and I told him, I said, "You son of a bitch, you. You ain't leavin' us till we find the guns."

He tells us, "Well, out here," and he gives us a location.

We get there, and this is when the guy really starts hemmin' and hawin'.

He says, "They're down a culvert."

You know culverts, you go down there, you can get drowned — some culverts are wet, some culverts are dry, some are half and half.

I figure, "I ain't goin' down this goddam culvert."

So what we did, is we grabbed him by his feet, took the handcuffs off him, and hung him down the culvert. And if you don't know it, in most culverts there's a ledge around the sides, down in the culvert.

And this bastard had laid two guns or three guns down on these ledges, down there.

We've got him by the feet, and he's screamin' murder, but nobody's listenin'. And he comes up with the guns, and they're still in the boxes with that waxed paper wrapped around them.

So we got more guns.

We don't really know how many guns were taken in this burglary, but we've got about seven or eight now. We take him in and we put him in the cell, and now we've got all these guns. So what we've gotta do is get in contact with this man that had the burglary.

Now he's in Yeadon, which is really out of our jurisdiction. It's comin' up morning time, so we motor out to Yeadon Police, and we ask them if they had a report on this gunshop.

And you tell 'em who you are, and so forth, and the guy on duty goes through the papers, says, "Yeah," he says, "We got a report of a burglary there," and gives us a list of the stuff that was taken.

There was more on that list than we recovered, but that's not unusual when it's an insurance job, and this guy had reported the theft to his insurance company.

Thomas M. Grubb & Allan "Lucky" Cole

So our next stop, we take a copy of the missing property. And we go out with the sergeant from Yeadon, 'cause, you know, it's out of our jurisdiction.

We explained to him what we recovered, and so forth, and he went out to the gunshop owner. We waited around, like, from nine o'clock in the morning till when he opened the place up.

We go in, we're talkin' to the guy, we check his records for the guns that he had on hand. And he's got all these listed out that are missing.

Well, we took a list of what he said was missing, and it sure as hell didn't correspond to what, y'know, we recovered. So we're screwin' around with this shop owner, and he's startin' to get like, sweats and nervous and pins and needles.

And we're explaining to him the property that's been recovered. I didn't even know what the hell calibers most of them were, 'cause we're just grabbin' 'em, and that was it. Stickin' 'em in the trunk of the car, and later we'd check 'em out.

Actually, this guy revised his missing list.

He said, "Oh," he said, "that was the original list I submitted," and this bullshit and that.

The burglary only happened, oh, a day or two prior to when we got our man to give us the information.

The sergeant from Yeadon was happy that the stolen property list dwindled down, and we told the owner he'd be notified what property was recovered, y'know, for insurance purposes. And we told 'im we'd be back eventually.

Now with the excess of guns that were still missing on this revised list that this guy put out, we went back to our man. We had him down at 61st and Thompson, that's a police station. And we got him.

By this time we really weren't so nice with this fellow, 'cause our asses were draggin'. We were dirty, we were hungry, and we were tired.

So I kinda stood him up a little bit, told him what we got, and how much was still missin'. Course he didn't wanta go for that, he didn't know nothin' more about that, and all this bullshit.

Thomas M. Grubb & Allan "Lucky" Cole

After we convinced him, he told us that he buried some out in the park, which is Cobb's Creek Park, right in their area. Well, off we go again.

Now it's pushin' noontime, and we're out in the friggin' park lookin' for where this guy thought he buried the guns. Well, we found 'em, we dig, we dug up the goddam guns, and we got four more of 'em.

This I was happy with. I felt that we did a good job and the hell with it.

We got most of 'em. In total I think there were eleven guns we recovered, so that left two unaccounted for. No doubt he sold these to somebody he wasn't gonna rat on, or they'd probably use the guns on him.

We got all of them in there, and when we got back to the district, we processed 'em, each one from the different district. And it turned out to be a real good arrest.

There used to be a great, old reporter called John Rawley, that used to follow the squad around. Any big pinch that was made, he would always have it on the news or in the paper.

So we hit the newspapers and the whole bullshit, y'know, John Rawley was down there with his recorder.

And it hit the newspapers — "Thirty-Six Hour Marathon Arrest".

We even had a commendation from the captain on the "Thirty-Six Hour Marathon Investigation."

But anyway, we got a good pinch out of it, and we made a lot of contacts. We didn't arrest everybody that was involved, simply because like I told you, you gotta let some off the hook to get information.

That's it for that pinch, Lucky.

Lucky, your Aunt Cass just told me I should explain to you what a culvert is. See, at the end of each block in the city, drainoff from rain or any spills of that nature goes down into an inlet called a culvert.

And they're covered over with heavy metal lids or a heavy metal grate. And that's what a culvert is. It's not like those canyons in California that all the water flows into. So I hope I made that clear to you, Lucky.

To get the grates off of them, that's a pretty heavy grate, maybe a hundred pounds. And you go down there, it's pitch dark and it's filthy. And that's where we held this guy down to get these guns, or some of them.

Actually, this is the first time I really ever stayed out that long from my home, and your Aunt Cass was in a panic thinking something had happened to me. And she had notified everybody in the family concerning my absence.

Before I got home the following day, the children, when they were getting up to go to school, actually saw something on the television concerning this arrest.

And it was in the newspapers by the time I got home, so everything was cool.

CHAPTER TWENTY–SIX
The Scolari Matter

I GUESS THE next big case I worked on was the Scolari murder. This was when two brothers named Scolari, who lived just around the block from us on Newkirk Street, just about one block away, went into a dry goods store operated by a fella named Max Gordon.

Now both your Aunt Cass and I knew this man, because we often frequented this store. He sold a variety of dry goods and sneakers and so forth, but he also sold money orders, cashed money orders, and accepted payment for the gas and electric bills.

These Scolaris only lived a half a block from the store, which was at Newkirk and Reed Street — they lived between Reed and Wharton Streets on Newkirk. Max Gordon used to live over the top of his store. We knew his wife, and he also had a daughter.

It seems that these two Scolari brothers, Tony and Dominic, went into the store, and they had a third guy with them, a black fella who was very light skinned, actually he looked like another white fella.

They held up the store, and in the process, I think one of them was gonna go upstairs, and this is when Max Gordon went for a gun.

And there was a shootout in the store, resulting in Max Gordon being killed. But he shot one of the perpetrators, and it happened to be this light-skinned black guy.

Now this happened like, in the late afternoon, and early that evening — I used to frequent the Earl Movies, which was just down the street from us — and I'm not sure, but I think I was gonna go see this show called "The Guns of Navarone."

I knew the ticket taker, Jack, and when I went into the movie, he said, "Gee, Tom, how 'bout all the excitement?"

I just passed this off, I said, "Yeah, how 'bout it, Jack."

And I went and I sat down.

I guess I was in there a half-hour or so, and the next thing I know, your Aunt Cass was down at the movie. And she's got me, tellin' me that the captain called on the phone, wants me to call him immediately.

Well, naturally I ran home and called the captain. He informed me of the robbery and killing, and told me to get my ass on the job right away, because I just lived around the corner. I lived around the corner, but I knew nothing about it so far.

I tried to call my partner, but this was one time I couldn't get ahold of him.

So I called my nephew, Tidge, and I told him, "C'mon over, want you to do something with me."

Tidge came over and we got in my car, and I went around to 29th Street, where the guys hung on the corner every night. And the thing was, I knew all these guys and they knew me.

We'd known each other since we were little kids. And it's a funny thing, these guys that hung on the corner, they were known as the Scumaleros, although they were pretty nice guys.

I asked 'em, I said, "Hey, what the hell's goin' on, what's happenin'?"

And one of the guys says, "I dunno, Tom," he says, "I hear there's a shootin'"

I said, "Yeah, whattya know about it? Gimme something."

And this one fella, Christ, I can't remember his real name, I only knew him as "Gunga" Dean.

"Gunga" Dean was a nice guy, he said, "Hey, Tom," he said, "I just seen the Scolari's fly by here 'bout a half hour ago." He said, "They were really barrelin'."

So I put two and two together, knowin' the Scolaris from the neighborhood, that they were the type of people that would do a thing like this.

One brother, Tony, who was also known as Tough Tony, had been in prison. I didn't know the other one that well, but my nephew did know these guys, and he told me, he said, "Uncle Tom," he said, "they're bad actors." He said, "They'd do somethin' like this."

Well, with this information I got from the guys on the corner, I flew out Snyder Avenue from 29th Street. And the logical thing was to cruise the neighborhood real fast, 'cause "Gunga" Dean gave me a description of the car. An old gray Chevy, and, y'know, beat up.

I toured around, down to Broad Street, back around, up and down the streets, lookin' for the car. And then I figured, "Now

Thomas M. Grubb & Allan "Lucky" Cole

where the hell would they go?" not knowing, but later learning they had gone to Broad Street, where they dropped this one guy off that Gordon had shot.

I didn't know this then, so I figured, "Now, where the hell else would they go?"

Next place I figured was, they'd make it over the South Philly Bridge — the Walt Whitman Bridge — to Jersey. And I took a ride over there, lookin' for the car.

I rode down, my brother happened to have a place in Clementon, and I rode down there. And at that time it was really isolated, a lot of dark roads and everything else. And I'm flyin' by, and I don't see a goddam thing.

So I come back, drop my nephew off, and called headquarters, told the captain what I suspected.

The next morning I went up to headquarters and had a discussion with the captain, told him what I had learned, and that was about it for the time being.

He told me, "This is your job. You follow it up, and you take care of it."

I told him, "Sure, captain, that's it."

The boss told me this was my job, and he expected results, so I didn't have anything else to do. I was relieved of any other responsibility, just to concentrate on this job.

So I did my thing, learned what I could. I learned a few things, that these guys used to hang out with a broad — Ida Iacca.

Well, that name stuck with me from when I worked in the district, because I had occasion one time to go up to 20th and Spring Garden, and she had an apartment over the drugstore.

I went up there, and I talked to some people, and they told me that she used to have a boyfriend, in the terms of the old days, who was called a "high yellow." This was a black guy, but very light skin, and this was her boyfriend, he had lived up there with her.

Ida was a, kind of a low-life, a prostitute at times, and a drug user also. I checked the record and found out all of this.

I was called up there from the district for a disturbance in the place, but, you know, a disturbance, you quiet it down and that was

Thomas M. Grubb & Allan "Lucky" Cole

it. But I did remember that name, though I did not remember the guy she was with. But I checked everything out and got records.

I guess it was within in the week — this happened on the weekend — I go up to headquarters, make my report, what I had learned, so forth, and the captain says, "You're on it."

Before I left the place, headquarters, the captain told me, "Just stay close to the phones. I may need you."

I didn't know what he meant about this, but I did go home that evening, and, I guess it was around dinnertime, I get a call from the captain.

And he tells me, "Get right over to this home on Reed Street, the home of Dominic's wife."

It seems that she had just recently had a child, and that he may be coming down there to see her before they take off, or whatever, maybe he's still in the area.

By then, naturally, they had a description of these guys, and photographs of them and all, and they were hot. Everybody knew that they had pulled this job.

I went over to this house on Reed Street — nice home, family home — a mother, a grandmother, and a sister living there. And he was married, this Dominic was married to the younger sister. I forget her name, but I know it was an Irish-sounding name.

Well anyway, my assignment was to get over to the house and stay there, and the captain had talked to the mother of this girl, and it was arranged that I would stay there.

Now by staying there, I don't mean overnight, but stay there as long as I could, for no determined amount of time.

I went to this house, met all the people that were there, and they were more than cooperative. They made me like a member of the family. And I was told that I would be relieved at certain times, and to just check into headquarters and so forth.

Anyway, I would go there, maybe noontime or so, and stay till maybe midnight or later, when I felt comfortable to leave. The people treated me well, and they understood why I was there.

The point being that they figured Dominic Scolari would contact his wife because of them just having a baby recently. The baby was,

I don't know, three months old or something of that nature, it was just an infant.

Well, I used to hang out there, and I would eat and everything else, the funniest thing being that detectives from the South Detective Division used to stop over frequently. And I would be sitting in the living room, watchin' T.V. or reading the paper.

And they would come in, and the mother would introduce me as a member of the family, and they'd look at me. And everything — y'know, they were suspicious, but they didn't know me.

That was the funniest thing, they really didn't know me, and so they just took it for granted I was a friend of the family, that's all.

This went on, oh, for the longest time, several weeks, maybe longer. And then one Sunday, early evening, I got a call at home from his wife, from Scolari's wife. And she told me that she had gotten a call from him, and he was supposed to come to the house.

I tore out of the house, grabbed my gun, and I'm on my way over to their place, and I get over there. And I spot the South Detectives' car sittin' down the street. I used to park my car around the block so they couldn't take the tag number, and I just walked up to the house.

Like I said, I spotted the squad car from South Detectives, but I just went right into the house, no problem. I met the mother and Scolari's wife, this little red-haired girl, I think her name was Kathy. Can't think of the last name.

Anyway, they told me they got a phone call from Dominic, and that he was comin' to see the baby, or get the baby. Well, this had them all shaken up.

I told them, "Don't worry, I'm gonna stay here," and I did.

I stayed there all afternoon, all evening, had dinner with the folks. Late into the evening there was another phone call, but there was nobody on the phone when she answered it.

I figured he was just checkin' to make sure she was there. So I got all set for him, and we heard some noises and stuff, but I knew there were detectives outside of the house and nothing was going down.

I guess he either came there, saw the car, saw the cops, and scooted, or else he didn't show up at all.

Thomas M. Grubb & Allan "Lucky" Cole

I thought I heard some noises on the roof and I went upstairs, and I'm waitin' for him — there's only one way to come in and that would be down off a side window off the roof. I waited there for a half-hour or so, but the noise turned out to be nothing.

So that was a false alarm, but it was enough to get everybody's adrenaline running.

It wasn't too much later after this that Ida Iacca somehow set herself on fire in a hotel room in Chicago while under the influence of drugs, and she actually lost an arm during this fire.

And with this, they kind of tied her in to the Scolaris, and it wasn't too much later that the Scolaris were apprehended in Chicago.

So that put the end to this case, and I was able to go home. That ended the Scolari matter.

But there was one thing I might add, that during the course of time, before I was assigned to watch this girl at her home, the father of the Scolari brothers passed away. And this was shortly after the incident occurred.

It was the night of his wake that this nut Carpasso and another guy from the squad came down, asked me to go over with them to the house. And actually, we went into the house durin' the wake to see if they would show up.

Well, Steve Capasso had his sawed-off shotgun in his coat while we were in the house, and naturally we were both armed.

But they knew we were police, and, y'know, there was a lot of grumblin' and shit. We went in and we looked around, and he was laid out in the house, which was how it used to be in those days, not in a funeral parlor.

And we saw nothing, we just laid around outside for most of the night, but they didn't show up — I guess they were in Chicago by then.

Also, the night that the incident occurred, this guy that Max Gordon popped, died. They took him in the car with 'em, and Ida Iacca had the apartment down on Broad Street at that time. And that's where he actually died, in that apartment.

194

Then they took him out in the car, and where the hell did they go, but right over the Walt Whitman Bridge, down by Clementon, and I think it was Ariel Road where they buried this guy.

As I said earlier, those were the two places I checked out, patrollin' in the area. Went down to Broad Street, not knowing that she lived there, and then I rode over to Clementon, which goes right by this Ariel Road.

It was just a shot in the dark, but here I missed them, maybe by minutes. And it's just ironic, I was right on their ass, but I couldn't catch them.

Thomas M. Grubb & Allan "Lucky" Cole

CHAPTER TWENTY–SEVEN
Good Pinches

AFTER THIS, LUCK, I was back on the regular duties of the squad, out junkie-huntin' with my partner, Sal DeLuca. And we went through our normal things again, scoopin' up any junkies that we saw, talkin' to them, seein' what we could learn, see if we could shake 'em down for information.

I'm going to tell you about a fella that we met. He was a junkie, he was what we call a skinpopper, and he would only pop on the weekends. Now it was the funniest thing how we got hold of this guy.

He used to work at Kelly's, up on Ranstead Street, that's off of Market and Ludlow. And he used to work in the seafood house, Kelly's Seafood.

Well, one night we were there in Center City, and I was talkin' to some old acquaintances that I met when I worked the district up there.

And this one young lady mentioned to me, "You see this guy comin' out of the restaurant?"

He was like a dishwasher or something, very menial job.

She said, "He's a junkie."

She was a prostitute, but that didn't make too much difference. We got many tips from prostitutes.

I said, "Yeah? How do you know that?"

She said, "I copped offa him once."

That was enough for me, so we snatched this guy up. I'm gonna give you his real name, it was Jimmy Price. Well, Jimmy was a junkie, no doubt about it, but he wasn't a mainliner, he was a skinpopper.

When we arrested Jimmy, I talked to him quite a bit, 'cause this is one guy that held down a steady job, worked like ten, twelve hours a day. And when he'd get off on weekends or whatever, that's when he would skin pop with the heroin.

I also learned that Jimmy was the sole support of his mother, an elderly woman, and he did take good care of her.

After learnin' all this about Jimmy, after we snatched him up and talked to him, you could see that he wasn't what you would call the average junkie. This was the first time he was ever arrested, to speak of.

And we got him so befuddled and everything, threatening to arrest him, send him away, and, y'know, he actually cried.

He said, "Nobody to take care of my mother," and this and that, and I believed him.

Well, I'm gonna tell you, he became one of our best, if not the best, source of information. Jimmy came up with, oh, maybe a dozen possession pinches for us, and nobody ever knew he was the informer that was givin' us these pinches. And like I said, Lucky, a possession pinch is a good pinch.

I had given Jimmy my home phone number and told him, "Anytime, you call."

And he called frequently. He gave us a possession pinch every week — ten days, two weeks at the latest — and we made some good ones.

We were catchin' 'em on the street, goin' in between places, and we always got stuff on them, and we got some good compensations, and it was always heroin.

Luck, I told you, every morning you would check the onionskins for who made arrests in the city on narcotics. The captain used to check them every morning, then they'd go on the board, so the guys could see them.

When we start comin' up almost every week with a possession pinch, y'know, the guys are, "Hey, whatta you got, whatta you got good?" And, "You never tell anybody what you are doing, nobody told us anything."

So we were lookin' real good then. Sal was walkin' around puffin' his cigar like he's the mayor, 'cause he thought that was really great.

Also at this time we had a narcotics squad in the city, and they work solely on narcotics, where we had the run of the city. Anything you wanted to work on, you did.

Well, the narcotics squad's startin' to get skeptical, 'cause they used to get a copy of all the arrests in the city, too.

Thomas M. Grubb & Allan "Lucky" Cole

And shit, me and Sal are beatin' their whole squad with possession pinches. Possession pinches are gold, they know that you made the hit, and you got the stuff.

With Jimmy Price workin' for us, we were really doin' fantastic work. As a matter of fact, we made one possession pinch, and the one we grabbed happened to be an informer for these two guys in the narcotics squad — Slater and Phil Nardi.

They didn't like that, because you used'ta carry cards around with your name and your squad, and you used to give 'em to your informers. If they ever got caught on the street doin' something, they would get a pass from whoever caught them.

And in this case, when we grabbed this one guy, he had this Nardi's card on him. So what we did, when we brought him into the district, courtesy — strictly courtesy — calls for you phonin' the guy whose card he has, 'cause they don't give them out that easily.

When I called Phil Nardi — Phil was a sergeant in narcotics, then — Phil came down.

And, y'know, we talked, he says, "Yo, Grubb," he says, "Can you give him a walk?"

I caught him, like, with a bag, so it wasn't real bad.

So I told him, I said, "Yeah, Phil, I'll give him a walk. You got somethin' for me?"

At that time he didn't have anything on tap, you know, so I said, "Look, Phil, courtesy," I said, "we work together," I said, "you got something for me? We both work narcotics, but anything else you may come up with, you can talk to me."

Well, that started a good relationship that lasted for years, just turnin' this guy loose. I gave him to Phil, and Phil talked to him. That relationship lasted a long time.

It was funny, after that, they saw we were makin' a lot of good arrests, and actually, this partner of Phil's, Slater, he used to actually try to follow us around to see where we were going.

It was comical — Center City, South Street, was the big hittin' ground for the narcotics users, the bars and so forth. And we would actually see him hangin' around down there, lookin' for our car. And a few times he tried to tail us, but that didn't work out too good.

Thomas M. Grubb & Allan "Lucky" Cole

There were several bars in and around Center City that I knew, that I had gone to and made arrests on prostitutes there. They never used to take me for a cop, Lucky. You know, you go in, you make your proposition, and then you pinch 'em.

Well, there were a couple there that I didn't arrest, I didn't do anything with 'em. Caught them, y'know, a right deal, they give you the price for this or for that, and then you arrest them.

But with these two women, I didn't arrest 'em, I told 'em, "You got a walk."

It's funny, with a prostitute, when you do that, they owe you. They will give you something eventually, 'cause they're the kind of women that get around to all the bad guys, and they know a lot of stuff.

One bar was the Bridge Bar up on Ray Street, and the other was the Dew Drop Inn, and these weren't too far from Chinatown, Luck. And there was always a lot of action going on up in that area.

With these girls, I used to give them my card, and it had my number on it, and I'd tell them, "You want me, you can get ahold of me. Just call me."

And they turned quite a few good pinches for me.

I guess the best one was the guy in Philly here, they had a rash of taxicab holdups. I mean this guy had hit maybe fifty cabs. And nobody could seem to catch him, I mean he'd hit 'em all over the city.

Well, this particular night, I'm in bed, your Aunt Cass and I are asleep. The phone rings, and here, it's one of these girls.

And she tells me, "Look, you know about the taxicab jobs."

"Yes, sure."

She said, "You want 'im," she says, "I can give him to you." She says, "I'm seein' him tonight."

She told me where and when, and this is like, God, it's gotta be two, three o'clock in the morning. So I got ahold of Joe, gave him a call, told him to meet me, and we drove up to Ray Street.

The girl had told me where she's meetin' this character, and she described 'im to us and everything else, so it wasn't that difficult. The thing was, this was a Chinese restaurant, and you got in the front as well as the back, there's like a side entrance.

199

So I told Sal, "You go in the back, I'll go in the front."

Well, when I went in the front, the first thing I look at is this girl, the one that called us. And I'm only maybe ten feet from this guy.

And he turns around, the first thing I did is whip out the gun and I put it right up to his head. 'Cause he was known to carry a piece.

Sal came right in, he saw me with a gun on the guy, and we got 'im out, called a wagon, sent him in to the district.

This guy went, not only for the possession of the weapon that he had, but also for the other cab jobs that he had done.

We also arrested the girl to make it look good. And we put up a phony charge of prostitution on her, but of course she walked.

But him, we got good.

I got a commendation for that, and again, I bumped into the detectives on this thing. 'Cause when it's a job like this, you gotta notify them, because after you take the guy into the district, he's gotta go down to — there, it was the Central Detectives.

Well again, it's a joke. At this time Yellow Cab used to give out rewards, y'know, for catchin' a guy stickin' up a cab. By the time this reward got split up with all the assholes that put their names on as an assistance in the arrest, I got fifty bucks outta the whole thing. Sal got fifty.

We also got commendations for it, but that's only a piece of paper. But it was a good pinch on our record. That was one good pinch that the prostitute gave us.

Now I'm gonna get back to Jimmy Price with you.

Well, with Jimmy Price, when we would meet, we picked out a spot down Third and Lombard, I think it was. It was really desolate down there. That's where the old food distribution center was close by, and it was really an isolated area.

Like I told you, Jimmy gave us a lotta good stuff. And soon as he would call me, I knew it was gold. We had a possession pinch.

We made a meet this night, Jimmy called, and I guess it was two o'clock in the morning, three o'clock in the morning. So I didn't bother tellin' Joe or anything, I just went down to the place where we'd meet.

I pulled up about a half a block away, three-quarters of a block, and I walked down. I walked down, it's like a triangular doorway where we used to meet, and I saw somethin' lyin on the step.

It's a body.

And I get up, and I turn him over. He's dead. Black guy.

Here, it's Jimmy Price.

Well, I was shocked, I tell you the truth. And I figure the first thing to do is call the wagon. Called the wagon, had the kid picked up, taken to the morgue, then I gotta go in and make out a report, Central Detectives.

And I told 'em who he was — "This is my informer."

Later on I learned that Jimmy got a "hot shot."

If you don't know what that is, it's when somebody injects battery acid into you, they mix it up with the heroin or whatever.

And from the autopsy report, it was quite evident that this shot that Jimmy had was right in the veins.

I knew Jimmy did not shoot mainline, he was only a skinpopper. He had no tracks on his arms or anywhere on his body.

I knew somebody killed the guy — murdered him, actually.

So that was my next project, to find out who did Jimmy in. No doubt somebody that we pinched might have seen him, or knew that he gave us information, or somehow they put the cap on him.

And they blew — y'know, they killed him.

Well, for the next six months, every junkie that we picked up we talked to, and the conversation always led around to Jimmy Price. It took six months, maybe a little longer, but we found the guy that used to supply him, and his street name was "Black Cat."

And eventually we went out lookin' for Black Cat.

And we got 'im.

We got 'im, and of course he wasn't gonna go for that, but we took him in the car, and we paraded him around all over downtown Center City, and let everybody get a look at 'im.

'Cause I sat in the back of the car with him and held him up while he was tryin' to fall on the floor to hide. And all the bullshit with him, and everything.

Thomas M. Grubb & Allan "Lucky" Cole

Now we got the word that he was the guy that did Jimmy, but we weren't sure, just the word. I figured this was the best thing to do with him, and we took him all over and let everybody see him.

That was the first trip.

And then the following day, we lay around and waited for him, and we got him again. Did the same goddam thing with him, rode him around, made sure everybody saw him. We even took 'im outta Center City — North Philadelphia, we took 'im all over.

By then, most people usin' or pushin' drugs knew our cars.

And it wasn't until maybe, oh, two weeks later, somebody did Black Cat.

Same deal, he got himself a hot shot.

We learned about this, we got his right name, which escapes me now, but it turned up in the paper, "body found." We checked the morgue and all that, and here, it was the son-of-a-bitch that did Jimmy Price.

So that made me happier, that he got the same thing he did to the other kid.

Lucky, I'm gonna talk about some information we got from Jimmy Price. We were told about a house that always had junk in it, it was a shootin' gallery.

A shootin' gallery is a place where junkies go get their stuff and shoot up right in there.

So we knew that there was stuff in this place. Like I said, when Jimmy told you something it was gold, you could take it to the bank. And we hadda get a few extra guys to hit this place.

We got another team of guys, and this was down in South Philly. Usually you didn't like to "eat where you shit," you know. Anyway, it was only a half a block away from the police station there, 20th and Federal.

So the four of us go down — I got a ticket for the place — and we go in, and we break in, y'know, we busted in the door and got in. Well, there were a few people in there, we declared who the owner of the house was, and with this we commenced our search, the four of us.

First of all we got the people, got the owner. When you've got the owner of a house, he takes the responsibility for anything you

Thomas M. Grubb & Allan "Lucky" Cole

find in there. We checked out who the other junkies were, got the wagon, coulda walked 'em down the street to the police station.

Then we started to search the place. And like I say, we just sent them into the station, y'know, with the wagon. Then we started to search the place.

Lucky, it's unbelievable when you start searchin'. I mean, these people keep these narcotics in such weird places that you just can't conceive of how they would hide 'em like that.

Now the normal thing is takin' out receptacles and lookin' at baseboards to see what's loose, and anything where you figure they might hide it.

We stayed in this place maybe two hours, and we really took it apart, Luck. Didn't find anything. So we keep goin' around there, and we get the lady in the house, and the baby — there was a baby in the house, in one of these bassinets, I guess you call it.

Well, the baby was all shitty and everything, and we knew that people come in there, they've gotta get the narcotics to sell them to them.

So we kept tearin' apart and tearin' apart, and then the kid starts cryin' and whinin'. And the woman was wantin' to go over to the kid, but we just couldn't let her.

Finally one of the guys, he says, "Somethin' ain't right."

So we went over to the bassinet. And in the kid's shitty diaper were about ten dime bags. There's where they put the goddam narcotics that they were sellin', so they'd have them readily available, y'know, pick up the baby, pull a bag outta the diaper.

Well, that was literally what we call a real shitty job. We got the stuff, but it was messy.

Luck, I'll tell you, you find junk in the weirdest places. We had hit another place, same thing, we went in and searched all over.

And there's a big German shepherd out in the yard, barkin' its goddam head off. At that time I had a German shepherd, y'know, and I really wasn't afraid of them, but this bastard was really vicious lookin'.

So we hadda get the animal, whaddya call 'em, like the S.P.C.A., we called. And the guy came down, and he got a noose on

Thomas M. Grubb & Allan "Lucky" Cole

the dog, and for some reason I said, "Let me search that goddam dog house."

They had the junk stashed in the doghouse.

People would come in to buy, they'd go out in the yard, go to the doghouse, grab the bag, sell it. Well, that was another good possession pinch, and that was also one of Jimmy Price's. Like I said, this kid was great for information.

Now I'll tell you about a hairy situation.

It was another raid, it wasn't ours, somebody else came in with the information. We're gonna hit this place off Ridge Avenue, second floor apartment.

So we get up there and it's, I guess about eight, nine, ten o'clock at night, and I don't know if this was Sullivan's job or another guy's job.

At that time we had a pretty good rep, so they used to call me and Sal to help them. So we're goin' and we hit this place. Well, we take the door, but that's down the first floor, leads right in off the street.

Then there's a flight of stairs going up. I don't know who was first or who was second, I was probably second or third, goin' up the stairs.

All of a sudden I see this arm come around, and next thing I know, BAM, BAM, BAM, BAM! I mean about ten.

And they're all hitting the curved ceiling above our heads, 'cause just the hand came around. And the guy doin' the shootin', if he had pointed the gun down, he'd have taken all of us out of the stairway.

But instead the gun was straight, and it was hitting the ceiling and the plaster was comin' the hell down on us.

Well no need to tell you, three bodies came floatin' down those stairs real quick.

And I was in the middle of them.

After that we hadda call the SWAT Squad, and they came out, and we got the shooter, but he didn't hit anybody. And it was a .22 that he was firing.

Thomas M. Grubb & Allan "Lucky" Cole

No need to say that the adrenaline was really flowin' by then. We wound up with a gun pinch, but we didn't find any narcotics, although the bastard that was shootin' at us was high as a kite.

Luck, I'll tell you the truth, I never liked that gun shootin', specially when I was one of the targets. I'll never forget that warehouse, where one popped off my badge. That always stuck with me.

Well, Lucky, we did maybe five or six of these convention hall raids, y'know, goin' out at night and pickin' up all the junkies that the undercover people had spotted and got warrants out on.

That was actually boring, and it was a big pain in the ass, but it was part of the job and you did it.

Thomas M. Grubb & Allan "Lucky" Cole

CHAPTER TWENTY–EIGHT
School Friends

LUCKY, I'M GOING to go back to when I was in the Special Squad, and relate a few incidents that stuck in my mind that you may be interested in.

It was one night I was working four to twelve, and I was in the South Detective Division, and went down to a house at 11th and Wharton Street. It was the Fourth Police District.

When I came in, I was just really going to make a call into headquarters to let 'em know where I was, in case there was an outstanding job they wanted to assign to me.

I've told you, unless you're on an investigation, you would make a call into headquarters every hour or so to let 'em know where you were and how you were.

Well, I came into this district, walkin' through, and I guess it was around, oh, ten thirty, eleven o'clock at night. Everything was pretty quiet.

When this lieutenant saw me, he said, "Hey, Tom," he said, "you got a minute?"

I stopped, went over and spoke to him, happened to be a lieutenant that I knew well and got along real good with.

He came out of his operations room, and he said, "Hey, Tom, I wanta tell you something."

He said, "Look," he said, "somebody saw you walkin' in here, and said, 'I know that detective. Can I talk to him?'"

I said, "Sure, who is it?"

Not knowing what it was — coulda been an informer, it coulda been a number of things, Lucky.

My concern was, "Christ, here it is, gettin' near goin' home time, and I don't want to get stuck with another job, if possible."

I went in to the operation room, and that's where the officers sit that take care of the district.

And back in the corner — he said, "Look," he said, "this is the one that wanted to talk to you."

I looked over, and I saw what actually appeared to be a bundle of rags. And I went over, didn't know if it was male or female, or what the hell it was.

But it was quite small, so I thought, "Maybe it's a kid."

Well, I went over and kinda bent down to talk to this individual, and this face came up and looked at me and, Christ, I knew it but I didn't know from where.

It was a young girl, or a young lady, and she said, "Tom, remember me?"

I said, "Sure, I remember you," not really remembering who it was.

And then she said her name, Ellen Murphy. Well hell, this was a girl that I knew when I was a kid, and Cass also knew her. We went to grade school with her.

She asked, "Can you help me?"

I didn't even know why she was there.

So I said, "What's the matter?"

She said, "I've been arrested," and, y'know, for drugs, is what it was.

I went over to the lieutenant and I spoke to him, and he said, "Yeah," he said, "she had a coupla bags of heroin on her, and she's dirty."

I asked the lieutenant for the 7548, which is the Incident Report from the officers that picked her up, and sure as hell, there was a notation that she was apprehended with heroin, two bags on her, two dime bags.

And that they picked her up because she was acting erratic — staggering, and so forth.

I went back and I talked to her, and I got her up on her feet, and took her over to a chair, sat her down, and it's a sin.

She was, oh, in bad, bad shape.

I talked to her, and I told her, "Ellen, I'll see what I can do, I can't promise you anything."

And then she's crying, and looking at me with big eyes that could melt you — this was a kid I remembered so well, when we were young.

Thomas M. Grubb & Allan "Lucky" Cole

She was the kind of little girl, she couldn't have stood more than five feet tall, very frail, used to wear these large, horn-rimmed glasses.

And she was just like a little sparrow that you'd see in the street.

Strictly harmless, and it struck me that, here, she's a drug user. Well, there're all kinda reasons to become a drug user, as you and I both know, but I couldn't believe that it would happen to her.

I told her, "I'm gonna ask the lieutenant to give you a chance to clean yourself up a little bit, get washed and whatnot."

Which I did, I asked Dutch, and he said, "Sure."

She went back, and she went over to a sink that's located back at the cellblock, and she cleaned herself up pretty good, and straightened her clothes, and whatnot.

But the truth of the matter was, there's really nothing I could do for her. She was an adult, and she was a junkie, and she was dirty from the drugs, and she was arrested while in possession of drugs.

While talking to her, I asked her the last time she ate and she was practically starvin', so I went out, went over to the restaurant, got some coffee, a sandwich, brought it back to her.

I talked to her while she was eating, and I learned that the report had already gone in to the Narcotics Squad, and a coupla guys were coming down to talk to her.

I waited and talked to the narcotics guys, and here, it was two guys that I knew from when I worked narcotics. Now the main thing was to ascertain where she got the drugs, and maybe that way they'd get a pusher, and make an arrest on that end.

While waiting for the two narcotics men to come to the station, I talked to her and I told her, I said, "You cooperate with these fellas that's coming down, and we'll see what we can do for you."

And she shook her head, yes, of course. By now she was lookin' like she was partially alive.

When the guys came in I was waitin' for them, and I talked to them, y'know, and they do you favors when they can. But here, she's dirty from the needle marks, and she's got a possession pinch against her already.

I talked to the sergeant in Narcotics, and I told him, I said, "Look, this is somebody I know. If it's any way possible that you

Thomas M. Grubb & Allan "Lucky" Cole

could give her a break, or, y'know, speak up for her in some way when you're gonna have a hearing," I said, "I would appreciate it."

These guys knew that I had done favors for them in the past, like they'd do favors for me. As far as informants were concerned, I'd always give them a break if I picked up one of their informants.

They knew this, and one guy right away said, "Sure, Tom," he says, "look, if we can make something outta this, we'll try to get her a break."

With this, I left while they interrogated her, and at this time she looked pretty decent.

I asked them, "Look, let me know what happens, willya?"

That meant, y'know, gimme a call later, after the hearing. And that was about it.

It wasn't until a while later — she was held for court, but these guys, they did speak up for her. She did have another arrest against her, only for use, and in the long run it worked out o.k., because they did me the favor.

They recommended that she be sent to Lexington, which was the drug rehabilitation center in Kentucky. And this is what she got.

I never heard from her again, and I never saw her again.

She did take the cure, that's as far as I know. It's an alternative sentence, either go to jail or go take the cure. And these guys told me she voted to take the cure. So that was a break in her behalf, and they did do me the favor.

You know, that's really a shock when you see something from your past, like, 15, 20 years later, from when you were a kid, with somebody you knew well, and went to school with, and everything else.

And then to see her in the condition she was in, and the type of girl that she used to be.

I told Cass about this, and we were pretty upset, you know, with something like this happenin' to an old friend.

There was another incident that occurred while I was in the squad, and it was down in the neighborhood. I was just hangin' around, and an old friend, guy I went to school with, came up to me and started talkin' about different things.

Thomas M. Grubb & Allan "Lucky" Cole

And he told me about another fella that we went to school with, I'll just say his first name — Pete. And Pete wasn't a bad guy in school, but everybody, when they grow up, does different things, goes different ways.

Well, it seemed that Pete was wanted for a holdup, and a shooting. And this particular individual, like I say, we went to school together and everything, and he was a friend of Pete's in school, also.

He was concerned about Pete, because it was reported that he had a gun, and so forth. And usually, when people are lookin' for you, the police are lookin' for you, and they know you've got a gun, chances are you may get shot.

He said, "Whattya say, Tom," he said, "could you do anything for 'im?"

I said, "What could I do for him?" I said, "I don't even know where he's at, but I heard of the particular incident he was involved in."

He said, "Well, look," he said, "if I tell you where you could find Pete," he said, "you wouldn't mention that I told you, wouldja?"

I assured him that I wouldn't.

He told me, he said, "Pete usually hangs out down at this certain bar outta the neighborhood, and this is where you could usually find him."

I decided — y'know, it was just outta the neighborhood where this bar was, and it was a pretty run-down joint, not too many people goin' there, and the ones that do go in there are usually older people. And it's not a place where you'd usually find a young guy.

Well, I went there, and I walked in the bar, naturally I was armed, and I hadn't seen Pete for a number of years.

But I knew I would recognize him, and sure as hell, there was Pete, standin' at the bar, about halfway down from the door.

I came in, and I saw where he was, and I walked down the bar to him.

I really didn't know if Pete knew I was a cop or not. But I talked to 'im, and he's lookin' and lookin' at me.

Thomas M. Grubb & Allan "Lucky" Cole

I told him, "Pete, I know you've got a piece on you," I said, "now I just wanta talk to you about givin' yourself up, and seein' if we can work this thing out."

And then he realized I was a cop. And I'm lookin' at him, and he's sort of leaning on the bar, his two hands are up on the bar. And he's sideways to me, while I was frontways to him.

I told him again, "Pete, look, I know you've got a piece. Why don't you just give it to me, or sit it on the bar, and, y'know, that's the end of it."

And he hemmed and hawed, and stuff like that.

I said, "Look," I said, "you don't want nothin' to happen to you, and I sure as hell don't want nothin' to happen to me."

I said, "But if you go outside, there's a coupla detectives out there, and they're gonna shoot you."

And he looked at me very oddly, in other words, like, "Well, are you gonna shoot me, or are we gonna shoot each other, or what the hell's gonna happen?"

I told him, "Pete, use common sense. I don't want to hurt you, you don't want to hurt me."

And in the long run — like I say, I was facin' him — and I just said, "Pete, just keep your hands on the bar."

I leaned over, and I saw he had a piece in his belt.

And I told him, "Pete, I'm gonna take your piece."

I had my gun in my hand, in my pocket. And I reached over and I lifted this .45 out of the waistband of his pants. And he just looked at me while I was taking it out.

Then I said, "Pete," I said, "I'm not gonna handcuff you or nothin'. Come along with me, and I'll take you in my car."

I said, "There's no squad cars outside or anything," I said, "and I lied to you about the two detectives outside, it's only you and me, Pete."

And he just looked at me and kinda laughed, and, y'know, he was tired of hiding.

He said, "O.K., Tom," he said, "I'll go with you."

Before we left, Pete had decided that he wanted a shot and a beer, and I had his gun, and he wasn't goin' anywhere then.

And we had a drink together.

211

Thomas M. Grubb & Allan "Lucky" Cole

I was really off-duty at this time, so, no big deal.

Well, Pete came outside with me and got in my car. And we talked about things and there was no question that he had done this robbery, no question at all, because there was a wanted out for him anyway.

I told him, "Pete, the best thing to do, I'll drive you down to South Detectives, you turn yourself in."

So we talked for a while in the car, and I said, "Look, it's not like I'm pinchin' you, Pete," I said, "it's much better you give yourself up, they'll go easier on you."

And, y'know, he's lookin' at me and he's talkin', and he's thinkin' about it, and I know he was thinkin' about it.

Anyway, we get down to South Detective Division, I said, "I'm not even gonna go in with you, Pete."

I said, "You go in, turn yourself in, not like you were arrested," I said, "you'll get a better break that way."

Well, ten minutes sittin' there, just talkin', and he decided, "Yeah," he says, "I guess I better."

He hadn't killed anybody, but he did use a gun in this robbery.

So Pete got outta the car and I watched him, I walked up to the steps with him. And he went in, and he went right to the operations room, which is just inside the door, and I could see him doing this.

Then a cop came outta there, all excited, and he put handcuffs on him. And then he started walking him towards the back, which goes up the stairs to the South Detective Division.

I was sure that everything was gonna be all right then.

As a result of turning himself in, Pete did get a kind of break. He went to jail, I think it was for five to ten years, but it was better than getting shot on the street by some cop.

I never really felt bad about this, although he was a friend from our school days. I figured I did him a big favor by doing this, and getting him to turn himself in.

Thomas M. Grubb & Allan "Lucky" Cole

CHAPTER TWENTY–NINE
The Numbers Squad

I GUESS I was in the squad maybe near three years, when one day I report in the morning, and the first thing, soon as I get near the check-in desk, the fella at the desk, the clerk, he said, "Grubb, the captain wants to see you."

It wasn't any big deal by then, it was old hat.

I said, "Sure. What's Lonnie want?"

He says, "I don't know, you see him."

So I went in and saw the captain. Like I told you, the captain had a little office in the back of our roll room, and there was an office next to him where this new sergeant used to keep himself, but I noticed he wasn't in the office.

When I spoke to the captain, he said, "Hey, Grubb," he said, "You're going to report to Sergeant Riggs."

And I looked at him, I said, "Where's Sergeant Riggs?"

He says, "He's in the next office."

So I took myself out, I went over, and here's this guy sittin' at the desk smokin' a pipe.

First thing I thought of, "Who the hell's this, McArthur?"

Here, it was this Sergeant Riggs. Looked like a pleasant enough guy.

I told him, I said, "I'm Grubb."

He said, "Oh yeah, Grubb. Come in and sit down, please."

Well, when the sergeant says "please," that kinda got to me, I said, "Wonder what the hell's goin' on?"

The first words out of his mouth, he says, "You're gonna be working for me."

I looked at him and I said, "Sergeant," I said, "I'm assigned to Captain Lonergan."

He says, "Oh, yes," he says, "but no longer. You're gonna be workin' with me."

I didn't even know this guy, never heard of him. So I said, "Well, I think I'd better tell the captain."

And he said, "Oh, the captain already knows."

So I figured, "Uh-oh, what's goin' on?" I figured, "Something's in the wind."

And I just said, "Sure, Sergeant."

He says, "Oh," he says, "in a little while you'll meet the fellas that'll be working with you."

Well, shortly thereafter two guys walk in, one guy — Bill Eisen, the other — Sam Ariola.

I just think to myself, "This is a good combination, an Irishman, a Jew, and an Italian."

I still didn't know what's going on, and the captain said, "You guys work with him."

These other two guys were not in the squad. I don't know where the hell they came from. So then the sergeant took us in.

And that was it, that was how I got in the numbers squad.

For some reason I became more or less Sergeant Riggs' chauffeur, and before we would go out on the street to hit anything, I used to always take him to City Hall.

He would go in, I never knew where he was going, and, oh, a half hour, forty-five minutes, an hour, he would be out.

And we would go to headquarters and meet the other two guys. Then we'd go out and knock down a place. Any place we ever hit, we all were in the same room where we searched and found whatever evidence we could gather to culminate in the arrest.

Well, Lucky, it was like, five years now I'm in the department, a little better. And I'd learned that, you know, you just can't take everything at face value.

I became suspicious of what the hell was going on, simply because we never really got good information to hit a place such as a bank, or at least a pick-up man.

The best you could do was roam the streets and find a coupla number writers, but that wasn't the thing that seemed to be the intention of the sergeant.

We always hit the big-time stuff, and we always hurt the people when we hit them.

You know, when they lose the receipts for a day, that could be in the thousands and thousands of dollars. And you never know what the hell somebody's gonna say — they had the number that day, or this — and it caused them a lotta problems.

Well Lucky, working with this one guy, I was kinda isolated from the other members of the special squad, and I no longer had my partner, DeLuca.

He used to always ask me, "What the hell's goin' on, Tom?"

What could I tell him, you know, "I'm workin' on the lottery, the numbers, with Riggsy."

He said, "I know that," he said, "Are you comin' back to the squad?"

I said, "Sal, you know as much as I do, I don't know a goddam thing."

And, you know, there were always rumors going around, what the hell was going on.

After working with this man for, oh, maybe six months or so, I didn't like it too much, and I didn't particularly care for the guys I was working with.

They had much more time in the business than I did, and I guess they had different ideas than mine.

Maybe they saw a quick buck somewhere or whatever, but it just wasn't what I was thinking about.

There were times when we'd make a hit early in the day, and the other two guys would say, "Well, whattya say we ride up to this guy and see him, or see this guy, or see that guy."

I'd tell 'em, "Hey, what the hell sense is it, going up to these places? The sergeant seems to have the information — where we're gonna hit — and we're his backup."

I mean, that's the way it looked to me.

I don't know what the hell these other two guys did when I left 'em, but when I got off for the day — we made a pinch or something, and I had off from maybe two or three o'clock in the afternoon — I went home.

That was my headquarters.

This stuff went on for, oh, maybe six months, and, y'know, I was really getting very suspicious that everything is coming — more or less, the information's coming from the sergeant.

Thomas M. Grubb & Allan "Lucky" Cole

We aren't doing anything, meaning me or the other two guys, as far as makin' number pinches. You brought in a guy that's a number writer, it was a joke.

What really got me was, this one particular evening, the sergeant called me at home. And this was the oddest thing, because it was in the early evening, maybe six or seven o'clock, and we had just finished dinner.

And he said, "I want you to come out and pick me up."

I just said, "O.K., Sarge, that's it."

I went out to his home, and I pulled up in front of his place, and soon as I pull up, here come the other two guys pulling up.

I said, "Oh, shit, this is something weird."

So we went in, and I talked to the sergeant, and he said, "Well, we're going to go out and make a visit to a place."

And he never tells us where we're going until the four of us are in the car and we're going. That way, nobody can get out and make a phone call, to tip somebody or anything of that nature.

That was all right with me, because I didn't give a damn, I wasn't tippin' anybody.

This particular evening, we go out to City Line Avenue, and we go in to one of the biggest hotels on City Line Avenue, very exclusive hotel.

And soon as we go in, naturally, one guy stayed with the desk clerk to make sure he made no phone calls.

The sergeant and I and the other fella, we go up to this apartment, he knew exactly where he was going.

When we got to this apartment he knocked at the door, and this gentleman answers, dressed to the T's. His smoking jacket, and underneath that was his tuxedo shirt and pants, and everything. Looked like a real classy guy. Somebody of some substance.

Well, the sergeant identifies himself — now we had no warrant or anything else. That is, as far as I knew. But we go in, and the sergeant did show him something. I guess it was a ticket, I don't know.

This gentleman just steps aside, and the sergeant says, "C'mon, fellas, we're gonna search."

We started searching room by room, all four of us in one room at a time. This was the sergeant's rule — nobody went on his own.

Well, no need to say, in this apartment, which was as big as any home I've ever lived in, we found various amounts of money, coin and paper money.

More money than I've ever seen in my life.

And it was all emptied out on the bed.

Well, this gentleman said, "Look, I don't know how much is there, and I don't care."

When this guy said that, I could see the other two guys' eyes light up and get big as golf balls.

I looked at the sergeant, and he just looked at me, and he said, "Well, fellas," he said, "just continue searching the room."

This man that we went to visit asked the sergeant, "Do you mind if I make a phone call?"

The man made a call, and then handed the phone to the sergeant. This seemed rather odd to me, but who am I to say anything, I'm not the boss. And after the sergeant talked to this fella on the phone, he gave the phone back to this man we went to see.

Then the sergeant said, "Well fellas, I think it's time to leave."

Nobody touched any of the money, nothing more was said, and we just left this apartment.

Now there was no numbers paraphernalia found in there of any sort. But this gentleman was very, very nervous, stating that he had guests arriving, and if possible, would we please leave before they arrive.

From the markers on the money, I've got to assume there was at least thirty to fifty thousand dollars in that apartment.

There was one thing, before we left, that sticks out in my mind — that this man, whose apartment it was that we went to search, showed us a wristwatch. And on the back it had an inscription, "To Dan, from (a name that was very influential in the City of Philadelphia)."

Well, we left that apartment, and I took the sergeant home, and I just went home myself, and the other guys got their cars and they left.

Thomas M. Grubb & Allan "Lucky" Cole

But when I got home I told my wife about this — Cass — and I told her the truth, what was on that watch.

Then I knew the reason for the sergeant going to City Hall every day.

The way it appeared to me was that the sergeant was going down to this person at City Hall, getting the various information of where to hit and who to hit and make arrests.

And maybe at a later time they would call him or somebody representing him, and say what occurred, and what they could do to prevent this.

At that moment I got very nervous and anxious, to tell you the truth. I figured somebody's going to one day drop the hammer on us.

It wasn't long after this — oh, maybe six months or more — that this squad was disbanded.

We had done our dirty work, as far as I was concerned, by hitting these people, the number bankers, and hurting them. And then the mediator would come in and make a deal, or whatever, to get us off the number backers' banks, and we were the fall guys in this whole goddam thing.

Like I say, it lasted so long and then we got off the train, and the next thing I know the entire squad, the special squad, was being disbanded. And this was going on while we were in the numbers squad of the Special Investigation Squad.

It took a while to disband all the forty men, transferring them back to one district or another. And I guess two-thirds of the squad went before my number came up.

I got the orders, you know, "Come in, see me, what district do you want to go to?"

And I told 'em, I said, "Look, I'll go to the First Police District."

You couldn't work in your own home district, and we lived in the 17th District. So I went down to the First District, at 24th and Wolfe, as a patrolman.

Well, by this time, Lucky, I was well-versed in the bullshit that goes on in the police department.

If you want to be naive, you think you're doing a great job, and all the time you're really being used.

And that really bothered me very much.

I had worked Vice for quite a few years now, and it bothered me to the point that — you're lucky, you're getting out of this without getting hurt. Like somebody saying you did something wrong.

That was the only comfort I got out of this whole thing.

Thomas M. Grubb & Allan "Lucky" Cole

CHAPTER THIRTY
Patrol (IV)

They gave me a few days to report to the First District.

And believe me, it was a little problem after several years — three, four years — to go back into the uniform when you finally learned how to operate out of the suit.

You may be curious why I chose to go to the First District, but I knew this was a district that, in the police department, was referred to as "The Old Man's Home," meaning very little happened in that district.

Now you might also be curious why I didn't go back to the district that I worked in before I went into Vice, in the Special Investigation Squad. Well, the explanation is simple.

Try to remember, did you ever see the movie, "The New Centurions," where the one old fella retired and started to go back to see his friends and so forth?

I'll explain. I did stop at the district — the Ninth District — a number of times, to see the guys that I had worked with and had been very friendly with, primarily my ex-partner, Johnny.

But when you get there, you might catch the guys and b.s. just a little bit before roll call, but then roll call comes. You get outta the roll room, no one's allowed there unless you're in the squad.

Then they're gone in their patrol cars, and so forth, and, you know, they've got a job to do.

And you say your goodbyes and that's about it.

I've done this on a number of occasions, and that's why I chose not to go back to the district, 'cause John had a new partner, who he introduced me to, and so forth. And he looked comfortable the way he was.

And you just can't ever go back to what used to be.

So I figured, "Let me go to a new district and start all over again."

I went down to this First District at 24th and Wolfe, which was also the headquarters for the South Detectives, which was on the second floor.

This was an old district, everything in it was old.

After a while, y'know, you get to know the squad you're being assigned to, and you get to know who's in it. The sergeant usually introduces a new guy, and that's about the size of it.

Well, the daily routine started. I was assigned to a car. And I had a partner, an Italian fella, older than me, who I'd never met before. We just introduced ourselves and started patrollin' around.

I had a very, very quiet sector, and that included League Island. If you remember, what you might remember callin' "The Lakes." And, you know, there was really nothing there.

After, oh, a week or so, goin' around with this guy, nothin' happenin', it was just boring. And one day, when I got on day work again, I got called in to headquarters, which was the district.

And I was told to report to the captain.

I had never met the captain before, not even when I got sent down there. You just report to the operations room and they assign you to a squad, and I met my sergeant. That was about the extent of it.

But when I met this captain, he had my records in there, and he gave me the b.s., "Oh, I see you just came from the Special Squad," and all this, "you've worked Vice for several years."

I said, "Yes sir, yes sir," y'know, standard answers.

Then he said, "Look, I want you to do somethin', Grubb," he said. "Do you have any civilian clothes here in the district?"

I told him, "No, I haven't been assigned a locker, yet."

He said, "Well, we'll take care of that."

He said, "What I want you to do," he said, "go home, get into some civvies, and then report back to me."

Well, livin' only about ten minutes from the district, it only took me a half hour to go home, change, and come back in civilian clothes.

At this time I went into the captain's office, and there's two guys in there, in civvies, who I didn't know. And he introduced me to them — they're two plainclothes men.

We said, "Hello," and normal greetings.

Then he said, "Look," he said, "I want you to go out with these guys, give 'em a hand."

I said, "Sure, Captain."

Thomas M. Grubb & Allan "Lucky" Cole

You don't refuse an order.

Then we went out, we got into one of the guy's cars.

So the first thing I asked him, I said, "Where're we going?"

One guy looks at me and he says, "Oh," he says, "we're going up to Coppers."

Well, Coppers I knew was a bar in the First District. From past experiences and knowledge I knew that it was a numbers place, and there was action going on in there.

So I told the guy, I said, "You got a warrant for this place?"

He says, "Yeah," he said, "I got one."

I said, "Let me see it, willya?"

Well, very hesitantly, y'know, he held back, he said, "Why, whattya wanta see that for?"

I said, "Look," I said, "you guys had the place under surveillance, no doubt."

See, it's a procedure, that before you hit a place, you've gotta have reasonable cause to hit it, and information that there's an illegal activity going on within that establishment.

After a lot of hemmin' and hawin' we pulled up to the place, and I ain't gettin' outta the car until I see the warrant. Well, he hands me the warrant, and I look at it, so forth, I see the normal b.s. that's written on it.

But at the bottom it's my name. That I had signed for this warrant and had given this statement.

Well, Christ, that was false. And I knew it was false.

And I just took the warrant and I ripped it up.

And the two guys had a fit.

So I told 'em, I said, "Look, guys," I said, "that's a lot of b.s."

I said, "I didn't get this warrant. I never had this place under surveillance. I don't know what in the hell's goin' on in here."

I said, "You can't middle me on this job."

The reason for this is, well, first of all, it was illegal. Second, I'd had the experiences of hitting places, and most of the time, the reasons for hitting them.

So these guys are really pissed, and they pull away from the bar, right back to the district, and in to the captain they go.

Well, I follow 'em in.

They tell the captain what happened, the captain looks at me and says, "What is wrong with you?"

Usin' a few curse words.

I said, "Captain, I have no knowledge of what goes on in that place, I don't know those places."

And he just was so pissed off that he told me, "Oh, get the hell outta here," he said, "I don't wanta see your face again."

I went home.

CHAPTER THIRTY–ONE
Beat Cop

NEXT DAY I report in to the squad, you know, eight o'clock in the morning.

And the sergeant says, "Well, c'mere."

I went up, I talked to the sarge, he says, "What the hell happened?"

One thing, you don't repeat anything that happens.

I said, "Sergeant, I don't what you're talkin' about."

He said, "Well, I've got orders to pull you off the car."

That didn't mean that much to me.

He says, "I'm gonna put you on a beat."

So I said, "O.K., Sergeant, whatever it is, it's o.k. with me."

Well, that's the first time I was really a beat cop.

I was assigned to a beat which was down on Oregon Avenue, I think it was a six-block beat street. And one side of the street was actually The Quartermaster, there was nothing on that whole side of the street.

I worked that beat for quite a few months.

I got to know the people down there, the various business people, the stores that were on one side of the street. And it was a pleasure. It wasn't bad at all.

When you walk a beat, you also get traffic posts and so forth. Well, during the day it was really a snap. At three o'clock I used to go over and direct traffic out of The Quartermaster, which was nothing.

It was really a soft job. I enjoyed it.

CHAPTER THIRTY–TWO
Patrol (V)

SEVERAL MONTHS PASSED by, and then the sergeant tells me one night, while workin' four to twelve, he said, "Hey, look," he said, "we got a new thing now."

He said, "Car assigned to that sector will pick you up, like at eight or nine o'clock, and you ride two to the car."

That was no big deal, it's fine with me. And that's what transpired.

And this guy that was on the car, he was a real weirdo. He used to like to go down into the Lakes, League Island Park, where lovers used to park.

And he used to like to break their balls.

He'd sneak up on the car and, you know, roust whoever's in the car, which I thought was very, very petty.

I told him as much, I told him, "Look, you're a police officer. What the hell are you botherin' those people for?"

And he would just laugh.

I was a little disgusted with this, and one night when we were checkin' off I told the sergeant, I said, "Hey, Sarge," I said, "I don't like workin' on this car." I said, "Can you do somethin' about it?"

The sergeant said, "I know what's goin' on," and he more or less said, "Just put up with him for a while," he said, "He's a creep, but what can I do?"

I did work with this guy for a while, and then there was an open car in the district. That means nobody was going to be assigned to this patrol car they had.

So the sergeant assigned it to me, and he said, "You'll be workin' a one-man car, Tom."

I said, "Fine, Sergeant," I said, "I've done it before. No problem."

Like I said, this was a very, very quiet district, and nothing really happened down there of any consequence, but from past experiences in the Special Squad, you get to learn things.

You get to see a car that's kinda low in the back and you've only got one person driving it, that's a suspicious vehicle. And it gives you probable cause to stop the vehicle.

Well, like again from experience, I knew that coming up — it used to be called Penrose Ferry Bridge in those days, and that comes up from the South from Maryland through West Philadelphia, Chester and so forth.

On Sundays, normally the quietest day of the week, you would get these people that would go down and buy liquor, or actually run the white lightning, which is bootleg whiskey. And they would carry it up to Philadelphia.

Just for the hell of it, I used to go down and sit at the end of my sector, which was like the approach to this bridge. And I would just sit there and watch the cars comin' over.

Sure as hell, every Sunday, one or two, maybe more, I would stop, the trunks would be loaded, the car would be all draggin' down in the back.

And I would have myself a whiskey pinch.

Sometimes it was bootleg whiskey, sometimes it was untaxed liquor, which they'd bring up from Baltimore, Maryland, or wherever. And that's a violation.

So I made a few liquor pinches, and, y'know, it was just somethin' to do while you're down there. You don't want to go through your whole tour of duty without doing anything.

Actually, these were the best arrests I made. Had a few stolen cars which were recovered, and like that, but they're pretty trivial.

Then there was this incident that really got me angry.

It was on a Sunday afternoon, oh, maybe one o'clock in the afternoon. I got called into headquarters by this specific lieutenant. And I guess he had a hard-on for me, but I really didn't know the guy.

I guess the captain gave him the word that, you know, I dropped a bomb on him by not servin' that warrant.

So this lieutenant tells me, he says, "Hey, c'mover here."

Our operations room was in the front of the building, where you could look out at these two small streets.

He said, "Whattya see?"

Thomas M. Grubb & Allan "Lucky" Cole

I looked out, and I saw nothing out of the ordinary.

There was — if you remember when you were a kid they used to have the hobbyhorses. That was a truck that had a carrousel on the back that used to go around, and the little kids would get on there and take a ride.

Now like I say, this was a Sunday, and the man that was operating it had the loudspeaker on with the music playing.

I said, "O.K., Lieutenant, what?" I said, "That's what I see, I don't see anything else."

He says, "Do you see anything wrong?"

I told him, "No, I don't."

He said, "Well, I want you to go arrest him. He's in violation of some city ordinance usin' the megaphone to solicit business."

I couldn't believe it.

I really could not believe this police lieutenant wanted me to arrest this man for running a hobbyhorse on a Sunday.

I — I just looked at him, amazed, but he gave me an order.

So I went out and I took this man, and I told him, I said, "Look, just drive the hobbyhorse back up the street and park it in front of the district." I said, "I've got to arrest you."

And here, the man had his wife with him. It happened to be an older Italian man and his wife.

When we get in to the district, I learned that his wife was just on release from the hospital.

Well, the lieutenant forced me to arrest this man and book him. Now that means you've got to go to a hearing in the morning.

The man pleaded with him to have somebody take his wife back to the hospital, at that time I think it was Byberry, and she was just out on a pass for the day.

And this sucker put the woman in a cab, and that's how she went back to Byberry.

The next day I went down in front of the magistrate, and I've got this poor man with me.

I was so embarrassed, Lucky, believe me.

I stood in front of the magistrate and I told him, "I was ordered by this certain lieutenant to arrest this man for violation of City Ordinance So-And-So and So-And-So."

The magistrate was somebody I knew from appearin' before him when I was in the Special Squad many times.

The guy got up and actually leaned over the desk, they're like in a pulpit, up in the air, and he said, "Are you kidding?"

I said, "No, sir, I'm not kidding."

And we had an arrest report that was made up, and he said, "This is utterly ridiculous. Discharged."

He said, "Take this man back," and he told 'em, "Release his vehicle," which was the hobbyhorses.

Well, I went back and I told the lieutenant, "Man was discharged."

And he was actually pissed off that this man wasn't held for some stupid violation of City Ordinance.

That was my dealing with this specific lieutenant.

Then the next day, the sergeant said, "Grubb, you're off the car again."

Thomas M. Grubb & Allan "Lucky" Cole

CHAPTER THIRTY–THREE
Beat Cop (II)

And then I was put back on my beat again.

Well, I really didn't mind it that much, Lucky. And I walked that beat, and I was very, very content.

It's really funny how — it was just like the service. If you had an officer above you in rank they could really screw you, and there wasn't too much you could do about it, but just smile and tell 'em, "Yes, sir."

Now my sergeant was a helluva nice guy. And he knew what was goin' on, he had found out about the original incident with the captain. And he thought more of me for that than anything else.

But then again, like I said, he was a nice guy and he understood, and he had plenty of time in the business. So he knew you couldn't be used, or if you were used, you were an asshole.

I guess I worked the district in uniform for approximately a year, and then I had a call from my rabbi.

Went over and talked to him, and as a result of this conversation, he told me, "You're going to be transferred."

I guess it was a few days later, the transfer comes over on the teletype, and I'm transferred to the Juvenile Aid Division.

CHAPTER THIRTY–FOUR
Juvenile Aid

JUVENILE AID DIVISION was a good unit, now that I look back on it. You were out of the uniform and you acted as a detective, same work as a detective, only you handled juveniles.

Our headquarters at that time was in the Board of Education building at 21st and the Parkway.

I did report to this unit, and of course you wore a suit and a tie, and you acted as a detective, only for the juveniles.

I met a lot of new people, guys I never met before, but it's a funny thing, your reputation precedes you when you go into various units.

The first day there I went in, I was called in to see the inspector, who welcomed me to the unit.

Then he said — y'know, he had my record in front of him — he said, "Oh," he said, "I see you've worked with the Special Investigation Squad and Vice," and this and that.

He said, "Well," he said, "You've gotta put all that behind you. This is an entirely different unit with entirely different work."

I got my introduction lecture and thanked him, and went out and reported to a sergeant.

This was an entirely new world for me.

Your job there was to get assignments, you would report to a division, really, that would include maybe two or three districts, or maybe even only one district.

You were called to come in for juveniles committing some offense or just making noise or anything, anything that the uniform men would pick these kids up for and bring 'em into a district and arrest them, or detain them, I should say.

Uniform people were not allowed to arrest juveniles. The only one that could arrest a juvenile was a J.A.D. officer, that's Juvenile Aid officer.

You would go to your division and you would make what we called a "pull" every hour. That means you would call into headquarters to see if there were any assignments for you.

At this time the men in the operations room of J.A.D. would tell you to go to a specific district and pick up an incident report.

Well, that's what you would do, Luck. You would go in and you would find the, oh, the sergeant there, at the district you were told to go to, and he would give you a 4548, which would be an Incident Report. And that would tell you, allegedly, what these kids had done.

You would talk to the kids and see if there was anything that would warrant an arrest. After this you would call their parents, whether you arrested the kids or not, for them to come in to the district and pick up their kids.

Like I say, it wasn't a real exciting job, but it was a job, and it had its benefits and its drawbacks. But you would find a lot of times you would have time on your hands, y'know, that you weren't that busy.

When you weren't on an assignment, then you would just have to patrol around the division you were assigned to.

Lucky, I'll explain to you what the Juvenile Aid Division is. This is an overall unit that handles all juvenile crime in the city.

Within the Juvenile Aid there is the Morals Squad, Juvenile Warrant Division, and a unit called Gang Control. These units all work separately with their own supervisors and personnel.

What I was assigned to was the Line Squad, which handles basically all the juvenile junk. While in this Line Squad of the unit you worked a rotating shift, that's the three shifts — eight to four, four to twelve, twelve to eight.

And it wasn't a bad job. I guess I was workin' it for perhaps a year when I had occasion to make arrests of youngsters for various things. Nothing really too serious, I guess most of that time it was stealing automobiles.

You would have to call the parent before you would release the kids to them, to appear at the Youth Study Center on the next day for an interview. With juveniles they don't call it hearings, they call it interviews.

Well, there's this one occasion, that one of the kids that was brought into the district, I had to arrest. And I called his parents, and his father came down.

Thomas M. Grubb & Allan "Lucky" Cole

His father was kinda odd looking, he was a guy that wore these milk-bottle type glasses, real thick, and he had a little mustache, and kinda balding.

It was the funniest thing, it brought back to my mind a person that I met who was very similar to this gentleman.

Now this has nothing to do with this particular case. That kid was just sent to the Youth Study Center and his father got him released.

But after talking to the father, I was just sitting in the, what we called the J.A.D. room, that was our room down there, where we conducted our business.

And I thought back after seein' this man, about another man that I had met before I came into the police department.

He was a psychiatrist.

Before you're accepted into the department, you go through all your various physical examinations and everything else, and your written examinations.

And then the last thing they do to you is have you be interviewed by a psychiatrist.

It happened that I got an appointment to go see this man, like seven or eight o'clock at night at City Hall.

Now, didn't mean anything to me, I went to City Hall, and at that time of night everything is closed in there, except the one elevator that took you where he was. I guess he had other appointments, interviewed other prospective police officers.

Well, City Hall is one of the lonesomest, dirtiest places you want to go to, particularly at night. I went up there, and it was either the seventh or eighth floor, to a specific numbered room.

And Christ, Luck, when you're walkin' through the halls up there, the rats are runnin' past you.

I got to this room and it was dark, and I walked in, I didn't see anybody, it was like an outer office. And then I could see this light in this inner office, and I knocked on the door.

And this guy calls me in, and he was the weirdest lookin' dude you've ever seen.

Thomas M. Grubb & Allan "Lucky" Cole

He had these thick, thick glasses on, and was sittin' behind this desk with this dim light in there. And then they ask you these stupid questions, like, "Did you wet the bed, do you like your mother."

Oh, I mean, real trashy questions.

And he kept you in there for maybe fifteen minutes.

And then he just says, "That's all."

Well, believe me, Lucky, I came home and told your Aunt Cassie about this guy.

I said, "I just met the weirdest bastard I've met in years."

We both had a big laugh about it, but meeting the father of this boy on that particular evening brought this all back to me.

I'll tell you about, I guess it's the biggest job I had while I was in the Line Squad of J.A.D.

I worked with a fella named Charles O'Brien. Now this was odd, because Charles O'Brien used to just live around the corner from me.

Actually, he went to the same school I did, but was a year or two ahead of me. And I remembered the name because Charlie was a football player, also. I never had occasion to play ball with him, but we hit it off real good when I was told I was gonna be workin' with him.

Well, like I say, we hit it off good, and Charlie was a hell of an investigator.

And we got this job — a missing kid.

All missing children are reported, naturally, to the police, and then it comes to J.A.D.

When you have a missing kid it's, you know, everybody that works that division in J.A.D. will go out on what we call a door-to-door search, lookin' for this child, in the streets, and anywhere else in his neighborhood.

This particular job was really weird.

I had an opportunity with Charlie to interview the father of this boy. Now the father's story was, he had the kid on Ninth Street, which is the Italian Market.

And I gotta describe it to you: any day in the week, this place is crowded, I mean particularly on Fridays and Saturdays.

It's belly to belly walkin' on the sidewalks, with the hucksters out in the street — fish, crabs, bakeries, clothes, you name it, they've got it. And I know it's not hard to lose a child there, if he wanders five feet away from you, outta your sight, you've got a problem.

Well, this father told us this is what happened, how he lost the boy.

No need to say, coupla days passed, we interviewed the parents, and we talked to the other kids in the family. And this happened to be a poor black family. We didn't get any new information, it was always the same story.

Naturally the newspapers picked this up, and the radio, and everything else. And we worked on this for the longest time, in between our other jobs that we were assigned to do.

And months passed.

The father of the child was brought in, was given a polygraph, which is the lie detector, and the man passed it. I think he had two of them, as a matter of fact, and he passed each time.

This job was, like I say, was assigned to Charlie and me, and we used to work on it whenever we had any spare time. If we didn't have another job to do, we'd work on that.

Quite a few months passed by, and occasionally we would stop at the house. And we got to recognize the mother, got to know her, and we got to know the other children in the family by sight. Also, we got to know just about every merchant along Ninth Street.

The way this whole thing broke open was, one afternoon, I guess it was around three o'clock when the kids would be comin' home from school, we were in the kid's neighborhood.

And we saw a little boy that we knew was the man's son coming up the street — not the one that was missing, but another one of his sons.

The kid didn't look too well, you know, for a little kid, they're always bouncin' around and everything. This kid was walkin' stiffly, and all.

Anyway, we stopped him, we talked to him. And no sooner we started to talk to the kid, he started cryin'.

Thomas M. Grubb & Allan "Lucky" Cole

We were asking, did he hear anything, and this and that — "We're your friends" — about what happened to your brother, and everything like that.

And then the kid just broke down, and he told me that his father had given him a beating.

Like I say, he was only a little kid, maybe seven years old, eight years old.

Then he repeated that he got a beating just like his brother got.

And that was it.

When we heard that the father had beaten the other boy that was missing, we started to really get into questioning this little guy. And then we took him home.

The old man wasn't there, but the mother was there. And of course, the mother was very upset when the kid was sayin' this.

The kid said, "You know how he beat" — I forget the child's name, that was missing.

Anyway, when we got this information, we got the old man in to the detective division, because he's an adult, awright?

The detectives got on him, started questionin' him in our presence, and the old man broke down. And when he broke down, he admitted that he had beaten the boy.

He beat him with a broomstick.

And unfortunately, while beating the boy, he killed him.

After he killed the kid, he put him in a seed bag, took him to 25th and Gray's Ferry, and he buried the kid by the railroad tracks.

With this information, the old man was immediately arrested. We went and confronted the mother with the information, and she broke down and she said, yes, the father had beaten the boy, and that was it.

We went up, and we took the old man up to where he said he buried the kid. And sure as hell, after three or four hours we got to the exact spot where he buried the kid.

We notified the proper people to come and dig up the area, and we found the kid in a seed bag. You know what a seed bag is, he'd just stuck the little kid in that and buried him.

Well, Lucky, that was the only big case that I worked on in the Line Squad of the Juvenile Division.

235

Thomas M. Grubb & Allan "Lucky" Cole

CHAPTER THIRTY–FIVE
Gang Control

IT WASN'T TOO long after this that I got transferred into what they call Gang Control. This was a more sophisticated unit, with only so many men in it, and usually they were all selected for whatever their talents might be.

I soon found out that Gang Control was an integral part of Juvenile Aid, and there were numerous gangs out in the streets at this time.

I learned that they were always killing each other for one reason or another, usually retaliation over territorial rights, or what have you.

In this Gang Control Unit we really only had one supervisor, and that was a sergeant.

I was partnered up with a guy named Bobby, and Bobby was a nice man, he was a good man. One of the most efficient typists that I've ever met, and we made a good combination, 'cause remember, I couldn't type worth a damn.

Anytime in Juvenile Aid or in this Gang Control Unit, you made your own arrest reports. And, Christ, that took you — half the time, instead of investigating, you'd be hangin' over a typewriter somewhere, tryin' to type up an arrest report.

Well, workin' with this guy, Bobby Annan, it was an experience in itself. He was the nicest guy you'd ever wanta meet. Great typist, great piano player, but a lousy goddam investigator. But we hit it off good.

Bobby had been in J.A.D. for a number of years, and he knew everybody, and this is a break. When you know everybody that's in a big unit like that was, you can get around pretty good, and you can get help when you need it.

This worked out very well, bein' partnered up with him.

In Gang Control, our purpose was patrolling around schools, primarily, or hangout corners where gangs congregated. You didn't get as many assignments as you did when you worked the Line Squad, because there you would handle any violation that a kid might commit.

But in Gang Control, the violation would have to be gang connected, so our assignments weren't as many as when we worked in the Line Squad.

When patrolling around the schools, you would watch the kids congregate, and almost without fail there'd be a fight — somebody might get stabbed or whatever — and that's when you took action, you went in and you arrested them.

Or you might get a call to a school, and they'd tell you about an incident where Joe Blow was stabbed by Harry Gump from some other gang. Well again, that's your kinda job, and that's what you would take.

Our assignment was to patrol in South Philadelphia, which suited me fine, because I knew every street, corner and alley down there.

I should tell you, Lucky, that the assignments we received in Gang Control were usually felonies of various degrees — aggravated assaults, stabbings, or shootings.

I should also mention at this time, the weapons of choice, you might say, between the gangs were zip guns, which they made themselves — various models, and so forth.

They were usually a one-shot affair. They weren't the automatic weapons that they have on the streets today, so it wasn't quite as bad.

Again, you're really in a learning process. Because I knew South Philadelphia, I knew that there weren't that many white gangs down there, a few but not that many. Possibly four at the most.

It was easy for me to get to know most of these kids, and just how bad they really were. The major things were the black gangs, of which there were many, because of the various projects in South Philly and Upper Central Divisions.

Our big problems were, when the transportation — when these kids used to leave school for some reason or another, they would get together.

And the various gangs would take one bus, another gang would take another bus, but sometimes they intermingled because of school transportation or public transportation.

Thomas M. Grubb & Allan "Lucky" Cole

Second, our big problem was the subways out of South Philadelphia.

In this squad we only worked the two shifts, but they kind of varied a little bit. You would start like, maybe at seven to five or from five to two.

This's because that's when the kids got together, and usually the gang activity was at its highest peak.

Though this was primarily kids, it was also intermingled with young adults.

Gang Control was rather a select unit, and you were selected by your sergeant or your captain to be assigned to this unit. At other times, even the inspector would pick a man to put in Gang Control.

Through various assignments you would receive, you would get to know the members of each gang, or get to know some of them.

Your main goal was to get to know the leader or his lieutenants, or the one who used to do the carrying. The guy that did the carrying was the one that usually had the gun or guns.

From time to time, in some of the shootings, there were real weapons used, such as .22's or .25's, and sometimes the bigger caliber weapons.

The prime purpose of our division was to not only catch the perpetrators, but to get these weapons off the street.

That was to know who the carrier was, because he was the guy that always stashed the guns somewhere, and got them before the gang was to take some sort of retaliation action against another gang.

It took quite a few months to get to know some of these guys out in the street, and to pinpoint where they were from. They usually identified themselves by the area in which they lived, such as Hawthorne, Southwark, Tasker, or by the street corners where they hung.

Also, while working these gangs, you went in to the various high schools in the area, and you got to know the principal, vice-principal, or disciplinarian quite well. Sometimes they were an excellent source of information.

But the only problem was, no one, and I mean no one, wanted to involve the students in any illegal activity or as the instigators of activity. On the whole, they were mostly all cooperative.

Thomas M. Grubb & Allan "Lucky" Cole

It was while working in this unit that we were moved from the Board of Education building at 21st and the Parkway, and they found us space in various abandoned schools.

We would go in there and set up shop, get old desks, chairs, or whatever. It was not very clean, or a place where you could really do your work comfortably.

It was on this one particular day while working with Bobby, that we were heading up from South Philadelphia, up to our headquarters, and had taken the Schuylkill Expressway.

It was sometime perhaps around two in the afternoon, or three — traffic was rather heavy.

While we're going up, on the radio we hear of a bank robbery, a security and loan office robbed by four men.

We were heading in the general direction, over the Vine Street Expressway, when we got another news flash that these four men had commandeered a taxicab and were heading West on Vine Street, which was — we were heading East on Vine.

We also got a flash message that police were in pursuit of this taxicab with the four men in it.

I told Bobby, "Let's move it, and maybe we can intercept them coming across Broad Street."

Bobby turned on the gas, we got up to Broad Street, but it was physically impossible to get across, due to the traffic.

I jumped outta the car, I told him, "C'mon, Bobby," I expected him to be right behind me.

I ran across Broad Street, ziggin', zaggin' between the cars, spotted the cab that the four perpetrators were in, and headed towards them. I guess I was maybe ten feet from them, or so.

I saw the other detectives that were following them, running up to the car.

I reached for my weapon, which I carried under my jacket, and much to my surprise there was no weapon.

I figured I'd better keep movin' anyway, I was this close. I ran up to the left side of the cab, toward the driver, and fortunately he was lookin' behind him at the guys approaching. They were really about to get out of the cab and run.

239

I grabbed the first guy, and just at this instant the other detectives that were after them came up on the other side of the cab. And they had their weapons out, and we made it a pinch.

It was pretty shocking to find out that I didn't have the damn gun, but my mind was racing.

I remembered in the morning I was late, I was hurrying, I left my weapon on a table near the doorway, but I didn't pick it up.

That's the last time, the first and the last time, I ever forgot to take my weapon with me on duty.

The other detectives were on the scene, called for a wagon, we transported the perpetrators into Central Detectives.

Although we didn't actually make the pinch, we were mentioned as assisting in the arrest of these perpetrators. No need to say, it looked good on the record.

It was a while after this that Bobby was reassigned back to headquarters, and I acquired a new partner, Paul Poletti.

Paul was a good cop and a good investigator, we hit it off real good. We worked together for several months handling various assignments and got along well.

As a matter of fact, Paul got to know my family well, as well as I got to know his.

It was interesting, 'cause Paul had a boy that went to Vietnam, I believe he was a gunner on a helicopter. He won several awards — the Bronze Star, Silver Star, D.F.C. — and he was quite a war hero, you might say.

Paul was very proud of him.

I recall an occasion when Paul said, "Tom, the kid asked me for a gun, a .38."

For some reason he wanted to carry that weapon, so Paul and I went out, and Paul purchased the Smith and Wesson .38 for his son and had it shipped over to him in Vietnam.

I think I should tell you how this Gang Control Unit was organized.

Our unit was broken up into two squads. There were 16 men to each squad. Of the 16 men, there were four white guys and the rest were black. Each squad had a sergeant.

The men were broken up into teams of two, and each team was assigned a certain section of the city, like West, Northwest, Central, East, South, North Central.

And they each patrolled their own area and handled assignments in their own area.

During this time while working with Paul, we handled a number of jobs — aggravated assaults, stabbings, shootings — and when we were fortunate enough to make an arrest, we would bring them in to the detective division where we made the arrest. It was then that we started our own typing of reports.

I want to explain to you what these detective divisions looked like, Lucky.

First of all, they used these old Underwood typewriters. If there were six or seven typewriters in the division, five of them were broken. And usually the other two were being operated by detectives trying to keep up on their reports.

Usually they were a shithole. You couldn't find the forms you needed to make your arrests, such as 7549's or 51's, which were continuation sheets.

After fighting that battle for a few months, I decided to buy my own typewriter. I got a Smith-Corona portable.

Fortunately, Paul was a better typist than I was, and we carried our own reports around with us. And when we went into a division, at least we could sit down with our own typewriter and type our reports.

Lucky, the best way I can explain any detective division, if you've ever seen the TV show "Barney Miller," that's the detective division. Each guy was doin' his own little thing, and there was no big emergency like you see on TV, where they run to a gun locker and grab rifles and shotguns and all that stuff.

That's a lot of bull. The only weapons these guys had were their own sidearms.

Usually in the evening the commanding officer would be a sergeant, or perhaps a lieutenant. There were no captains on duty then.

Well, having our own typewriter and stuff, we used to get through our reports pretty quickly, and this was a big help.

241

Thomas M. Grubb & Allan "Lucky" Cole

Some nights you might handle one job, some nights you might handle five jobs. The rule was, if you got a job an hour before quitting time, that was your job and you saw it through.

You didn't pass it off to the next shift coming in — particularly if you were working the late shift, which was up till midnight or two o'clock in the morning.

So many nights you worked — well, it wasn't overtime in those days. You got compensatory time, hour for hour, no money.

Paul and I, we did our job. We got along pretty good, and we used to handle our stuff alone.P

Thomas M. Grubb & Allan "Lucky" Cole

CHAPTER THIRTY–SIX
Sergeant

IT WAS DURING this time that my sergeant, who happened to be a guy I knew from the academy, got himself jammed up and subsequently was suspended.

It was the day after this happened, my inspector called me into his office, and he told me, "You are now the sergeant in your squad."

This was all well and good, and when I came on duty that particular evening, the guys learned that I was their sergeant, and that kinda threw a different complexion on things.

Knowing some of the men that I worked with, I had asked for some replacements. I more or less picked some guys I knew that I wanted to work with me. And they were transferred into the squad after the others were transferred out.

On the whole I thought I had the better squad, because they were all good men and they knew their jobs.

It was during this time that our unit was receiving some complaints of brutality, that some of the kids were struck, or this or that, or they weren't treated right.

So I created a situation where, when they were brought in, we would take photographs of the individuals we brought in — just how they looked, and photographs when we let them go.

Well, if you don't know it, you weren't allowed to photograph juveniles. There were no mug shots of juveniles. And there was a little static over this, but our boss, our inspector, figured it was a good idea.

We didn't publish these photographs, we kept them in a file. And eventually this became a very, very important part of our work.

For the next year or so we constructed quite a file on gang members — these were gang members only. We got to know street names, which were very, very important, as well as some of their real names.

We got to know who were the leaders of the gangs, who were the lieutenants, who were the carriers, who were the warlords. And this was very beneficial to us, that is to our unit only.

In the next year or so, while building this up, we had quite a success in clearing cases that otherwise would not have been cleared.

I want to tell you about a story, where it happened that this particular evening, a gang member who had been shot was being laid out in West Philadelphia.

When this occurs, that's a signal to go to the wake with your whole squad, or nearly all your squad, and patrol the areas.

Because sure as hell, you knew there was gonna be some retaliation from the gang of the boy that was killed.

Sure enough, on this particular job, while we're patrolling around, we hear a radio call of a shooting. And we get a location, and the guys that are out there all pile up to that location, find out what's goin' on.

And here, we get up there, we find out it's two cars involved, they're shootin' at each other.

We got a wagon, and we take three in to the hospital — two from the gang of the kid that's killed, and the other one is from the gang that did the original shooting.

I barrel over to the hospital with the two guys that were workin' West Philly, and they happened to be two of the better guys I had working in my squad. In the hospital, the first thing you want to try to do is get the identity of the shooters.

In this case a pistol was used, as well as a shotgun.

Two kids from the gang of the boy that was being viewed that night only received shotgun pellets, so they were in pretty good shape. The other kid from the shooter's gang had got hit with a .38.

He wasn't hit that bad, but he didn't know that, and finally one of the doctors gave us permission to talk to him.

We went in and we talked to 'im, and the point was to find out if he was the shooter or who he was with that did the shootin'.

Well, without sayin', he ain't gonna tell you anything, this was the normal code among these kids.

We did our thing, and then the doctor told us, "You gotta leave."

We just begged for a few minutes more, and the doctor walked outta the room.

And this one detective with us, he went over close to the kid's head and whispered in his ear. And then he kind of bent the

Thomas M. Grubb & Allan "Lucky" Cole

intravenous line that was going into his arm, at least I think it was bent, I'm not sure.

But this kid started raisin' hell, and he was talkin' to this detective quite freely.

And we walked out, didn't take but maybe 30 seconds, 45 seconds.

Once outside, this one detective who did this turned around to me and said, "Sarge," he said, "We've gotta go pick up an individual known as 'Little Man,'" and another one with another particular name.

From our detective's knowledge — he knew who "Little Man" was, he had his name in our nickname file. And we went out to where they usually hung out, and we lay around there for, oh, an hour or so.

And finally these two that we're lookin' for decided to go to their homes, and that's where we snatched 'em.

We took them to our headquarters and interrogated them, and with the information we had received from the kid in the hospital, we had them cold.

But what we wanted were the guns that were used in the incident.

This guy gave us the names of the other two kids that were in the car, and also the kids that were in the car of the boy whose wake we were guarding.

All in all, we made six arrests, and we cleared up that case.

Over the next few months we made numerous arrests for felony charges with these gang kids. On the whole we had an excellent average of clearing cases. I think our percentage was about 93 per cent clearance of cases.

In the police department, this is exceptional.

During my years with Gang Control we had a number of assignment, one involving, I believe he was a state legislator.

It seems that his son was on his way home from school, and he was surrounded by a group of black kids — he was black also — and they beat him with what appeared to be a piece of telephone cable.

Although he was not seriously injured, his father threw a fit and wanted somebody arrested for this incident. His father brought a lot

Thomas M. Grubb & Allan "Lucky" Cole

of weight against the police department, and like they say, shit runs downhill.

It went from the commissioner's office down to the inspectors, and eventually wound up in our unit.

I was called in and it was explained by the inspector that somebody's gotta make a pinch on this case.

Well, myself along with one other guy, we went out and worked on this case alone for, oh, maybe three, four days. And finally, by talking to some of the kids that we knew from various gangs around the area, we got a name.

And with the name, we picked up a kid, and lo and behold, we were able to break the case. It wasn't that great a case, but we all got commendations for catching the kids that beat this other boy up with the cable.

It just goes to show, when you've got some political influence you can get a lot of things done real quick.

I guess the next big incident was, when Paul and I were patrolling in South Philly, we ran into what was a real gang fight. There hadda be fifty goddam kids on Point Breeze Avenue, battling.

And there were kids gettin' cut, and whatnot.

Well, other Gang Control cars came down, and subsequently one of our guys got hit by a zip gun. The bullet bounced off his ribs, broke a rib, but he was o.k. Later on we shipped 'im to the hospital.

But we got the son-of-a-bitch that shot him.

And we must have arrested thirty kids that night.

Like I told you earlier, these zip guns all fired .22 caliber bullets.

With the passing of time, we had collected numerous homemade weapons used by these gang guys. And we had made up a rather impressive display, along with other articles.

Gangs were pretty well running rampant in the city at this time, and more and more, our unit was called on for assistance by various detective units, and also by Homicide.

It got so that we were assigning a man to detective divisions as well as Homicide as liaison, to assist them in their cases where they might suspect a juvenile was involved.

I myself worked closely with Homicide as liaison, and we worked on numerous cases. Sometimes the juveniles were involved, sometimes they weren't. You would have an eighteen year old, or perhaps nineteen, they're still running with the gangs.

And these were the guys, we had them in our nickname files for years under various names and addresses. And that's when our files became beneficial in tracking some of these guys down and associating them with the crime at hand.

I'll tell you now about another incident that occurred in Broad Street subway, where a young lady was gang-raped by a group of juveniles.

And where a sailor — I don't know if he tried to intervene, or he just happened to be on the platform at the same time — well, these guys beat him up, also.

This was a big case, with the girl being gang-raped, and also with this serviceman bein' beaten pretty badly.

I happened to be on duty when this occurred, and we were advised by the lieutenant on duty to handle the case, which we did. And in doing so, we had to call members of the other squad in to work also, because this was going to be an all-hands effort.

The decision was to round up all the gang members that we knew, and that meant an all-night job, which we did. All our guys went out and rounded up the guys that were in that area that we knew as gang members.

As a result of doing this, we had our headquarters full of kids, I guess we had a hundred of them in there or more.

After interrogating all these gang kids, we came up with a lot of names, and therefore our guys hadda go out and pick up others. And we worked like, oh, 20 hours on this, 22 hours, all through the night and the day.

And finally concluded with an arrest. We did arrest a numerous amount of kids that were involved, the onlookers as well as the guys that did the raping.

This case was carried, I guess what you would call in the national news, it went clean across the country, with photographs of myself and the sailor involved, and other photographs.

Thomas M. Grubb & Allan "Lucky" Cole

As a result of this we got a unit commendation, as well as individual commendations. Our lieutenant was honored, and our captain, so everybody felt good about it. We got the right guys, and we got some recognition out of this arrest.

After this, I was ordered by my inspector to go to F.B.I. Headquarters and give a seminar on gang-related incidents, and present the weapons that we had gathered from the juvenile gangs, and just tell the way they operate.

I didn't particularly care for this, but I went down anyway, to F.B.I. Headquarters, I believe at that time it was in the Widener Building.

And a group of F.B.I. guys, you'd give them an hour's seminar, let them see what the hell the kids were using in the streets and how they were set up in their various gangs.

Like I already told you, you had your chief, your boss, you had your lieutenants, you had your carrier — that's the kid with the weapons — and you had your warlord.

This was the guy that would go from one gang to another gang, then make arrangements that they were gonna have a war, or whatever they were gonna do.

This was well-accepted by the F.B.I., and I think I received a letter of commendation from the F.B.I. concerning these seminars.

I should tell you, about that gang-rape in the subway, we had all these people into headquarters, and it was like, three, four o'clock in the morning.

And it was bedlam, believe me. Our guys were workin' over the ones they were talkin' to, to get some information on this case.

They finally did get it, but some of these possible offenders tripped and fell down the stairs, y'know, or went into the men's' room and slipped on the floor.

As a matter of fact, I guess one guy that accidentally slipped down the stairway from the second floor to the first, he rolled down just as our inspector was comin' in the door.

Now that was very odd, at four o'clock in the morning, for our boss to be coming in.

He said, "Geez, what happened? Did he fall?"

Thomas M. Grubb & Allan "Lucky" Cole

And of course, the Gang Control man that was there said, "Yeah, boss, he fell."

By now, Lucky, I had passed my twenty years in the department.

I saw a lot, did a lot, and this is when you've got to look back and say, "Did I do my job? Did I earn my pay?"

Well, I decided to myself that I did my job and I did earn every penny of my pay.

We had a pretty good grip on everything concerning the gangs in the city, and I had the men that could really handle the whole situation.

Like I said, we were often assigned to homicide, to try and help them out in some cases they had, which we did. When it came to the juvenile offenders, everyone was interested in the nickname files that we had constructed. And more than often, we did clear up some of their cases.

Also, at times we were assigned to South Detective Division, and going down there, helping them with some cases where they suspected juvenile offenders, our nickname files were very beneficial.

Plus, some of the guys that were down there looked at me very suspiciously, and began to wonder, "What the hell had I been doing over there in the house, waiting for the Scolari's to come in?"

On a few occasions, some of the old-timers asked me, "Didn't I see you over there?"

It was comical, I'd say, "No, I'm sorry, you didn't see me."

That's when I was assigned to the Special Investigation Squad, and more or less was guarding the wife of one of the Scolari's, which I told you about on the previous tapes.

This was just one of the funny things that occurred.

Thomas M. Grubb & Allan "Lucky" Cole

CHAPTER THIRTY–SEVEN
Riots

THE NEXT TWO things I'm gonna tell you about are when I was in Gang Control.

The first thing is the Columbia Avenue riots.

This was back in the sixties, and at that time Frank Rizzo, our former Commissioner and Mayor, was a police inspector.

As I understand it, when these riots started, he requested all of Gang Control to report up to Columbia Avenue, to him.

Well, I happened to be working four to twelve when all this happened, and I guess we got the radio call somewhere, oh, around seven or eight o'clock at night.

And the riots were in full bloom then.

Different guys that were patrolling, you know, responded to the radio call, and we met up at Broad and Columbia. And then we talked to the inspector, bein' I was a sergeant, and he told us what he wanted, we're gonna clean off Columbia Avenue and Ridge Avenue.

Well, that was it.

Now mind you, we were dressed — I've got a suit on and everything, and the other guys were dressed — we all wore suits of some sort. And we went along with the inspector.

And man, it was a madhouse up there.

The neighbors, or residents of that area, and the gang boys were up there, and they were breakin' into places, and throwin' rocks through windows, and what have you.

We went up there, and as we were goin' up, we had a wagon behind us. Matter of fact, two wagons.

We went down the street, sidewalks and street, and we started, and of course there was a great deal of opposition.

And it was more or less — clubs were trump.

Meaning, when you went up there, you had your nightstick in your hand, or jack or whatever, because you knew you were gonna need it. It's as simple as that.

These rioters were fighting back, and there was stuff being thrown out windows and off the roofs — bottles, bricks, stones, whatever they could throw out — and quite a few guys got hit with things.

In the first four hours we cleaned the street off — nobody was on the street. I mean, we went all the way down Columbia Avenue and Ridge Avenue, and it was cleaned up pretty good. Now it was maybe midnight, one o'clock in the morning.

A lot of our guys, including myself, got some lumps, you know, nothin' for a hospital, but enough lumps. Some got stitches or what have you, later.

And the situation was quelled.

Then we all reported back to the boss, who was Rizzo. And we regrouped back at, oh, Broad or 15th and Columbia. At this time some of the big brass had come down, and I was close enough to hear the conversation that went on after that.

The conversation, from what I could understand, was Deputy Inspector Rizzo was relieved of the duties there at Columbia Avenue.

He got into an argument with the commissioner — there was some hostility in the voices — and the commissioner relieved him of his duties right there.

You know, in other words, "You did this, now that's the end of it."

And he was dismissed.

After he was relieved, it got to be a joke.

The rioters came out again, started with the robbing and stealing, and the gentleman who was commissioner — now, I'm not quite sure, if my memory serves me right, it was O'Leary.

His theory was, "Just identify who you can with these incidents," you know, who's stealing televisions out of stores, radios or what have you, refrigerators, "don't take any action."

This was a joke. You can't go near those people while they're robbin' stuff and just not arrest 'em.

Well anyway, we didn't get outta there till, oh, maybe four or five o'clock in the morning, at daybreak, I guess, if you want to call it that. We were up there like, 12, 15 hours.

Then we were relieved, and all uniform men started to come in. And that was the end of the riots.

Thomas M. Grubb & Allan "Lucky" Cole

Actually, we didn't make a single arrest, not our group. But we could see some of the people that were involved, and we knew some of them, maybe for a later time.

That was the Columbia Avenue riots.

It was more or less a farce, in the end, not to arrest anybody. And really, it wasn't worth while to arrest 'em, because all you'd do is go to court, and they'd have some kind of a story, that it wasn't them, it was three other people.

That was a wasted effort, as far as I was concerned, in those riots. We got lumped, we lumped some of them, and that was about the end of it.

It was my understanding — much later we understood that this whole situation occurred because a black woman was stopped in her automobile and given a ticket. Now how true that is I'll never know, but that was the story we got later on.

Lucky, it wasn't like Watts in California, but it was bad enough for right here, y'know, in Philadelphia. It was quite an experience, and it didn't turn out any better than Watts, which occurred much later — matter of fact, it wasn't nearly as bad as Watts.

Nobody got burned out or anything of that nature, but it was bad enough.

Our group, Gang Control, was assigned to a number of civil disobedience actions, where these protesters would come to a school, surround the school, not let anybody in or out, and we would have to disburse them in an orderly manner, as the saying goes.

Well, some of these things backed up on us and some people got hurt, and there's not much you could do about it.

All you were there for is, along with the Civil Disobedience Squad and the Labor Squad, is to identify any of the protesters that you could for later information. Also, to identify anyone that was involved or you arrested in any scuffles of any kind.

There were a number of these in the sixties and seventies, and then came Girard College.

This is when Attorney Cecil Moore broke the Will of Girard College — this was to admit black children.

Well, no need to say that we were sent up there, our entire squad, and we worked twelve hour shifts. You were in an unmarked

252

vehicle patrolling the areas to prevent problems. There had been some problems up there, such as throwing of bottles and whatnot, and protesting, which was every day.

The lines were completely around Girard College, and sometimes the protesters would get over the walls, or carry on in some way.

Our job was to stop this — now they had uniform guys all around the place, but we were on the perimeter. And our tour was twelve hours on, twelve hours off.

In this squad car were two Gang Control people, and at least one, what they called Line Squad J.A.D. guys.

And we just rode around and rode around. If we saw any trouble spots, or something that appeared to be trouble, we would try to calm them down, if not, arrest them for disorderly conduct or whatnot.

This went on for months and months.

It got so that, Christ, you didn't know if it was daytime or nighttime, you worked so many hours. You rarely changed your clothes, because you're in a car most of the time, just patrolling around.

And you've gotta remember — summertime — we had no air conditioners in the cars, so you cooked yourself in them while you were just rolling around.

There were actually no places to get anything to eat up there, so what they did, they sent in something called the "Second Alarmer," which is a truck.

They were distributing sandwiches or coffee or Kool-Aid, and if you were fortunate enough, it would come over the radio.

As I was saying, if you were fortunate enough to get to that truck, you would be given a sandwich and a glass of Kool-Aid.

Well, the sandwiches were horrendous, to say the least, y'know, one slice of meat and mustard, or whatever, on it. Actually, you had to take three or four sandwiches to make one.

And this is what we did, this was the only food you were getting in your twelve-hour shift.

And you can imagine, when the radio announced the location of this truck, any other cars that were in the vicinity, including the average police patrol car, would get over there, and you were lucky to get anything.

You ever see a bunch of hungry people converge on someone that's giving out food, well that was it.

Also, Lucky, if you're in the car with the same guys twelve hours a day and not getting any breaks, after a couple of weeks, I mean, everybody's on edge.

There's no more pleasantries, really, talked about or spoken. And you would lapse into silence for a couple of hours at a time.

And this really started to get on everybody's nerves.

Also, you were always driving in the same area you were assigned to, and this went on for months.

Actually, it was some of the lousiest duty I ever had.

When my shift was over, y'know, it would be an hour to get home, and the first thing you wanted to do was go to bed, take a bath, or what have you.

I wished some of the guys I was in the car with had decided to do the same thing and take a bath, because in that heat, sometimes the car would get rather rank.

You would turn around and ask 'em, "Which one of you didn't take a goddam bath?" or "Which one of you didn't use a deodorant?"

No need to say, after a coupla weeks I was so constipated from eatin' dry sandwiches and Kool-Aid that — it was really a tough, tough assignment.

Well, in the end it concluded, and the black kids got into Girard college, and we didn't do anything to prevent anything, really, except patrol around and break up small groups of people that were potential troublemakers.

It was great to be relieved up there and go back to your normal duties, and at the time, like I say, it was Gang Control.

Thomas M. Grubb & Allan "Lucky" Cole

CHAPTER THIRTY–EIGHT
Court Liaison

AFTER TWENTY TWO years on the street, I got this young guy that came into our squad. Actually, I didn't ask for him, he was put there by the inspector.

He was a white fellow, and he was a college kid, and I was more or less instructed to teach him how the squad ran, kinda cut him in on all the information we had.

And have him ride with me, get to know the men. And sort of like indoctrinate him to everything that was going on.

He was well placed, he had a helluva rabbi, and I could see the writing on the wall, that my time was short-lived there.

Within a matter of six months or so, maybe a little longer, I was called in to the inspector's office and advised that this young man was going to become the sergeant of Gang Control and take over my squad.

This was no surprise, this happens in a lot of places.

So the boss just told me, he said, "Look, Grubb, where do you wanna go?" he said, "What's on your mind?"

In other words, I had my pick of assignments, right then and there.

I had been workin' shift work for 22 years, and I told him, "Boss, I'll take a day-work job. What's open?"

At that time, we decided that the District Attorney's Office, Court Liaison, was the assignment that I wanted.

And that's exactly what I got.

This was a pretty good deal as far as I was concerned. I had enough time on the streets, I didn't care for any more.

It was 20 years plus, and then I finally hit an eight to four or nine to five job — weekends off, holidays off. That was pretty good.

So I accepted it, and this young fella that I was breaking in took my slot as sergeant in gang control, one of the squads.

I went back and I told the guys what was going on.

At this time half the squad said, "Shit, you're goin' Sarge, I'm gettin' out, too."

Half the guys actually went in to the inspector and asked for transfers. You know, you make up a slip and then you give a verbal request for transfer.

I appreciated this, because I had some good guys workin' with me, and we got along well, and we did the job better, I think, than anybody else coulda done.

Well, no need to say that these guys didn't get their transfers, because they were doing too good a job in the squad.

I went down to 1801 Vine, met with the D.A. down there. This was Municipal Court, this was where they handle all the juveniles.

I was told by one of the A.D.A.'s, Assistant District Attorneys, just what my duties were.

He told me, "Look," he said, "this is a breeze, you haven't got a thing to worry about."

At this time I knew the guys who were workin' down there, all but one, and he had been an old timer that was down there, I guess, from the first time this Court Liaison group was originally instigated.

Besides 1801 Vine there was the Youth Study Center and the people that were assigned down there.

We had a choice, you worked three days at one place and two at the other, then the next week you reversed it, worked three days at the Center and two days at 1801 Vine.

At 1801 Vine you worked with District Attorneys, who presented the Commonwealth's case, and you had a judge on the bench. At the Youth Study Center you did the same thing, but you presented the case instead of the A.D.A.

And what you would do, you had what they called an interviewer behind the desk. This man was a probation officer.

He would make the decisions on the cases presented, and find out whether they had enough merit to be transferred to 1801 Vine, to the Juvenile Courts.

This Youth Study Center also housed some of the kids that had been arrested, and they would be in there either awaiting an interview or awaiting time to go to court.

Our primary job was to take a report made by the arresting juvenile officer, which could be one, two, three or four pages, and actually condense that down to maybe one-quarter of the report.

Take out all the unnecessary stuff and only present the meat of the report to the interviewer or to the sitting judge.

At 1801 Vine, you didn't always go into court day after day, but you would be working on all these reports that would come in, and try to condense 'em down to a few paragraphs.

And at 1801 Vine, instead of the A.D.A. that was there, the Assistant District Attorney, you would read the police report.

This helped by keeping all the arresting officers out of the courtroom — you represented the arresting officer, and you read the condensed report to the judge.

It was more like making a pony — you remember a pony from school, for cheating?

You would just have so much on the "pony," to let the judge know what occurred. Then the A.D.A. would take over the case.

Well, that was good, up to the point where we kept all the arresting officers out of court. That was the main purpose for the Court Liaison Officers.

You did get to know a lot of the judges, the majority were pretty good guys, and you got to know them on a personal basis.

There was only one old judge there who was a real pain in the butt, he wanted to hear everything about everything and, y'know, that just prolonged the cases.

Where the other judges might hear ten cases in a day, he heard three or four, so you didn't want to get into his courtroom that much.

At the Youth Study Center it was a little different. You got a report on every arrest that was made in the previous 24 hours, so there were a number of reports that you had to go over. There were three guys assigned to the Youth Study Center, two beside myself.

You had to split up the reports which you marked in the morning, which ones were going to which interviewer. And then you would present the cases, after you condensed them.

Then the interviewer would make his decision — whether the case should go further, on to the Juvenile Courts at 1801 Vine.

When you were assigned to the Center you always had more action, because some of those little suckers would be in the room, they would have a parent or stepmother or an aunt or grandmother with them.

257

And some of them were pretty belligerent, y'know, for the more serious crimes. And they would try to get away.

You had to sit at a desk with the interviewer, and sometimes you would sit as close to the door as possible, and you would intercept these kids while they were trying to make it out.

Sometimes they did make it out the door, and you chased them down a hall filled with people and apprehended them if possible.

There were even occasions when some of these little suckers would just jump up from their seat and jump out the window. Kick the screen out and go right out the window.

The Youth Study Center was not air conditioned, so you had to open up the windows for a little air, and that was it, the way it worked.

Over at 1801 Vine it was a little better. You were actually in a courtroom with a judge, and there was a cop outside the door, so very, very rarely did anybody make a break, to try to get away.

There were occasions where some did, but it was rare.

After the first six months or so, I got together with the guys, and I asked 'em, "Look, what do you say we pick a permanent team to work at the Center and one to work at 1801 Vine?"

It wasn't too hard to do, and we did break the guys up, and we put three permanent guys at the Youth Study Center and the rest stayed at 1801 Vine. I decided to go to the Youth Study Center — I had my reasons for this.

I found that while working at 1801 Vine, you were always there till four or five o'clock, and sometimes later if a case was going on, you couldn't get up and walk out.

Whereas, at the Center you did have a lot of cases, but the normal day, with the three guys with three interview rooms, we were through at three o'clock or earlier. And of course, if you were through, you left.

This suited me just fine. Although the work was repetitious and sometimes monotonous, you knew that at three or four o'clock at the latest, your duty day was done and you could leave.

I will tell you about one thing that I had knowledge of, but I wasn't the guy to take the action.

Thomas M. Grubb & Allan "Lucky" Cole

This was with a murder in Dante's Inferno. This was a nightclub, I believe it was on Walnut Street if I'm not mistaken, where a man and woman were shot to death, by someone allegedly burglarizing the establishment.

I knew about this from the beginning, simply because a guy that I worked with in the First District who became a detective was assigned to the case. And knowing him — I knew that he was an ass, simply because of an incident one time when I was down at that district.

He stopped a stolen car, and he told the driver of this car, "Follow me into the district."

Now that is an utterly ridiculous thing for a police officer to say.

He preceded the stolen car to the district, and the guy that was drivin' the stolen car never showed up.

I happened to be in the operations room that night when he came in.

And the sergeant of the operations room just looked at him and said, "What an ass."

Well anyway, this guy was assigned to the case and, Christ, it, I don't know, it lasted a year or so.

Down the street from me, downtown, was a club called the Southwark Club. I knew the guys that ran it, Monk Cox used to run the club. And I guess you'd call him the bouncer, was a kid named John Silver.

I knew both of 'em, I played football with Monk Cox, and John Silver, I went through grammar school with him. John was a kid with one eye, and one of the toughest kids I ever knew.

As far as I knew, as he got to be a man he was still just as tough, or tougher.

I knew — I used to stop down the club once in a while, because it was the neighborhood, and most of the guys that went there, I knew.

And this guy Phelan used to go in there. I really didn't know him, he wasn't from our neighborhood. But he was the kinda guy, he was a big guy, not bad lookin', and had the rep of being a tough guy only if he could get behind you.

Thomas M. Grubb & Allan "Lucky" Cole

Well, I know for a fact that John Silver bounced him outta the club several times, y'know, for whatever — makin' a pass at a girl or just gettin' outta hand.

He had the rep of bein' a pretty nasty guy, but as time went on and you read the newspapers, it was really odd. They couldn't break this case for boo.

Later on, I learned through different things that, y'know, they're lookin' for this guy, they're lookin' for that guy, and whatever. And I don't even know if Phelan's name was ever mentioned or not.

But he disappeared for a few months, and then he showed up at the club again. And he did his usual thing, mouthin' off and this and that.

And some guys got the impression that he had done something that he was trying to say but wouldn't say — just tryin' to make himself a big deal.

When the story finally broke, it was the manager of the club had hired Phelan to kill his wife, who was supposed to be in the club. You know, he gave him all the details — when to come in and whatnot.

And the husband's real plan was — he would be there also, and instead of payin' Phelan off for killin' his wife — I don't know who the other guy was — but it was the woman's husband that had made the deal with Phelan.

And he was gonna do Phelan, when Phelan came in to do them — Phelan would kill them — then he was gonna kill Phelan. But somehow, Phelan got either scared or whatnot, and the husband was unable to get to Phelan.

Well anyway, Phelan was arrested for these murders.

And they used to call him "Birdman," Birdman Phelan, because he was big — big arms and whatnot.

Thomas M. Grubb & Allan "Lucky" Cole

CHAPTER THIRTY–NINE
Nicky Blue

On many occasions you saw kids from your own neighborhood, and you saw their mothers, who, God, you knew since you were 15, 16 years old.

And they recognized you, y'know, they'd always kind of look for a favor, what could you do to help, and this sort of thing and that.

Well, there were hundreds of occasions when this occurred, and if something wasn't too serious, you could help. And usually I did, if I knew the families and so forth, and this worked out rather well.

'Cause you could give a kid a break for something trivial, and he wouldn't have to go to court.

Now you have to remember, every juvenile that was arrested had to come through the Youth Center Study first to get a determination — whether his particular case was bad enough to be certified to 1801 Vine, which was the big court.

You had a judge and so forth there, and usually from there they received a sentence. We did not sentence anyone in the Youth Study Center, we just referred them to 1801 Vine.

There was one particular kid that came through the Center, I knew his mother quite well from when we were kids.

This kid got into all kinds of trouble, usually trivial stuff, but you could almost bet every couple of months he would wind up in the Center.

And it really got to be a habit.

Most of the time he was let go, and he would just go out and do something else dumb, y'know — drinking, breaking bottles, carrying on, and all that kinda dumb stuff. Nothing really serious, until later on in his career.

Each time he came in I would try to help him out, simply because of his mother, and sometimes she would have a local politician there who would kinda tell her, "Gee, why don't you see Tom, maybe he could help you out."

And that's the way it would go.

Of course it wasn't my decision to just let the kid go, I would have to talk to the interviewer, who decided whether to go on to court or not. In this kid's case, I did talk to the interviewer on several occasions.

Then, finally, he came in on something that was very serious, and the mother cried and everything else. And, y'know, when you help a kid along, trying to get him straight, and they keep foulin' up. . .

The decision at this time — I think he was 17 years old when he came in, and I talked to the interviewer.

He said, "Look," he said, "let's get this guy into the Army, or something."

Vietnam was going on then, and the kid conceded, if he got a break he would go into the army.

Actually, the kid did go into the service, and over the next months I got letters from him. He wrote me a letter and told me he was doin' well and all this stuff.

The kid's in Vietnam, and you know what that was, that was a hellhole. And this was only a slightly-built kid, he wasn't a big guy or anything, he was just one of the grunts in the Army.

Sometimes it pays off to help another person, and this kid distinguished himself in the Army. He must have gotten leave, because one day I'm working and he came up in his uniform, and the kid really looked good.

He had the Bronze Star, he had campaign ribbons, and, you know, he looked like a real soldier.

He thanked me for everything he was doin', and gettin' him a break, and told me he's got his head together now.

His mother was with him, and what could you say — "Just keep yourself straight, you'll do good, you're on the right road."

Well, we went through that, and I had told Cass about this kid, and she knew the parents, they were from the neighborhood.

It was quite a while later, he had signed up, he had done two or three tours in 'Am, I'm not quite sure. But anyway, we read in the paper that he was awarded the Silver Star for bravery.

This was a big award, this was next to the Congressional Medal of Honor. And the kid distinguished himself over there quite well.

Then it was, oh, some time later, I don't know how long, Lucky, we read in the paper that he was killed in Vietnam.

Thomas M. Grubb & Allan "Lucky" Cole

He had gained the rank of sergeant. And I don't know if it was his mother that came and told me — I had read it in the paper — but she had gotten letters from him, and the kid always mentioned me in his letters.

I felt — I felt good about him doing the right things, but then I felt bad — Christ, here's the kid, he's dead. And he's still a very young man.

So sometimes you got things going in the right direction, but then something happens and you're sorry for what you originally did.

Maybe he'd have been better off going to jail for a couple of years, I don't know.

I got thanked a hundred times by the kid, and I felt real good when I saw him. Unfortunately, the war got him, and that was it. But he certainly did distinguish himself while he was in the service.

There was another occasion, this captain of police came up to the Youth Study Center — I didn't know the man — and he identified himself, who he was.

We used to have a room where just the policemen sat and talked, or we had our coffee or whatnot, before the cases really started, when you would arrange everything for the various rooms.

Well, this captain came over to me, he said, "Look," he identified himself, he said, "My kid's up here," he said, "maybe you could give 'im a break."

So I got his name and I went in and I pulled the report, it wasn't in my room. But I talked to — I read the report, and the kid was in for some, I think it was marijuana. It wasn't serious, but he had been up there a couple of times for marijuana.

And the captain realized, you don't come up two or three times and avoid going to court for that.

So after reading the report, I said, "Captain, I'll see what I can do for you."

The kid was released from the Youth Study Center, again, meaning he didn't have to appear before a judge. Now this would have been embarrassing for a police captain, to say the least, and actually we got to be friends, this captain and me, later.

263

But subsequently, oh, maybe a year or so later, this kid, the captain's son, killed the captain and his mother, his father and his mother.

I don't know if he chopped their heads off, or what. He killed them with an ax.

And so, you know, you do things for people at their request and it doesn't always turn out right. A lot of things we did, by giving kids a second break, turned out real good, but this one, it was maybe a year or two later, when I guess he got on to more serious drugs or whatever.

And he actually killed his parents.

Before I forget this, I've gotta tell you about a certain young man that I came across while he was just a little boy, like maybe fourteen, fifteen years old. His name was, his street name was "Nicky Blue." That wasn't his real name.

I came across him, this was a white kid of Italian descent, and just as tough as nails.

The first time I came across him, he was brought into the district when I was in Gang Control.

It seemed that he had cut a gang member in one of the schools. Nicky was not, as you would say, a gang person, but he was so tough every white kid would kinda get next to him if possible, to be his friend. 'Cause they knew he was a tough son-of-a-gun.

Well, Nicky was an arrogant kid, I mean really arrogant. Anything you'd say to him, he'd curse you or something, and I used to slap the hell out of Nicky, I'll tell you the truth.

I got him, oh, several times, on different assaults and what have you. And I would arrest him. I would arrest him, and he'd go to court, and he used to get out.

Nicky attended a school that was primarily black, like 85 per cent. And Nicky, bein' the kid he was, he was as tough as any kid I ever met.

His theory was, if somebody pulls a knife on him, he's gonna pull a bigger knife. And if somebody got a gun, he's gonna have a bigger gun. And he meant every word he said.

I guess I came in contact with Nicky a dozen times, and he was gettin' up to the age where he's gettin' to be an adult, he's like 17.

And every time somebody's pinch him for corner lounging' or something, he'd come in and he would see me

Well, he knew what was coming.

On the first few occasions I'd tell him, "Put your hands up," and, y'know, "If you wanta fight back, you fight."

But I used to tune him up pretty good.

It was kind of a shame, simply because Nikki's father, you know, came from the other side. And I won't say the man was illiterate or anything else, he could just about speak English.

When he'd come in, when I would release Nicky, he would always say, "You fighting again?"

And I would tell him, "Take 'im home."

That's when I didn't arrest him.

Several times I had to go into this school to take Nicky out because of something he did in the school, fighting usually. Sometimes he'd have something a little more serious, somebody would get cut, or whatever.

I'd have to take Nicky in, and if there was proof enough I would arrest him. But he always got slapped in the head before he got arrested.

Nicky turned 18, and of course after 18, I wouldn't see him again as far as Gang Control was concerned or Juvenile was concerned, because he was considered an adult.

But from all the stuff I heard, I used to check every now and then, he wasn't being arrested by anyone.

And then there was this occasion, your Aunt Cass and I were going to the Broadway movie, and we're drivin' down Broad Street and I stop in front of the movie, lookin' for a place to park.

And this pick-up truck pulled up beside me, and this guy's yellin' out to me, "Hey, Mr. Grubb, Mr. Grubb."

I looked around, and Cass says, "They're callin' you," and here's a young lady in the truck, and this guy.

Here, it's Nicky Blue.

And he's motioning' to pull over, pull over, and I pulled over.

He parked, and he jumped out of the truck, and I figured, "Now, what's this guy gonna do? Is he gonna shoot me, or what the hell is he gonna do?"

He's a young man, mind you, and he came over, and he leaned in the window, and he's tryin' to grab my hand, and I figured, "What's he tryin' to grab — my gun, or what?"

And he's sayin', "I want to thank you, I want to thank you," and here, he stood there and he told us, oh, for fifteen or twenty minutes. And he's tellin' Cass, "He used to beat me up every time he found me."

He said, "Now I've got my own business," he said, "you know, I'm goin' straight."

And here, he was a contractor, and he was doin' great, and he told me that. And he told me, "This is my girlfriend, we're gonna get married," and all of this.

And, you know, I just looked at the kid — now he's a young man — and I figured to myself, well, here was one good thing. He got bounced around enough as a young kid, and into and out of a lot of trouble, but he got himself straight, and here he is, with his own business.

That made me feel very good. And your Aunt Cass remembers that to this day. If you ever mention Nicky Blue to her, it's just like sayin' your nephew, or your cousin, or something.

I felt good about this, because here's a kid who found the right road and he traveled it well.

Thomas M. Grubb & Allan "Lucky" Cole

CHAPTER FORTY
Epilogue

Well, Luck, I finished up my last few years at this Court Liaison job, and it was more like coasting out of the police department. You did your twenty-some on the street, and then you did your last few years on a softer job.

You really didn't get out on the street to have to take much police action.

I'm gonna wrap up these tapes shortly, but I want to tell you this, Luck. In the department you meet such a variety of men and women, and I always managed to get along with the majority of them, 99 per cent of them.

You know, you give a little bit and you take a little bit.

But even till today, when I go to meetings at the Fraternal Order of Police, I meet some of the old guys that I used to work with.

They've always got a good word to say, nothing like, they ignore you or, you know, you weren't a good guy and all this stuff and that.

And that means a lot to me.

I always found, all my time in the department, you treat people like you would have them treat you. If they were fair and spoke well, and did not give you a hard time, you treated them the same way.

On the other hand, you had the asses that would start out just by cursing you for any reason and, you know, giving you a hard time in general.

And then you had to put your gorilla suit on and you treated them the same way.

This seemed to work out for me, I guess it worked out for a lot of other guys.

I've tried to impress on you in many of the tapes, Lucky, that being a police officer is really operating in a state of boredom a lot of the time, particularly when you're in uniform. You ride around, day after day, night after night, really nothing going on.

And you think to yourself, "Is this the job that I should be in? Why did I ever leave my last job? How far am I gonna go on this job?"

With the situation, the way things are, or were then, you could be accused of something that you were never involved in. And there's always a chance that they'll blame you for something you didn't do.

I always remembered my old sergeant, when I was a rookie, that one time I called him for advice.

He just looked at me and he said, "Look, you are a policeman. You make your own decisions. Right or wrong, you make your own decisions."

I never forgot that, Lucky.

I'll say one other thing — that your Aunt Cass, when I used to moan and groan sometimes about the job, she would always say, "Tom, you do the best you can. Things will work out right."

The ultimate goal of any policeman is to stay married to the woman you are married to. There are temptations out there that get many, many cops into difficulty, and they wind up losing their home or their wife or their family.

The second goal of any police officer is to get their time in, and get their pension, and get out.

This is gonna be about the end of these tapes, Lucky, and the end of my "sermons" about being a cop. I hope you can make some head or tail out of it, kid, and anything you do is all right with me.

Take care, and good luck with everything, Lucky.

THE END

Thomas M. Grubb & Allan "Lucky" Cole

About the Authors

Thomas M. Grubb (Jan. 6, 1929 - Feb. 20, 2005) The son of Irish and German immigrants, Mr. Grubb was a native of Philadelphia. He joined the police department in 1953. Prior to that he was a technician at Dupont and served in the Navy in Post World War II Europe.

Honored many times during his thirty-year career as a police officer, he retired from the department in 1983. Afterwards, he used his hard-won detective skills in the insurance adjustment business, which he owned along with his two sons.

Mr. Grubb and his beloved wife, Cassie, were blessed with five children, fifteen grandchildren and five great-grandchildren.

A recording secretary for the Philadelphia Retired Police Officer's Association, he was also active in the Fraternal Order Of Police and was a delegate to the national convention in 1999.

Allan Cole is a best-selling author, screenwriter and former prize-winning newsman who brings a rich background in travel and personal experience to his work. Raised in Europe and the Far East, Cole attended thirty-two schools and visited or lived in as many countries.

Rejecting invitations to become a CIA operative like his father, Cole became an award-winning reporter and editor who dealt with everything from landmark murder cases to thieving government officials. Since that time he's written twenty five books, many of which have become international bestsellers, as well as numerous screen and television dramas. He currently lives in Boca Raton, Florida, with Kathryn, his strongest supporter.

For more information about Allan, and to contact him directly see his homepage at http://www.acole.com. Or visit his popular blog - My Hollywood MisAdventures:http://allan-cole.blogspot.com/. Links to all versions of this book, and Allan's other books can be found at: http://tinyurl.com/47l2l4l And be sure to listen to the radio interview he participated in on American Heroes Radio, honoring his "Uncle Tom." Here's the link: http://tinyurl.com/66dscxt

Glossary

Backer - Money man underwriting numbers games.

Bank -"Calculates all the numbers that were played and declares a winner out of the lot."

Big Apple - Weekend off.

Byberry- Pennsylvania state mental institution.

Bye - Person released from custody without being charged, i.e., "he got a bye."

Came from the other side - Emigrated to the United States.

Carrier - Gang member responsible for holding weapons.

Clothes - Plainclothes detectives, i.e., "he worked clothes."

Corner lounger - Person hanging around on street corner.

Dirty - Person under the influence of or recent user of narcotics, i.e., "I got this guy, and I got him dirty."

Drop the hammer - Inform on.

Fish - New man.

Floater - Body found in river.

Ginks - Internal Affairs.

Give him a walk - Release from custody without charging, bye.

Going up the golden stairs - Policeman going to City Hall to be suspended from duty.

Gorilla suit - Tough demeanor, i.e., "put on a gorilla suit."

High yellow- Light skinned African-American.

Hit - Raid.

Hot shot - Fatal shot of heroin.

In service - Patrolman available for calls.

Kettle - Part of still

Knock down - Raid.

Last out - Police shift, 12:00 midnight to 8:00 A.M.

Lottery Squad - Police unit specializing in numbers game arrests.

Mainliner - Heroin addict, one who shoots heroin into veins.

Mary Jane - Marijuana (archaic).

Middle - Put someone in the middle, i.e., "You can't middle me."

Nickel or dime bag - Heroin costing $5.00 or $10.00.

Onionskins - Daily arrest reports.

Pick-up man- Guys that pick up the stuff [money and bets] from all the writers and then take it to a bank or to a drop."

Pinch - Arrest.

Pull - Hourly report of beat officers.

Put the boots to - Have intercourse with, i.e., "he put the boots to another man's wife."

Quartermaster - Area in Philadelphia, former Army supply depot.

Rabbi - Mentor. "Somebody politically [connected] who can help you get a transfer and a unit."

Red ass -New man.

Runner - Bootlegger carrying illegal alcohol.

Second Alarmer - Fire truck supplying food, etc, to officers on duty.

Shooting gallery - Place to purchase and do drugs, usually heroin.

Skinpopper - One who shoots heroin under the skin only, not into veins.

Still - Homemade machine for making bootleg liquor.

Taking the action - Taking bets.

Taste - Drink of alcohol, i.e., "I had me a taste."

Ticket - Warrant.

Walk - Release without charges, i.e., "give the suspect a walk," bye.

Warlord - Gang member responsible for making battle arrangements.

White lightning - Bootleg alcohol, white whiskey.

White whiskey - Bootleg alcohol, white lightning.

Windows - Police detail checking store windows in business district for breakage or burglary.

Writer - Person writing down numbers bettor wishes to play and taking money from bettors.

Zip gun - Homemade gun, usually one shot, made and used by gang members.

Thomas M. Grubb & Allan "Lucky" Cole